The Making of the Modern Homosexual

The Making of the Modern Homosexual

Edited by

Kenneth Plummer

Lecturer in Sociology, University of Essex

Barnes & Noble Books
Totowa, New Jersey

First published in the USA 1981 by
Barnes & Noble Books
81 Adams Drive
Totowa, New Jersey, 07512

ISBN 0–389–20159–6

Printed in Great Britain

A *species* comes to be, a type becomes fixed and strong through the long fight with essentially constant *unfavourable* conditions.

F. NIETZSCHE, *Beyond Good and Evil*

The nineteenth-century homosexual became a personage, a past, a case history, and a childhood, in addition to being a type of life, a life form, and a morphology, with an indiscreet anatomy and possibly a mysterious physiology. Nothing that went into his total composition was unaffected by his sexuality. It was everywhere present in him: at the root of all his actions because it was their insidious and indefinitely active principle; written immodestly on his face and body because it was a secret that always gave itself away. It was consubstantial with him, less as a habitual sin than as a singular nature. We must not forget that the psychological, psychiatric, medical category of homosexuality was constituted from the moment it was characterized – Westphal's famous article of 1870 on 'contrary sexual sensations' can stand as its date of birth – less by a type of sexual relations than by a certain quality of sexual sensibility, a certain way of inverting the masculine and the feminine in oneself. Homosexuality appeared as one of the forms of sexuality when it was transposed from the practice of sodomy onto a kind of interior androgyny, a hermaphroditism of the soul. The sodomite had been a temporary aberration; the homosexual was now a species.

M. FOUCAULT, *The History of Sexuality*

The consciousness of class arises in the phenomenology of domination. Black or Jewish or gay identity arises from no intrinsic or biological quality in itself. Intrinsically they are nothing. Only the image of self reflected by *others' ability to influence or control one's life or survival*, necessarily organises the self's priorities and orientations.

B. ADAM, *The Survival of Domination*

Contents

8 *Contents*

Appendices

Contributors

Gregg Blachford gained his BA from Queen's University, Kingston, Canada in 1971 and his MA from Essex University in 1978. He 'met' GLF while in Australia in 1972, and subsequently was involved in the Gay Left editorial collective in England (1975–7). He is currently a teacher.

Annabel Faraday gained her BA from Essex University in 1975, and was a research officer there until 1979. She has researched into transvestism and female sexuality, and is currently a Ph.D student examining the historical construction of lesbianism.

Dave King gained his BA from Portsmouth Polytechnic and has undertaken postgraduate study at the Universities of Keele and Essex. He is currently a lecturer in social work at Liverpool University and is engaged in a SSRC-supported project, 'Conceptions of gender deviance'.

John Marshall gained his BA from the University of East Anglia, and since 1977 has been researching into homosexuality at Essex for a Ph.D.

Mary McIntosh gained her BA from Oxford and her MA from Berkeley. She has taught at Leicester University and South Bank Polytechnic, and is currently a senior lecturer at Essex University. She has researched a wide range of subjects including prostitution and professional crime, and is currently studying the family and the welfare state in relation to the position of women. She is the author of *The Organisation of Crime*, co-editor of *Deviance and Control* and has written a number of articles.

Kenneth Plummer gained his BSc. from Enfield College and his Ph.D from the London School of Economics. He has taught at Middlesex Polytechnic, and is currently a lecturer at Essex University. He is researching into a range of different sexual experiences – including paedophilia and masochism, and is the author of *Sexual Stigma: An Interactionist Account* and a number of articles.

Jeffrey Weeks gained his BA from London University, and has held research posts at both the London School of Economics and Essex University. He is a founder editor of *Gay Left*, a consulting editor of the *Journal of Homosexuality* and has co-authored five volumes of *Sources in British Political History*. His study of the gay movement, *Coming Out*, won the *Gay News* literary award in 1978.

Preface

Homosexual experiences in the Western world appear to have undergone somewhat dramatic transformations since the early 1960s. Where once male experiences were largely banished by law, now – increasingly but cautiously – they are being decriminalized. Where once all homosexual experiences were viewed as pathology and sickness, now – increasingly but cautiously – they are being demedicalized. Where once 'homosexuals' would do anything to conceal their stigma from public gaze, now – increasingly but cautiously – they are coming 'out of their closets' to make themselves visible and known about. Where once homosexual experiences would only lead to heads bowed with shame, now – increasingly but cautiously – such experiences are being seen as joyful and fulfilling. Where once 'gays' saw themselves passively as downtrodden and downcast, now – increasingly but cautiously – they see their oppression as squarely political and have organized to fight back through gay and feminist movements. Where once the female homosexual community was denied any existence, now a world of intimacies both emotional and political between women is increasingly prominent. Where once the male public homosexual 'world' was fragmented and composed largely of hidden bars, furtive toilets and exploitative hustling, now it has become a massive social scene – with its own discos, newspapers, religious organizations, political groups, switchboards, counselling services, community centres and holiday resorts. Indeed in some parts of America – at least – gays have almost established an all-embracing ghetto. In sum the age of a new homosexual would seem to be arriving.

While this may be so, it is *not* the argument of this book; only history will allow us to judge the significance of these events. It is difficult sometimes to resist the feeling that the current situation, the current 'struggle' or the current 'crisis' is the lynchpin to dramatic social change, but resist it we must. For the evolution of the modern homosexual is a process that began a good way back – quite when is uncertain – and it is a process that is likely to continue some while into the future. It is with these broader changes that this volume is concerned.

At base, all the contributors to this book would argue that the homosexual is *not* a type of person that has been with us – in various guises – throughout time and space; he and she are not simply 'beings' that we are slowly discovering and understanding better. On the contrary, our starting point contends that specific ways of experiencing sexual attraction and gender behaviour are bound up with specific historical and cultural milieux. Indeed in some such environments 'sexual attraction' and 'gender' may not even be sensible categories; to the members of those worlds such a way of seeing may lie outside their frame of possibilities. We can no more compare what happened between 'men' and 'boys' in ancient Greece with the happenings in a San Francisco sauna bath than we can compare the dying of a starving Kampuchean with the poverty found in the United Kingdom in the 1970s! We can group (or construct) threads that hold them together – 'sex', 'poverty' – but it must be appreciated that there is no uniform essence that connects them. They are constructed, they evolve and may finally fade away within specific historical and cultural settings. The 'homosexual' then is an invention, and the problem for this inquiry is to chart what is so far known about this invention – its origins, content and functions – and to pose questions that should be asked about it.

The first section gives the background orientation by providing a brief history of the sociology of homosexuality and by reprinting the classic article to formulate the problem of homosexual categorization: Mary McIntosh's 'The homosexual role'. Since the publication of this article in 1968, McIntosh has changed some of her views and these are presented in an afterword.

Part Two attempts to develop some of these ideas analytically and thereby to provide some directions for future empirical research. Plummer charts a framework of issues generated generally by labelling theory; Weeks discusses both historical issues involved in the 'construction' of the homosexual category and the theoretical disputes entailed in understanding the 'construction' of the homosexual experience, while Faraday argues against the misogyny of homosexual research to date and for an approach which firmly grounds any analysis of lesbianism within feminist concerns.

The third section of the study contains a series of exploratory empirical researches which, taken collectively, present an interesting picture of the way in which 'masculinization' is becoming a central feature of the *new* male homosexual experience and how the extremely feminized experiences that once might have been seen as 'homosexual' have now been hived off into new categories, the 'transvestite' and transsexual'. Marshall's article sees 'homosexuality' as a form of control to keep men behaving like men, first, by stigmatizing all men who didn't behave like men as 'pansy' and 'gender invert' and, second, by shaping 'homosexuals' to behave more like men. Central to his argument is the separation of gender-role from sexual attraction in the homosexual category – which he tentatively suggests occurred during the 1950s. King picks up the argument by considering how new categories of effeminacy evolved during the early part of this century – first through the category of 'transvestism' and since the 1960s through the category of 'transsexual'. The last article is distinctly more 'modern'; it analyses aspects of the English gay world at the end of the 1970s. In it Blachford continues with the theme of masculinity and shows how it is crucial in thinking about the contemporary gay bar and disco scene. He is, however, less concerned with describing this scene and more concerned with showing how such masculinity is linked to the dominant culture. His account draws from the conceptualization of the Birmingham Centre for Contemporary Cultural Studies, and shows that the homosexual sub-culture may be simultaneously conservatively reinforcing the dominant culture and radically innovative in devising its own strategies.

The study therefore is a whole and not a mere collection of essays. It moves from a clarification of the intellectual origins of the problem in Part One, to a discussion of conceptual problems and directions for research in Part Two, to concrete exploratory empirical studies within this framework in Part Three. It also moves from historical considerations of the homosexual role in the eighteenth century to an analysis of its most contemporary manifestations today.

All of the contributors have been, or still are, researchers in the sociology department at the University of Essex, England, and in large part the book should be viewed as a collective effort in clarifying the theoretical and empirical problems involved in approaching 'lesbianism' and 'male homosexuality' as historical and sociological concerns.

Finally, our thanks go to the secretarial staff in the sociology department at Essex who helped prepare the final typescript – in particular, Lynda George, Eleanor Hunter and Janet Parkin.

Part One
The Making of a Sociology of Homosexuality

1 Building a sociology of homosexuality

Kenneth Plummer

The history of sociological inquiry into homosexuality is a very limited one. It spans little more than thirty years, is almost wholly 'male' and American, and – until the 1970s – has been built upon one broad, generally tacit viewpoint: that of 'labelling'. Most approaches to homosexuality – dominated in the past by medicine, psychology and psychiatry – have focused on the core problem of aetiology (to find out what makes a person homosexual), have worked from the core assumption of heterosexual superiority (by which homosexuality is always some kind of problem) and have aimed at providing remedies (usually treatment) (see Morin 1977). But these have not been the concern of those few sociologists who have studied the area. Rather, their concern – manifested in diverse ways – has been to show *how historically produced stigmatizing conceptions surrounding same-sex experiences have had dramatic consequences for those experiences.*

The formalization of these concerns into something known as 'labelling theory' did not really happen until the mid 1960s, but the focus was nevertheless present in earlier studies. Thus, for instance, Kinsey – albeit no sociologist but nevertheless producing the first major social study in 1948 – could not only urge the abolition of the term 'the homosexual' in favour of talking about 'individuals who have had certain amounts of heterosexual experience and certain amounts of homosexual experience' (Kinsey *et al.* 1948, p. 617), but could also signpost the potential damage caused by labelling. In a striking passage he wrote:

One of the factors that materially contributes to the development of exclusively homosexual histories, is the ostracism which society imposes upon one who is discovered to have had perhaps no more than a lone experience. The high school boy is likely to be expelled from school and, if it is in a small town, he is almost certain to be driven from the community. His chances of making heterosexual contacts are tremendously reduced after the public disclosure, and he is forced into the company of other homosexual individuals among whom he finally develops an exclusively homosexual pattern for himself. Any schoolteacher and principal who is faced with the problem of the individual boy should realise that something between a quarter and a third of all the other boys in the same high school have had at least some homosexual experience since they turned adolescent. [1948, p. 663]

We would now identify this as a rather vulgar, simple statement of the labelling position, primarily because of its focus on the overt, direct labelling mechanisms and not the covert, symbolic ones (see Warren 1974). Nevertheless the seeds of this perspective were sown.

In America these ideas were taken up in the 1950s through the popular work of Cory (1953, 1963 and 1964) on male and female homosexuality, the social psychology of Hooker (1956, 1958 and 1969b) and the sociology of Leznoff and Westley (1967), who produced the first contemporary 'community studies' of the male gay world. That hostility and stigma structured the features of this world was clear throughout. Thus Leznoff and Westley remarked:

The subjection of homosexuals to legal punishment and social condemnation has produced a complex structure of concealed social relations which merit sociological investigation. [1967, p. 185]

Hooker's work was of special importance in highlighting the psychological 'normality' of the homosexual.[1*] Using standard psychological tests (for example, Rorschach, Thematic Apperception, Make-a-Picture-Story) and comparing small groups of heterosexuals and homosexuals, she suggested that homosexuality as a clinical entity did not exist and its forms were as varied as those of heterosexuality. It was a perspective that was to be replicated many times on men and women and was ultimately to lead to the rather eccentric position that 'homosexuals may be healthier than straights' (Freedman 1975).[2]

In England little of sociological significance appeared until 1965. Indeed it is tempting to suggest that until that time all the

*Superior figures refer to the Notes on pages 241–52.

sociological insights, apart from the rather eccentric 'sociological report prepared for the Home Office' in 1958 by Richard Hauser (1962), grew from the work of one man: Michael Schofield, writing under the alias, Gordon Westwood (1952, 1960).[3] Again his position increasingly highlighted the labelling view so that by his 1965 study he could produce the following general theory:

Homosexuality in itself has only a minor effect upon the development of the personality. But the attitudes, not of the homosexual but of other people towards him create a stress situation which can have a profound effect upon personality development and can lead to a character deterioration of a kind which prohibits effective integration with the community. [Schofield 1965, p. 203]

It was about the same time – which corresponded to the formal recognition of the labelling perspective in American sociology (see Spector 1977) – that a number of studies emerged in America which made a direct link between labelling and homosexuality. Schur, for instance, studied the impact of legislation and argued that 'society's reaction (both informal and formal) significantly shapes the problem of homosexuality' (1965, p. 113),[4] while Kitsuse studied students' responses to homosexuals and posed a central sociological problem:

what are the behaviours which are defined by members of the group, community, or society as deviant, and how do those definitions organise and activate the societal reactions by which persons come to be differentiated and treated as deviants? [1962, p. 88]

By the early 1960s, then, the tacit influence of labelling ideas was being publicly recognized, and moves towards a clearer statement of the problems of a sociology of homosexuality were under way.

Two versions of labelling

Once detected within the sociology of homosexuality, it is possible to see 'labelling' approaches moving in two directions. One could be called the *labelling theory* and the other, the *labelling perspective*.[5] The labelling *theory* is largely a product of the critics who present the theory in a few very limited propositions, and then subsequently show that they can be readily falsified or that they are overly narrow. The labelling *perspective* is usually presented as a defence against critiques; it argues that labelling is not a specific theory, but a paradigm shift that can be used to reorientate research to more useful areas. As Scheff puts it in his defence of the labelling theory of mental illness, it is an attempt to

transcend the traditional classifications and models that imprison thought. It is an attempt to jostle the imagination, to create a crisis of consciousness that will lead to new visions of reality. [1975, p. 22]

The labelling *theory* – hailed by Tittle as a 'stringent and more interesting form' and by Schur as an 'unnecessarily narrow and somewhat less interesting form – centres around testing two key propositions, with labelling as a dependent and independent variable. These may be crudely (but not without too much distortion) stated as:

1 Deviant labels are applied (in formal settings, overtly) without regard to (or independent of) the behaviours or acts of those labelled.
2 Labelling produces (stabilizes or amplifies) deviants and deviant behaviour.

The labelling *perspective* – hailed by Schur as being 'so incontrovertible, so well established and so central to the sociological enterprise as to be undeniable', and castigated by Tittle as the 'weak and essentially non-novel form',[7] centres around asking four sets of related questions about labels and deviant categorizations. These are: (1) What is the nature of deviant labels? (2) How do they arise? (3) Under what conditions do the labels become attached to conduct? (4) What are the consequences of such labelling – both for the individual and the wider society? There are many answers to these questions – they serve as a massive research programme – but the underlying premise of this work may be simply if rather generally put. It holds that no adequate understanding of deviant experiences (for example, homosexuality) is possible without a consideration of the stigmatizing meanings in which these experiences become enmeshed. These stigmatizing meanings therefore must always serve as a focus of analysis, if not the central focus.

The labelling perspective does not entail a commitment to a specific brand of theory (like interactionism), nor does it try to establish a set of restricting hypotheses. Any number of theories and propositions may be brought to bear on these distinctive problem areas. An assessment of the labelling perspective on homosexuality then will entail considering the usefulness of the questions the perspective generates, and the value of the research programmes that flow from it. It does not require that one looks at the testability of the labelling *theory*, only that a series of useful ideas which would enhance our understanding of the nature of homosexuality should be generated.

Labelling and homosexuality

It is possible to see these two traditions of labelling as theory and perspective unfolding in the late 1960s through the key sociological studies of homosexuality of that time. Briefly, the work of the Kinsey Institute (Bell 1973, 1976b; Bell and Weinberg 1978; Weinberg and Williams 1974) sets up a tradition of 'testing' labelling propositions (the labelling theory), while the work initially of Mary McIntosh (1968) and Simon and Gagnon (1967), and latterly of the gay movement, sets up a tradition of reorientating research problems to a wider set of labelling concerns. I will discuss each tradition briefly in turn.

The labelling theory of homosexuality

The instigators of this approach were Weinberg and Williams,[8] though many have followed in their wake (Farrell 1971; Farrell and Morrione 1974; Farrell and Hardin 1974; Farrell and Nelson 1976; Harry and DeVall 1978; Steffensmeier 1974; Tanner 1978). The former researchers have produced the two most systematic statements of the labelling perspective on homosexuality, and have gathered much empirical data which in general tends to work against the narrow labelling theory of homosexuality. The first of their studies is an extended Ph.D thesis, *Homosexuals and the Military*, and compares homosexuals who receive a less than honourable discharge from military services with homosexuals who receive an honourable discharge. The crucial variable here is the imposition of the stigmatizing label 'less than honourable discharge'; the study attempts to look at labelling as both an independent variable (how people come to be labelled) and as a dependent variable (the consequences of being labelled), concluding that homosexuals are not usually labelled independently of their homosexual experiences and that 'less than honourable discharge' labelling does not necessarily have negative consequences for the individual. Although this small empirical study – which the authors themselves say is not a test of the labelling theory (Williams and Weinberg 1971, p. 2) – seems to refute labelling theory, such a conclusion would be premature. For their work, while a model of clarity, is inadequate both in terms of sample size and representativeness and in terms of the highly specific label which they study. Thus the 'less than honourable discharge' label is in no way comparable to the all pervasive, powerful, denigrating label of homosexuality that exists abroad in American society generally. All homosexuals, irrespective of whether they are less than honourably discharged or not, are subject to this particular form of labelling. In other words *it is abstract societal symbolic labelling that is more important than the specific formal labelling of the military*. To show that *specific* direct labelling has little impact misses the point; it is the whole weight of cultural hostility that counts.

In order to allow, therefore, for the impact of societal labelling, the second study by Weinberg and Williams (1974) – which again they stress is not really a test of the theory, but simply a framework of analysis (1974, p. 8) – attempts to provide a cross-cultural comparison (Denmark, Holland and USA) of homosexual adaptations. By choosing three cultures in which it is alleged the hostility of the homosexual label is at variance, they can chart the differential adaptations that homosexuals may take within these different cultures. The prediction is clear; in cultures which are highly hostile towards homosexuals – as in America – the negative adaptations will be greater than in those cultures where homosexuality is more accepted. Thus the authors compare homosexual adaptations in several American cities (New York and San Francisco) with those in several (supposedly more tolerant) European cities (Amsterdam and Copenhagen). They use very much larger samples than their earlier study, and the conclusion once again is fairly negative for the labelling theory, for they find that:

There are no major differences amongst the three societies with regards to our respondents psychological problems, despite differences in the socio-cultural reaction. [Weinberg and Williams 1974, p. 136]

This is not, of course, what labelling *theory* would predict. But then it is a rather naive and oversimple prediction in the first place, and not one the labelling perspective would endorse (see Chapter 3, page 75). Even on simple empirical grounds, one is at a loss to see why Weinberg and Williams believe that San Francisco (traditionally a homosexual 'mecca') should be more intolerant than Copenhagen.

The labelling perspective on homosexuality

This does not aim to address clear propositions, but rather seeks to establish new questions and problems of wider significance. Two crucial papers to do this were those by McIntosh (1968) and Simon and Gagnon (1967).

McIntosh's paper (reproduced in this book) examines 'the homosexual' label and argues that this conception of 'the homosexual' should 'in itself, [be] a possible object of study'. She suggests then that once a particular conception such as 'the homosexual' becomes part of an existing social order, the members of that social order start to act in terms of that conception. The implication of this argument is that homosexuality as we now know it simply did not exist prior to the seventeenth century, nor will it be found to be structured in a similar fashion in other cultures. Homosexual experiences may be universal; specific homosexual roles are not.

Her article is brilliantly suggestive, but it is only that. Like all landmark articles, it raises many more questions than it resolves. One problem centres around the empirical observation that the homosexual role emerged at the end of the seventeenth century – an idea which has been partly disputed by both the work of Jeffrey Weeks and John Marshall in this volume. Likewise McIntosh fails to consider the evolution of related roles like 'lesbianism' (a topic which is focused upon by Annabel Faraday in Chapter 5) and 'transvestism' (a topic discussed by Dave King in Chapter 7). Further it is arguable that her conception of role suffers from all the deficiencies of mainstream structural–functional role theory: reification, over-determination, consensual absolutism. Her suggestion could have been enhanced through the utilization of the more dynamic version of role theory found in the interactionist writings of Turner or Strauss (Turner 1962; Strauss 1969). Finally she fails to discuss the links between personal labelling and public role. Nevertheless McIntosh's paper is central to the labelling perspective precisely because it raises the crucial question of homosexual categorizations.

The other central paper from Gagnon and Simon should be seen as part of their wider work – their account of sexuality drawing heavily upon the writings of social learning theorists and symbolic interactionists and their account of sexual deviance drawing heavily from the work of labelling theorists. One of the central ideological thrusts in their writings is their wish to take the study of human sexuality out of the realm of the extraordinary and replace it where they believe it belongs: in the world of the ordinary. Sexuality is not to be seen as something special; it is not to be seen as a powerful drive shaping the universe or the personality; it is not to be studied by special theories which endow it with a further added significance. Instead it should be seen as an unremarkable phenomenon which can be studied in unremarkable ways using unremarkable theories.

John Gagnon summarizes this perspective in the following way:

In any given society, at any given moment in its history, people become sexual in the same way they become everything else. Without much reflection, they pick up directions from their social environment. They acquire and assemble means, skills and the values from the people around them. Their critical choices are often made by going along and drifting. People learn when they are quite young a few of the things that they are expected to be, and continue slowly to accumulate a belief in who they are and ought to be throughout the rest of childhood, adolescence and adulthood. Sexual conduct is learned in the same ways and through the same processes; it is acquired and assembled in human interaction, judged and performed in specific cultural and historical worlds. [Gagnon 1977, p. 2]

If this is the case for sexuality in general, then it is true for homosexuality in particular. If we have devised 'peculiar theories' to deal with homosexuality in the past, then it is only because our stigmatizing culture has blinded us to its 'ordinariness'. As they say:

We have allowed the homosexuals' sexual object choice to dominate and control our imagery of him and have let this aspect of his total life experience appear to determine all his products, concerns and activities.

. . . It is necessary to move away from an obsessive concern with the sexuality of the individual, and attempt to see the homosexual in terms of the broader attachments that he must make to live in the world around him. Like the heterosexual, the homosexual must come to terms with the problems that are attendant upon being a member of a society. . . . [Simon and Gagnon 1967]

The reorientation of questions is thus set up: discard the socially imposed label and seek the overlap and continuity of homosexual experience with everyday life. The labelling theorist's awareness of the relativity of labels permits this distancing process.

Enter the gay militant: from 'pathology' to 'oppression'

The problems and perspectives established by sociologists during the 1950s and 1960s became empirically and conceptually clarified during the 1970s. The early gay community studies led to detailed investigation of every nook and cranny of male homosexual life – from sex in the sauna (for example, Weinberg and Williams 1975; Styles 1979) to homosexual drive-ins (Ponte 1974; Levine 1979b) and to some exploratory work into the lesbian community (for example, Wolf 1979). The early concern with societal reactions led to studies which documented – and sometimes tried to explain – the hostility towards homosexuality (Levitt and Klassen 1974, Lehne 1975). The discussion of the 'homosexual role' led to a turn away from questions of aetiology and pathology to an increasing concern with adult homosexual socialization patterns and 'coming out' (Dank, 1971).

It would be quite wrong, however, to see all the recent work flowing out of the 'labelling concerns' of the 1960s. There has been significant discontinuity – brought about by the eruption of the gay and feminist movements during the late 1960s – and a new, avowedly political set of issues have been brought into focus. At the early meetings of the gay movement in England, for instance, the realization that one was collectively oppressed rather than individually disturbed set new and urgent questions. What forces were at work in our oppression? For how long had this been going on? Why had nobody done anything about it before? Why did the majority of gays still refuse to 'fight'? Was there any connection between capitalism and gay oppression? How did the evolving analysis by feminists of patriarchy and sexism relate to gay oppression? What were the best tactics to resist and overthrow oppression? Looking back – a decade later – the questions seem a little naive. Yet while all kinds of 'answers' may now have been given to each one,[9] they have generally been highly personal and polemical. Only a few studies – Altman's *Homosexual: Liberation and Oppression*, Week's *Coming Out*, Katz's *Gay American History*, Hocquenghem's *Homosexual Desire* and Adam's *The Survival of Domination* among them – have been sufficiently sustained and balanced to qualify as social science. What has nevertheless happened in the past decade is a significant enlargement of the inheritance bestowed by labelling theorists. And in many ways it is a major indictment of the professional elite of academic sociologists whose epistemological, methodological and theoretical disputes are a far cry from the daily struggles of oppressed minorities all over the world. The academic's ultimate duty may be to provide balance, equivocation and delay among vastly competing urgent claims to 'truth' (see Halmos 1979), but if he or she is unable even to grasp certain sides of the debate and to raise certain problems in the first instance (and arguably 'the homosexual's' side has only recently been heard), then that level of balance which is the academic's task must remain an impossibility. We should be clear then that it was only once the sociologists got near to the gay movement and heard the debates going on (and in many cases – myself included – 'gays' and 'sociologist' became synonymous) that they were able to pose the additional questions of 'gay oppression'. It is interesting to ponder whether sociologists would have asked such questions had a gay movement never occurred.

Sociology and homosexuality: the future

In briefly chronicling the past thirty years of sociological inquiry into homosexuality and the significant problems it has raised largely in opposition to the dominant clinical paradigm, I have perhaps failed to make clear just what a minority concern such research is within sociology. A selective account like mine could lead the reader to suppose that the world of sociology is peopled with many investigators into homosexuality, but such a perception would be a serious distortion. Look at any textbook in sociology, review any course reading lists (even those dealing with 'deviance' or 'sexual divisions'), go to any sociological conference. Rarely, if ever, will you hear homosexuality mentioned; almost never would you hear a sustained discussion. Although a few American sociologists – through the Gay Sociologists' Caucus[10] – have tried to counteract this 'heterosexual hegemony', it remains overwhelmingly true that homosexuality is largely hidden from sight.

Many sociologists would argue that such neglect was most appropriate. Some would do so for the suspect reason that homosexuality was a 'contaminated' and invalid area of study, but most would probably simply assert that there were other, more pressing theoretical tasks at hand and that in any event 'homosexuality' simply does not constitute a coherent field of inquiry.

I have some sympathy with this latter view point. It may well be that to study homosexuality is to reinforce its separate existence in the world and to remain blind to the connections between homosexuality and other forms of oppression, domination and categorization. A sociology of homosexuality may be a necessary half-way house on the road to understanding wider issues of social meaning, social order and social change, but it should not be an end in itself.

Several paths of study can hence be predicted for the future, paths which hopefully more sociologists will be willing to confront. The first – and most apparent – lies in the field of feminist thought and sexual divisions (see Faraday, Chapter 5). The last decade has thoroughly documented that every aspect of sociology in the past (including gay research) has been coloured by its vantage point of masculinity; women, like gays, have been hidden and of little concern. Yet it is also true that the past decade has seen the emergence of a vast area of inquiry into 'sexual divisions', 'women's studies' and the like – courses, investigations, theories and journals which aim to clarify multiple aspects of the gender stratification system. Same-sex experiences show, fleetingly, a world where sexual divisions as we know them are somewhat transformed: women loving women, men loving men. Does 'homosexuality' as currently defined lead to a reinforcement of sexual divisions – passivity amongst women, dominance amongst men – or does it lead to a glimpse of a future where equal relationships are possible – where two contemporary women may engage one another in equal but 'objectificatory' sex for pleasure because both are equal in a way that men–women relationships are currently not?[11]

A second line of inquiry has been heralded by Barry Adam's *The Survival of Domination: Inferiorization and Everyday Life* (1978). In this study he acknowledges that his main intellectual problem is that of 'order', but his special concerns lie with 'inferiorized, dominated or subordinated' groups: with the ways in which their life chances are structurally restricted, their mental lives devalued and with the strategies they employ to cope with domination and/or resist it. These are not new themes; most sociology routinely confronts such problems through its discussion of class. But Adams hardly mentions this obsession of most sociologists – for him, the groups of concern are blacks, Jews and gays – and he challenges sociologists to continue ignoring these other immense sources of suffering:

If radical theory is not to ossify into yet another ideal straightjacket contorting the material world, the historically changing political relationship founding suffering and alienation cannot be ignored. Particularization of the politics of oppression to the ideal type of the nineteenth-century English working class fails to recognize the universality of capitalism as a system of domination. This narrowness has contributed to notorious neglect by the 'Left' of oppressed classes such as those examined here (viz. blacks, gays, jews). [Adams 1978, p. 129]

'Sexual divisions' and 'systems of domination' are then two problematics worthy of expansion which can incorporate homosexuality into their analysis at a central point.

There are many other perspectives from which this may be done, and one more should be mentioned here since it is closest to my own area of inquiry, informs much of this book and brings my discussion full circle. It is the problem of labelling.

Labelling and ambiguity

There is nothing so unthinkable as thought, unless it be the entire absence of thought.[12]

Labelling theory has slowly developed into a received wisdom in sociology, but in their attempts to render it operationable, sociologists have often lost the core of its problem. For the root issue, for me, is to grasp the way in which the world is simultaneously necessarily contingent upon orderly categories through which we may grasp it and how simultaneously such categories invariably restrict our experiences and serve material forces of domination and control. We cannot live without them but living with them is a horror! Categorization is paradoxical: it aids and it destroys.

The category 'homosexual' is only one of a gallery of sexual types; 'paedophiles', 'transsexuals', 'fetishists', 'sado-masochists' are others that have been invented over the past century (see Foucault 1979). And with all these categorizations comes the paradox: they control, restrict and inhibit whilst simultaneously providing comfort, security and assuredness.[13] On an even wider scale, categorizations are attempts to order and structure the chaotic, complex and undifferentiated. To search for complexity is to undo categorization; to search for order is to categorize. Both seem necessary and thereby hangs the twist.

This book is actually lodged in that twist. It persistently strains to debunk the category of 'homosexual', to show its relativity, its historical sources, its changing meaning and – overwhelmingly – its damaging impact on human experience. Yet *at the current moment* it also tacitly finds it hard to believe that 'liberated, joyful homosexuals' could ever have attained their 'liberation' without that label. It is a theme which haunts this book and will probably haunt inquiries to come.

2 The homosexual role*

Mary McIntosh

Recent advances in the sociology of deviant behaviour have not yet affected the study of homosexuality, which is still commonly seen as a condition characterizing certain persons in the way that birthplace or deformity might characterize them. The limitations of this view can best be understood if we examine some of its implications. In the first place, if homosexuality is a condition, then people either have it or do not have it. Many scientists and ordinary people assume that there are two kinds of people in the world: homosexuals and heterosexuals. Some of them recognize that homosexual feelings and behaviour are not confined to the persons they would like to call 'homosexuals' and that some of these persons do not actually engage in homosexual behaviour. This should pose a crucial problem, but they evade the crux by retaining their assumption and puzzling over the question of how to tell whether someone is 'really' homosexual or not. Lay people too will discuss whether a certain person is 'queer' in much the same way as they might question whether a certain pain indicated cancer. And in much the same way they will often turn to scientists or to medical men for a surer diagnosis. The scientists, for their part, feel it incumbent on them to seek criteria for diagnosis.

Thus one psychiatrist, discussing the definition of homosexuality, has written:

I do not diagnose patients as homosexual unless they have engaged in overt homosexual behaviour. Those who also engage in heterosexual activity are diagnosed as bisexual. An isolated experience may not warrant the diagnosis, but repetetive (sic) homosexual behaviour in

*This essay first appeared in *Social Problems*, vol. 16, no. 2 (Fall 1968) and is reprinted here with permission of *Social Problems* and the Society for the Study of Social Problems.

adulthood, whether sporadic or continuous, designates a homosexual. [Bieber 1965, p. 248]

Along with many other writers, he introduces the notion of a third type of person, the 'bisexual', to handle the fact that behaviour patterns cannot be conveniently dichotomized into heterosexual and homosexual. But this does not solve the conceptual problem, since bisexuality too is seen as a condition (unless as a passing response to unusual situations such as confinement in a one-sex prison). In any case there is no extended discussion of bisexuality; the topic is usually given a brief mention in order to clear the ground for the consideration of 'true homosexuality'.

To cover the cases where the symptoms of behaviour or of felt attractions do not match the diagnosis, other writers have referred to an adolescent homosexual phase or have used such terms as 'latent homosexual' or 'pseudo homosexual'. Indeed one of the earliest studies of the subject, by Krafft-Ebing (1965), was concerned with making a distinction between the 'invert' who is congenitally homosexual and others who, although they behave in the same way, are not true inverts.

A second result of the conceptualization of homosexuality as a condition is that the major research task has been seen as the study of its aetiology. There has been much debate as to whether the condition is innate or acquired. The first step in such research has commonly been to find a sample of 'homosexuals' in the same way that a medical researcher might find a sample of diabetics if he wanted to study that disease. Yet after a long history of such studies, the results are sadly inconclusive, and the answer is still as much a matter of opinion as it was when Havelock Ellis's *Sexual Inversion* was published seventy years ago. The failure of research to answer the question has not been due to lack of scientific rigour or to any inadequacy of the available evidence; it results rather from the fact that the wrong question has been asked. One might as well try to trace the aetiology of 'committee chairmanship' or 'Seventh Day Adventism' as of 'homosexuality'.

The vantage point of comparative sociology enables us to see that the conception of homosexuality as a condition is, in itself, a possible object of study. This conception and the behaviour it supports operate as a form of social control in a society in which homosexuality is condemned. Furthermore the uncritical acceptance of the conception by social scientists can be traced to their concern with homosexuality as a social problem. They have tended to accept the popular definition of what the problem is, and they have been implicated in the process of social control.

The practice of the social labelling of persons as deviant operates in two ways as a mechanism of social control.[1] In the first place it helps to provide a clear-cut, publicized and recognizable threshold between permissible and impermissible behaviour. This means that people cannot so easily drift into deviant behaviour. Their first moves in a deviant direction immediately raise the question of a total move into a deviant role with all the sanctions that this is likely to elicit. Second, the labelling serves to segregate the deviants from others, and this means that their deviant practices and their self-justifications for these practices are contained within a relatively narrow group. The creation of a specialized, despised and punished role of homosexual keeps the bulk of society pure in rather the same way that the similar treatment of some kinds of criminals helps keep the rest of society law-abiding.

However, the disadvantage of this practice as a technique of social control is that there may be a tendency for people to become fixed in their deviance once they have become labelled. This too is a process that has become well-recognized in discussion of other forms of deviant behaviour, such as juvenile delinquency and drug taking, and indeed of other kinds of social labelling, such as streaming in schools and racial distinctions. One might expect social categorizations of this sort to be to some extent self-fulfilling prophecies: if the culture defines people as falling into distinct types – black and white, criminal and non-criminal, homosexual and normal – then these types will tend to become polarized, highly differentiated from each other. Later in this paper I shall discuss whether this is so in the case of homosexuals and 'normals' in the United States today.

It is interesting to notice that homosexuals themselves welcome and support the notion that homosexuality is a condition. For just as the rigid categorization deters people from drifting into deviancy, so it appears to foreclose on the possibility of drifting back into normality and thus removes the element of anxious choice. It appears to justify the deviant behaviour of the homosexual as being appropriate for him as a member of the homosexual category. The deviancy can thus be seen as legitimate for him and he can continue in it without rejecting the norms of the society.[2]

The way in which people become labelled as homosexual can now be seen as an important social process connected with mechanisms of social control. It is important therefore that sociologists should examine this process objectively and not lend themselves to participation in it, particularly since, as we have seen, psychologists and psychiatrists on the whole have not retained their objectivity but have become involved as diagnostic agents in the process of social labelling.[3]

It is proposed that the homosexual should be seen as playing a social role rather than as having a condition. The role of 'homosexual', however, does not simply describe a sexual behaviour pattern. If it did, the idea of a role would be no more useful than that of a condition. For the purpose of introducing the term 'role' is to enable us to handle the fact that behaviour in this sphere does not match popular beliefs: that sexual behaviour patterns cannot be dichotomized in the way that the social roles of homosexual and heterosexual can.

It may seem rather odd to distinguish in this way between role and behaviour, but if we accept a definition of role in terms of expectations (which may or may not be fulfilled), then the distinction is both legitimate and useful. In modern societies where a separate homosexual role is recognized, the expectation, on behalf of those who play the role and of others, is that a homosexual will be exclusively or very predominantly homosexual in his feelings and behaviour. In addition there are other expectations that frequently exist, especially on the part of nonhomosexuals, but affecting the self-conception of anyone who sees himself as homosexual. These are the expectation that he will be effeminate in manner, personality, or preferred sexual activity, the expectation that sexuality will play a part of some kind in all his relations with other men, and the expectation that he will be attracted to boys and very young men and probably willing to seduce them. The existence of a social expectation, of course, commonly helps to produce its own fulfilment. But the question of how far it is fulfilled is a matter for empirical investigation rather than *a priori* pronouncement. Some of the empirical evidence about the chief expectation – that homosexuality precludes heterosexuality – in relation to the homosexual role in America is examined in the final section of this paper.[4]

In order to clarify the nature of the role and demonstrate that it exists only in certain societies, we shall present the cross-cultural and historical evidence available. This raises awkward problems of method because the material has hitherto usually been collected and analysed in terms of culturally specific modern Western conceptions.

The homosexual role in various societies

To study homosexuality in the past or in other societies we usually have to rely on secondary evidence rather than on direct observation. The reliability and the validity of such evidence is open to question because what the original observers reported may have been distorted by their disapproval of homosexuality and by their definition of it, which may be different from the one we wish to adopt.

For example, Marc Daniel (1965) tries to refute accusations of homosexuality against Pope Julian II by producing four arguments: the Pope had many enemies who might wish to blacken his name; he and his supposed lover, Alidosi, both had mistresses; neither of them was at all effeminate; and the Pope had other men friends about whom no similar accusations were made. In other words Daniel is trying to fit an early sixteenth century Pope to the modern conception of the homosexual as effeminate, exclusively homosexual and sexual in relation to all men. The fact that he does not fit is, of course, no evidence, as Daniel would have it, that his relationship with Alidosi was not a sexual one.

Anthropologists too can fall into this trap. Marvin Opler, summarizing anthropological evidence on the subject, says:

Actually, no society, save perhaps Ancient Greece, pre-Meiji Japan, certain top echelons in Nazi Germany, and the scattered examples of such special status groups as the *berdaches*, Nata slaves, and one category of Chuckchee shamans, has lent sanction in any real sense to homosexuality. [1965, p. 174]

Yet he goes on to discuss societies in which there are reports of sanctioned adolescent and other occasional 'experimentation'. Of the Cubeo of the North West Amazon, for instance, he says, '*true* homosexuality among the Cubeo is rare if not absent', giving as evidence the fact that no males with persistent homosexual patterns are reported (Opler 1965, p. 117).

Allowing for such weaknesses, the Human Relations Area Files are the best single source of comparative information. Their evidence on homosexuality has been summarized by Ford and Beach (1952), who identify two broad types of accepted patterns: the institutionalized homosexual role and the liaison between men and boys who are otherwise heterosexual.

The recognition of a distinct role of *berdache* or transvestite is, they say, 'the commonest form of institutionalized homosexuality'. This form shows a marked similarity to that in our own society, though in some ways it is even more extreme. The Mojave Indians of California and Arizona, for example, recognized both an *alyhā*, a male transvestite who took the role of the woman in sexual intercourse, and a *hwamē*, a female homosexual who took the role of the male (Devereux 1937). People were believed to be born as *alyhā* or *hwamē*, hints of their future proclivities occurring in their mothers' dreams during pregnancy. If a young boy began to behave like a girl and take an interest in women's things instead of men's, there was an initiation ceremony in which he would become an *alyhā*. After that he would dress and act like a woman, would be referred to as 'she' and could take 'husbands'.

But the Mojave pattern differs from ours in that although the *alyhā* was considered regrettable and amusing, he was not condemned and was given public recognition. The attitude was that 'he was an *alyhā*, he could not help it'. But the 'husband' of an *alyhā* was an ordinary man who happened to have chosen an *alyhā*, perhaps because they were good housekeepers or because they were believed to be 'lucky in love', and he would be the butt of endless teasing and joking.

This radical distinction between the feminine, passive homosexual and his masculine, active partner is one which is not made very much in our own society,[5] but which is very important in the Middle East. There, however, neither is thought of as being a 'born' homosexual, although the passive partner, who demeans himself by his feminine submission, is despised and ridiculed while the active one is not. In most of the ancient Middle East, including among the Jews until the return from the Babylonian exile, there were male temple prostitutes

(Taylor 1965a; Henriques 1962, pp. 341–3). Thus even cultures that recognize a separate homosexual role may not define it in the same way as our culture does.

Many other societies accept or approve of homosexual liaisons as part of a variegated sexual pattern. Usually these are confined to a particular stage in the individual's life. Among the Aranda of Central Australia, for instance, there are long-standing relationships of several years' duration between unmarried men and young boys, starting at the age of 10 to 12 years (Ford and Beach 1952, p. 132). This is rather similar to the well-known situation in classical Greece, but there, of course, the older man could have a wife as well. Sometimes, however, as among the Siwans of North Africa (Ford and Beach 1952, pp. 131–2), all men and boys can and are expected to engage in homosexual activities, apparently at every stage of life. In all of these societies there may be much homosexual behaviour, but there are no 'homosexuals'.

The development of the homosexual role in England

The problem of method is even more acute in dealing with historical material than with anthropological, for history is usually concerned with 'great events' rather than with recurrent patterns. There are some records of attempts to curb sodomy among minor churchmen during the medieval period (May 1938, pp. 65, 101), which seem to indicate that it was common. At least they suggest that laymen feared on behalf of their sons that it was common. The term 'catamite', meaning 'boy kept for immoral purposes', was first used in 1593, again suggesting that this practice was common then. But most of the historical references to homosexuality relate either to great men or to great scandals. However, over the last seventy years or so various scholars have tried to trace the history of sex,[6] and it is possible to glean a good deal from what they have found and also from what they have failed to establish.

Their studies of English history before the seventeenth century consist usually of inconclusive speculation as to whether certain men, such as Edward II, Christopher Marlowe, William Shakespeare, were or were not homosexual. Yet the disputes are inconclusive not because of lack of evidence but because none of these men fits the modern stereotype of the homosexual.

It is not until the end of the seventeenth century that other kinds of information become available, and it is possible to move from speculations about individuals to descriptions of homosexual life. At this period references to homosexuals as a type and to a rudimentary homosexual subculture, mainly in London, begin to appear. But the earliest descriptions of homosexuals do not coincide exactly with the modern conception. There is much more stress on effeminacy and in particular on transvestism, to such an extent that there seems to be no distinction at first between transvestism and homosexuality.[7] The terms emerging at this period to describe homosexuals – Molly, Nancy-boy, Madge-cull – emphasize effeminacy. In contrast the modern terms – like fag, queer, gay, bent – do not have this implication.[8]

By the end of the seventeenth century, homosexual transvestites were a distinct enough group to be able to form their own clubs in London.[9] Edward Ward's *History of the London Clubs* (1896), first published in 1709, describes one called 'The Mollie's Club' which met 'in a certain tavern in the City' for 'parties and regular gatherings'. The members 'adopt[ed] all the small vanities natural to the feminine sex to such an extent that they try to speak, walk, chatter, shriek and scold as women do, aping them as well in other respects'. The other respects apparently included the enactment of marriages and childbirth. The club was discovered and broken up by agents of the Reform Society (Taylor 1965b). There were a number of similar scandals during the course of the eighteenth century as various homosexual coteries were exposed.

A writer in 1729 describes the widespread homosexual life of the period:

They also have their Walks and Appointments, to meet and pick up one another, and their particular Houses of Resort to go to, because they dare not trust themselves in an open Tavern. About twenty of these sort of Houses have been discovered, besides the Nocturnal Assemblies of great numbers of the like vile Persons, what they call the Markets, which are the Royal Exchange, Lincoln's Inn, Bog Houses, the south side of St James's Park, the Piazzas in Covent Garden, St Clement's Churchyard, etc.

It would be a pretty scene to behold them in their clubs and cabals, how they assume the air and affect the name of Madam or Miss, Betty or Molly, with a chuck under the chin, and 'Oh you bold pullet, I'll break your eggs', and then frisk and walk away. [Taylor 1965a, p. 142]

The notion of exclusive homosexuality became well established during this period:

> two Englishmen, Leith and Drew, were accused of paederasty. . . . The evidence given by the plaintiffs was, as was generally the case in these trials, very imperfect. On the other hand the defendants denied the accusation, and produced witnesses to prove their predeliction for women. They were in consequence acquitted. [Bloch 1938, p. 334]

This could only have been an effective argument in a society that perceived homosexual behaviour as incompatible with heterosexual tastes.

During the nineteenth century there are further reports of raided clubs and homosexual brothels. However, by this time the element of transvestism had diminished in importance. Even the male prostitutes are described as being of masculine build, and there is more stress upon sexual licence and less upon dressing up and play-acting.

The homosexual role and homosexual behaviour

Thus a distinct, separate, specialized role of 'homosexual' emerged in England at the end of the seventeenth century, and the conception of homosexuality as a condition which characterizes certain individuals and not others is now firmly established in our society. The term role is, of course, a form of shorthand. It refers not only to a cultural conception or set of ideas but also to a complex of institutional arrangements which depend upon and reinforce these ideas. These arrangements include all the forms of heterosexual activity, courtship and marriage as well as the labelling processes – gossip, ridicule, psychiatric diagnosis, criminal conviction – and the groups and networks of the homosexual subculture. For simplicity we shall simply say that a specialized role exists.

How does the existence of this social role affect actual behaviour? And, in particular, does the behaviour of individuals conform to the cultural conception in the sense that most people are either exclusively heterosexual or exclusively homosexual? It is difficult to answer these questions on the basis of available evidence because so many researchers have worked with the preconception that homosexuality is a condition, so that in order to study the behaviour they have first found a group of people who could be identified as 'homosexuals'. Homosexual behaviour should be studied independently of social roles, if the connection between the two is to be revealed.

This may not sound like a particularly novel programme to those who are familiar with Kinsey's contribution to the field. He, after all, set out to study 'sexual behaviour'; he rejected the assumptions of scientists and laymen:

> that there are persons who are 'heterosexual' and persons who are 'homosexual', that these two types represent antitheses in the sexual world and that there is only an insignificant class of 'bisexuals' who occupy an intermediate position between the other groups ... that every individual is innately – inherently – either heterosexual or homosexual ... (and) that from the time of birth one is fated to be one thing or the other .... [1948, pp. 636–7]

But although some of Kinsey's ideas are often referred to, particularly in polemical writings, surprisingly little use has been made of his actual data.

Most of Kinsey's chapter on the 'Homosexual outlet' centres on his 'heterosexual–homosexual rating scale'. His subjects were rated on this scale according to the proportion of their 'psychologic reactions and overt experience' that was homosexual in any given period of their lives. It is interesting, and unfortunate for our purposes, that this is one of the few places in the book where Kinsey abandons his behaviouristic approach to some extent. However, 'psychologic reactions' may well be expected to be affected by the existence of a social role in the same way as overt behaviour. Another problem with using Kinsey's material is that although he gives very full information about sexual behaviour, the other characteristics of the people he interviewed are only given in a very bald form.[10] But Kinsey's study is undoubtedly the fullest description there is of sexual behaviour in any society, and as such it is the safest basis for generalizations to other Western societies.

The ideal way to trace the effects on behaviour of the existence of a homosexual role would be to compare societies in which the role exists with societies in which it does not. But as there are no adequate descriptions of homosexual behaviour in societies where there is no homosexual role, we shall have to substitute comparisons within American society.

Polarization

If the existence of a social role were reflected in people's behaviour, we should expect to find that relatively few people would engage in bisexual behaviour. The problem about investigating this empirically is to know what is meant by 'relatively few'. The categories of Kinsey's rating scale are, of course, completely arbitrary. He has five bisexual categories, but he might just as well have had more or less, in which case the number falling into each would have been smaller or larger. The fact that the distribution of his scale is U-shaped, then, is in itself meaningless (see Table A).

It is impossible to get direct evidence of a polarization between the homosexual and the heterosexual pattern, though we may note the suggestive evidence to the contrary that at every age far more men have bisexual than exclusively homosexual patterns. However, by making comparisons between one age group and another and between men and women, it should be possible to see some of the effects of the role.

Age comparison

As they grow older, more and more men take up exclusively heterosexual patterns, as Table A, column 2 shows. The table also shows that *each* of the bisexual and homosexual categories, columns 3–8, contains fewer men as time goes by after the age of 20. The greatest losses are from the fifth bisexual category, column 7, with responses that are 'almost entirely homosexual'. It is a fairly small group to begin with, but by the age of 45 it has almost entirely disappeared. On the other hand, the first bisexual category, column 3, with only 'incidental homosexual histories' has its numbers not even halved by the age of 45. Yet at all ages the first bisexual category represents a much smaller proportion of those who are almost entirely heterosexual (columns 2 and 3) than the fifth category represents of those who are almost entirely homosexual (columns 7 and 8). In everyday language it seems that proportionately more 'homosexuals' dabble in heterosexual activity than 'heterosexuals' dabble in homosexual activity and such dabbling is particularly common in the younger age groups of 20 to 30. This indicates that the existence of the despised role operates at

Table A *Heterosexual–homosexual rating: active incidence by age*

	% of each age group of male population having each rating								
	(1) X	(2) 0	(3) 1	(4) 2	(5) 3	(6) 4	(7) 5	(8) 6	(9) 1–6
Age									
15	23.6	48.4	3.6	6.0	4.7	3.7	2.6	7.4	28.0
20	3.3	69.3	4.4	7.4	4.4	2.9	3.4	4.9	27.4
25	1.0	79.2	3.9	5.1	3.2	2.4	2.3	2.9	19.8
30	0.5	83.1	4.0	3.4	2.1	3.0	1.3	2.6	16.4
35	0.4	86.7	2.4	3.4	1.9	1.7	0.9	2.6	12.9
40	1.3	86.8	3.0	3.6	2.0	0.7	0.3	2.3	11.9
45	2.7	88.8	2.3	2.0	1.3	0.9	0.2	1.8	8.5

X = unresponsive to either sex; 0 = entirely heterosexual; 1 = largely heterosexual but with incidental homosexual history; 2 = largely heterosexual but with a distinct homosexual history; 3 = equally heterosexual and homosexual; 4 = largely homosexual but with distinct heterosexual history; 5 = largely homosexual but with incidental heterosexual history; 6 = entirely homosexual.

Source: Based on Kinsey *et al.* (1948), p. 652, Table 148.

all ages to inhibit people from engaging in occasional homosexual behaviour, but does not have the effect of making the behaviour of many 'homosexuals' exclusively homosexual.

On the other hand, the overall reduction in the amount of homosexual behaviour with age can be attributed in part to the fact that more and more men become married. While the active incidence of homosexual behaviour is high and increases with age among single men, among married men it is low and decreases only slightly with age. Unfortunately the Kinsey figures do not enable us to compare the incidence of homosexuality among single men who later marry and those who do not.

Comparison of men and women

The notion of a separate homosexual role is much less well developed in women than it is for men, and so too are the attendant techniques of social control and the deviant subculture and organization. So a comparison with women's sexual behaviour should tell us something about the effects of the social role on men's behaviour.

Fewer women than men engage in homosexual behaviour. By the time they are 45, 26 per cent of women have had some homosexual experience, whereas about 50 per cent of men have. But this is probably a cause rather than an effect of the difference in the extent to which the homosexual role is

Table B   *Comparison of male and female heterosexual–homosexual ratings: active incidence at selected ages*

| | | \% of each age group having each rating | | | | | | | | |
| | | (1) X | (2) 0 | (3) 1 | (4) 2 | (5) 3 | (6) 4 | (7) 5 | (8) 6 | (9) 1–6 |
Age										
Male	20	3.3	69.3	4.4	7.4	4.4	2.9	3.4	4.9	27.4
Female		15	74	5	2	1	1	1	1	11
Male	35	0.4	86.7	2.4	3.4	1.9	1.7	0.9	2.6	12.9
Female		7	80	7	2	1	1	1	1	13

Source: Based on Kinsey *et al.* (1948), p. 652, Table 148, and Kinsey (1953), p. 499, Table 142. For explanation of the ratings, see Table A.

crystallized, for women engage in less non-marital sexual activity of any kind than men. For instance, by the time they marry, 50 per cent of women have had some pre-marital heterosexual experience to orgasm, whereas as many as 90 per cent of men have.

The most revealing contrast is between the male and female distributions on the Kinsey rating scale, shown in Table B. The distributions for women follow a smooth U-shaped pattern, while those for men are uneven with an increase in numbers at the exclusively homosexual end. The distributions for women are the shape that one would expect on the assumption that homosexual and heterosexual acts are randomly distributed in a ratio of 1 to 18.[11] The men are relatively more concentrated in the exclusively homosexual category. This appears to confirm the hypothesis that the existence of the role is reflected in behaviour.

Finally, it is interesting to notice that although at the age of 20 far more men than women have homosexual and bisexual patterns (27 per cent as against 11 per cent), by the age of 35 the figures are both the same (13 per cent). Women seem to broaden their sexual experience as they get older whereas more men become narrower and more specialized.

None of this, however, should obscure the fact that, in terms of behaviour, the polarization between the heterosexual man and the homosexual man is far from complete in our society. Some polarization does seem to have occurred, but many men manage to follow patterns of sexual behaviour that are between the two, in spite of our cultural preconceptions and institutional arrangements.

Conclusion

This paper has dealt with only one small aspect of the sociology of homosexuality. It is, nevertheless, a fundamental one. For it is not until he sees homosexuals as a social category, rather than a medical or psychiatric one, that the sociologist can begin to ask the right questions about the specific content of the homosexual role and about the organization and functions of homosexual groups.[12] All that has been done here is to indicate that the role does not exist in many societies, that it only emerged in England towards the end of the seventeenth century, and that, although the existence of the role in modern America appears to have some effect on the distribution of homosexual behaviour, such behaviour is far from being monopolized by persons who play the role of homosexual.

Postscript: 'the homosexual role' revisited

Jeffrey Weeks and Kenneth Plummer interview Mary McIntosh

PLUMMER: In writing 'The homosexual role', how much were you influenced by the specific circumstances of the period, the debate around the campaign to change the law on homosexuality in Britain?

MCINTOSH: I was very much concerned about that because it seemed to me that the work I was doing and the position I was taking up ran counter to the arguments that were being put for law reform at the time. People like Leo Abse, who was the spokesman for law reform in the House of Commons, were adopting a sickness perspective. They were putting forward the view that homosexuals could not help being homosexual; it was just how nature made them, or at least something that happened in very early childhood and that all societies have their homosexuals, so there should not be laws against homosexual behaviour. Certainly Leo Abse held that view in a very developed sort of way. I remember writing a letter to the Homosexual Law Reform Society at one stage, supporting the cause in general, but saying that I had a lot of reservations about the nature of the argument that they were putting forward because I could not really accept the view that homosexuality was a sickness. And they wrote back and said they had a lot of sympathy with my position but that at that time they had to use the arguments that were suited to the moment. I quite understood that; in fact I was doing some work on Parsons's theory of legitimation, and I wrote a seminar paper around that time about types of legitimation in which I compared the type of legitimation that the gay world adopts with the type of legitimation that the homophile movement adopts. It argued that the homophile movement had to seek what Parsons calls 'total legitimation', that is legitimation in terms of the general value system; whereas what the gay world does is to seek legitimation in terms of the sub-culture and simply say 'we don't care what the rest think about us, in terms of our sub-culture being gay is ok' (cf. McIntosh 1965). So I could quite understand why the homophile movement had to use that kind of analysis. I had also read a lot of the American homophile movement's literature – the Mattachine Society and so on – and I could see the same thing going on there. So I felt very diffident about actually publishing anything, because I thought I was right but, on the other hand, this was not the moment to be going round talking about it. It would not contribute to the political developments of the time to say that sort of thing. I think that may be partly why I submitted it to an American journal rather than an English one, because the debates did not have quite the same form there. There wasn't such a hopeful movement for law reform in America at the time. But there is also the fact that I would not have known what journal to publish it in in this country.

PLUMMER: *Social Problems* was presumably very sympathetic to that kind of article at the time?

MCINTOSH: Yes, *Social Problems* was the main forum for labelling theory, though of course my article does not in fact use labelling theory except in a very mechanical way.

PLUMMER: Did your experience of the gay liberation and women's liberation movements affect the way you now see your article?

MCINTOSH: I suppose it did, partly in the sense that I now see it as a very academic article, about men without ever actually saying so. This was because more of the things that you read seem to be about men and it is all much more clear cut. I never really challenged that at all, and that is why I think Annabel Faraday's paper in this volume is so important. She is actually trying to take up that issue, and it is extremely difficult to break away from the existing model. Just as the generic term 'man' applies both to men and to people in general, so the term 'homosexual' applies both to male homosexuals and to homosexuals in general. The assumption always is that we can use the same theories and concepts for female homosexuality but that, for simplicity, we can just talk about men and assume that it applies to women. I now see how unsatisfactory that is.

PLUMMER: But would that mean that with hindsight now you would like to write an article on roughly the same lines called 'the lesbian role', or would you in fact want to write something totally different?

MCINTOSH: It would be totally different. Because I now think that what needs to be understood is heterosexuality and that you can't understand homosexuality without locating it in sexuality in general. When I say heterosexuality I mean marital heterosexuality, which is a core around which everything else must be seen as revolving, either in contrast to it or as a subsidiary form. What I did then was to take heterosexuality for granted, and so accept the whole deviance paradigm and the idea that what needed to be studied was the deviance, even if you recognized deviance as socially constructed too.

PLUMMER: So that, even if you were studying male homosexuality now you would want to study it in terms of masculinity and the family rather than homosexuality?

MCINTOSH: Yes, exactly.

PLUMMER: In a way, though, that is what Gagnon and Simon did say about lesbianism in their article on femininity in a lesbian community, where they said lesbians have much more in common with women than with homosexuality (see Gagnon and Simon 1967b).

MCINTOSH: Yes, but what they don't say is that male homosexuals have much more in common with men than with homosexuality. That is the thing that is taken for granted: the specificity of men and of masculinity is never made problematic. It certainly isn't in my article, and I don't think it has been sufficiently since then. The part that sexuality plays in that specificity of masculinity is quite different from the part that sexuality plays in the specificity of femininity. This does not mean that you need a whole different theoretical baggage for women; what it means is that the theoretical baggage that we have used so far for men is inadequate. Looking at women reveals that, and it should take you back with further questions in relation to male homosexuality. There are also specific research problems about lesbianism, just as there are about women's history in general. Women's place in the private sphere tends to make them relatively invisible so there are problems of documentation, evidence and so on. It also makes interviewing more difficult as there is probably less articulation about sexuality. It is easier to think about male sexuality because it is more separate. But the fact that it is socially conceived as separate, that sexuality for men is socially seen as somewhat separate from the rest of life, does not mean that it is sociologically separate, and does not mean that it is not in fact structured by that very separateness.

WEEKS: Another related problem about your approach is a possible latent essentialism. When you talk about other cultures, for example, the transvestite sub-cultures of a North American Indian tribe, the *berdache*, you imply that transvestism is a role which a homosexual man can fall into as if there is a pre-existing homosexual man that can fall into a transvestite role. The other interpretation that can be drawn from this is that for these tribes the man who dressed in women's clothes and who adopted the women's role wasn't adopting a woman's role as such; he was *actually* a woman in terms of that culture. There's no need for a notion of the homosexual; the transvestite was actually the gender he or she was adopting, a cross-dressed gender.[13] So in a sense there's no homosexual role there, there's no place for the homosexual; it's actually a place for someone who just happens to be a biological man who lives the life of a woman and becomes a woman, where all the myths legitimate his becoming a woman so he can conceive and go through the rituals of giving birth and so on.

MCINTOSH: I think that's true; I think the way I was operating was starting with a very schematic definition of what the modern homosexual role was and going round looking for it in history. In a sense this was very much what I was accusing anthropologists and historians of having done, only I was looking rather more sceptically because I was prepared to find that homosexuals, in the sense of my three characteristics, did not exist as well as that they did exist. But one ought to look at a situation like that of the Mojave Indians in their own terms, that is, not from the perspective of how they differ from us – that's not the most relevant thing to be said about them. I'm not quite sure why that is latent essentialism, though.

PLUMMER: Because it implies that if you look back through history you can pin-point things that seem to have some kind of common core that makes them readily identifiable. But we need to question, what is it that holds all these things together? Why should one even begin to contemplate the notion that the *berdache* has anything at all to do with homosexuality in our terms?

MCINTOSH: Yes, it is like the work of Foucault (1979); it is the history of modern homosexuality. It is only the concern with modern homosexuality that brings those things together, so it is not really history or anthropology, but a use of comparative material to illuminate a contemporary Britain. I think that can be justified to some extent, though I think people need to be very aware that that is what they are doing, and not see it as what anthropology or history ought to be doing or at least not the only thing that anthropology or history could do. It is rather like nineteenth century anthropology, which has quite rightly been rejected by functionalist anthropology.

PLUMMER: As well as the essentialism of anthropologists and historians, there is surely also an essentialism to be found in contemporary clinical work: the assumption that homosexuality is a basic way of being. This view – and it's put forward by sociologists like Whitham – is surely one you'd reject.[14]

MCINTOSH: That's right, he goes back to what he calls homosexual orientation, but it seems to be pre-given somehow. He locates it too early for people to have realized that there's a sub-culture or a role out there. He almost seems to be implying – although he doesn't actually come out and state it – that if it happens that early, if people experience feeling they are gay that early, then it must be pre-social. I would reject the idea that because something happens when you are 2, it is pre-social, because I think what happens to children when they are 1 is social.

PLUMMER: So the fact that a large number of studies of adult homosexuals now point to the idea that as boys and girls they seemed to know at very early ages that they were sexually different would not imply an essential homosexuality?

MCINTOSH: I think it is a really interesting problem. Jeffrey has certainly said this to me, and I imagine that you have experienced the same thing when you have asked people about their life histories, and people do say 'but I knew very early'. It is seen as a fact about themselves, as if they had looked in the mirror and found they had red hair or something. The fact that people do so firmly experience it that way, as some transsexuals say that they do as well, really does seem to me a bit of a problem. But I still don't think that the way people experience things, however strongly it seems to be the case, is evidence that it's essential.

WEEKS: It does highlight the point that Ken mentioned earlier, and you also mention: the necessity of seeing all sexual variations within, in a sense, a controlling form. What we need to look at is gender and sexual arrangements at the societal level, on which all these other parts are in a sense dependent. Possibly the reason that in our culture we feel very strongly at an early age that we are heterosexual or gay may be related to these other social organizations, like the relations between men and women in the culture – so the *berdache* amongst the Mojave Indians might very well have different influences on early childhood which impel people in different directions not to see the need for a separate homosexual role in your terms. There are only men and women. Quite straightforward.

MCINTOSH: I agree, but that is not the end of the question; it is the start of a new one. We have to question what *are* men and women, and not treat that as unproblematical.

Part Two
Directions for Inquiry

3 Homosexual categories: some research problems in the labelling perspective of homosexuality

Kenneth Plummer

This article is primarily concerned with a cluster of recently invented categorizations that purport to locate coherent phenomena. To the scientist such categorizations include 'the inverts', whether 'absolute', 'amphigenic' or 'contingent' (Freud 1977) and 'the homosexual', whether 'pre-oedipal', 'oedipal' or 'pseudo' (Socarides 1978). To the lay person such categorizations include 'queer', 'bender', 'dyke', 'pansy' and 'faggot'. To a small group of people the category now is 'gay'. There is a considerable difference between the first two – which are largely negative and 'other-created' – and the latter – which is positive and 'self-created'[1] – but they all nevertheless point to an external empirical referent which is supposed to be identifiable. I am not at all sure that it exists. Certainly the categories exist; they are applied now (willingly or unwillingly) to millions of people throughout the world, and indeed are also today applied to large numbers of people throughout history. Certainly there is considerable political intent behind the making of such categorizations – to order, control and segregate in the name of benevolence (Gaylin 1978). Certainly too these categories have rendered – in the main – whole groups of people devalued, dishonourable or dangerous, and have frequently justified monstrous human atrocities and the denial of human rights.[2] But these certainties about the categories should not be confused with certainties about the phenomena to which the category refers.

In this article my concern lies with presenting some research suggestions for studying the category *not* the phenomena, and in doing this I am drawing heavily from the labelling *perspective* outlined in Chapter 1. Thus four broad questions need detailed exploration:

1 What is the nature of the homosexual categorizations?

2   When and how did such categorizations emerge?
3   How do they come to be bestowed upon certain behaviours and people?
4   What kind of impact do they have on people once bestowed?

These are large and significant questions which signpost a dramatic turn away from clinical concerns with the phenomena itself. In what follows, I can only treat each question selectively.

The nature of the 'homosexual' category

The starting point of all labelling research must lie with rendering the very categories we use as a problem. In this case we need to know the nature of the diverse and ever changing meanings which people bestow upon 'same sex emotional and erotic encounters',[3] from those who are formally and informally engaged in their control through to those who find the meanings applied to them. What meanings are imputed by specific groups? How do such meanings change in different contexts? What part do such general features as 'stigma' (the devaluation of people) and 'essentializing' (the translation of doing into being) play in the assembling of such meanings? What is the relationship between what people *say* about 'homosexuals' and what people do to them? Answering such questions will turn the researcher away from an oversimplified version of both uniform hostility and identifiable 'types' to a view of the world that is more empirically valid, because it will highlight the multi-tiered, changing, conflicting, confused and contrasting social meanings surrounding same-sex experiences. What is called for here, then, is an ethnography of societal reactions to same sex experiences, a task that has hardly begun.

The issue from above that I would like to consider more fully here concerns the problem of 'essentializing' – of the ways in which 'doing' and 'experiencing' can become consolidated into 'being' through categoric labelling. For two recent trends can be discerned in the clarification of homosexual categories: an essentializing trend from homosexuals themselves and an opposite trend from social scientists.

Essentialism and the gay movement

Most of the articles in this volume agree that a distinct 'homosexual role' now exists in Western capitalist societies which did not exist in earlier historical periods and which does not exist in other cultures now; they differ primarily on *when* that role emerged, *what* its precise content is and *how* it gets translated into people's actual lives. Thus McIntosh sees it emerging in the late seventeenth century, Weeks in the late nineteenth century and Marshall in the mid twentieth. McIntosh focuses on the expectations that 'homosexuals' would be sex-focused, boy-molesting effeminates, Weeks highlights the medicalization of homosexuals, and Marshall links medicalization with the separation of gender from sex.

None of these discussions, however, consider the role and its constitution in the 1970s (although this is Blachford's concern). Yet this is a curious omission for something unusual is happening: the expectations of homosexuality being a 'condition', which were generated in the past by clinicians, are today being sustained and reinforced by gay radicals. It is true liberationists would reject the effeminate, boy-seeking, 'sick' expectations of earlier role portraits, but they still sustain the view that gays are types of being. Indeed Dank has even argued – rightly I believe – that:

the reality constructions created by persons overtly committed to homosexual liberation perform the same functions as the reality constructions of the traditionalists. Specifically, their reality constructions function to homogenise and dehumanise homosexually oriented persons often through the process of deification and at the same time they construct *the* heterosexual as an alien being. Just as the traditionalists have created *the* homosexual and *the* heterosexual so have other persons done so while invoking the rhetoric of homosexual liberation. [Dank 1976, pp. 14–15]

Here, then, Dank extends the McIntosh–Weeks–Marshall argument by showing that the liberationists themselves have started to become key definers of a homosexual role and hence ironically have started to become their own source of regulation. 'Homosexuals' were once regulated and defined by 'experts'; now these experts need no longer do it, for the homosexual has assumed that role for himself or herself. Ghettoized and reified, 'the homosexual' remains firmly under control in 'liberated' capitalism. He and she are being 'pushed' further and further down from the mainstream of society – establishing their own colonies and ghettoes (see Levine 1979a; Humphreys 1979b),[4] rendering their 'gay identities' as increasingly pivotal to their personal world and creating a proliferation of separatist groups, until both mentally and spatially 'the homosexual' exists as a highly restricted and confined species. And even within this world, 'gays' cut themselves off further from each other through the construction of further types: 'men' with 'men', 'women' with 'women', 'effeminates' with 'effeminates' 'S-Ms' with 'S-Ms'. It forms a heady spiral of ever-increasing *self*-categorization as types anticipate an ever increasing self-imposed segregation.[5]

I do not want to be too pessimistic about this trend, for it can be rightly counter-argued that this increasing categorization and segregation, far from being harmful, may have very positive consequences for 'homosexuals' because it is *self*-created and *self*-controlled. Better to live in a self-imposed ghetto than a state-imposed concentration camp! However valid this may be, one should at least be aware that the history of many labels has shown a passage from a benevolent origin to a malevolent consequence, where ostensible humanitarianism has led to a straightjacketing and closure of opportunities to whole groups of people (Gaylin 1978).

The research questions generated by these brief observations are especially crucial for 'radical/critical' criminologists. For they remind us, sociologically, that 'radical' and 'liberating' social movements are never just that; they will always bring their own forms of control. 'Total' freedom and 'total' liberation can only exist in the revolutionary's mind; they are sociological nonsense. And the question that needs asking is whether these movement-based forms of control can be seen to complement or even extend the wider societal forms of control. In this case, as homosexuality appears to be entering a new phase of 'liberation' and 'acceptance' in the Western world, could it be that the control processes prevalent earlier are simply being more firmly extended – only now in a more private manner – by 'homosexuals' themselves?

Decategorization and deconstruction

Along with this invention, classification and expansion of the 'homosexual role' first by clinicians and latterly by homosexuals themselves, another process has been taking place which perpetually aims to subvert the idea that homosexuality is a condition or type of person. It is an underground tradition, yet it is rooted in both classical thinking (which highlighted free will) and more recent sex research. While the 'condition' viewpoint is completely congruent with the mainstream criminological positivism which dominated thinking from the mid nineteenth century to the mid twentieth, this alternative aims to subvert that kind of viewpoint by stressing that *homosexuality is a complex, diffuse experience that anyone may have*. A number of strategies can be located which attempt to reconstruct homosexuality in this fashion. Four such processes can be briefly identified:

1 polymorphous perversity
2 the continuum
3 the normalization
4 the pluralization of identity

Human nature and polymorphous perversity   Although Freud's writings helped in the constitution of 'perverted' types, his underlying imagery – of bisexuality and polymorphous perversity – helps subvert them. For it provides a portrait of people who at least initially are open to a broad range of experiences, who harbour the potential for masculine and feminine conduct, as well as a diffuse sexual pleasure seeking with multiple aims and objects. Of course in Freud's account it is necessary for such world-openness to become canalized, but in the writings of others such restrictions of experience are too high a price to pay (Brown 1959; Marcuse 1955; Altman 1971). In this imagery homosexuality is one component of a more general 'desire' that exists in us all.

Desire emerges in a multiple form, where components are only divisible *a posteriori*, according to how we manipulate it. Just like heterosexual desire, homosexual desire is an arbitrarily frozen frame in an unbroken and polyvocal flux. [Hocquenghem 1978, p. 36]

The belief in this 'diffuse desire' constantly strains against the view that homosexuality is a condition, since this desire is present in us all (see Stambolian and Marks 1979).

The homosexual continuum and homosexualities   It was Kinsey who first clearly argued that 'the world is not to be divided into sheep and goats' and stressed the need to view homosexuality as a seven point continuum with the scaling classification running from zero (exclusive heterosexuality) to six (exclusive homosexuality). The baseline for such a continuum was Kinsey's own empirical findings – based on 16,000 white Americans living in the first decades of this century – who clearly showed the mix of homosexual and heterosexual experiences found in many people's lives. Thus while only 4 per cent of his male population was exclusively homosexual from puberty onwards, 37 per cent experienced homosexuality leading to orgasm at least once in the period between puberty and old age. Further, 30 per cent had at least accidental homosexual experience or reactions during a period of at least three years between the ages of 16 and 55; 25 per cent had more than incidental homosexual experience or reaction during a period of at least three years between the ages of 16 and 55; 18 per cent recollected at least equal amount of homosexual and heterosexual experience during a period of at least three years between the ages of 16 and 55; 13 per cent had more homosexual than heterosexual experience over a period of at least three years; 10 per cent of the men were more or less predominantly homosexual during a period of at least three years between 16 and 55 years, and 8 per cent were exclusively homosexual during a period of at least three years between the ages of 16 and 55. These figures – despite weaknesses – are of homosexual experiences at a time when they were strongly taboo, but they convey the flux, change and diversity of homosexual experiences in human life very well (Kinsey *et al.* 1948 and 1953). Not surprisingly, the more recent 'Kinsey study', specifically focused on homosexuals in the early 1970s in California, reasserts and strengthens this diversity. Bell writes:

In regard to how they (adult homosexuals) rated themselves during adolescence, less than a third of the males rated themselves exclusively homosexual in their sexual behaviours during this entire period; about one third of them were predominantly *heterosexual* in their behaviours at that time. About a third of the males classified themselves as exclusively homosexual in their feelings during the adolescent period, and more than a quarter of them were predominantly *heterosexual* in their feelings at that time. 40% of the males had changes in their feelings and behaviour ratings during adolescence and about one half of them recorded some degree of discrepancy between the two different ratings . . . . Clearly a homosexual is not a homosexual when it comes to their past and present sexual feelings and behaviours. Again, going back to the adolescent career, almost two thirds of both males and females experienced heterosexual arousal; smaller but still relatively large numbers of them did not know what it was like to be aroused sexually by a person of the opposite sex. Among the males who reported both homosexual and heterosexual sexual arousal prior to young adulthood, 54% were sexually aroused by males before they experienced sexual arousal by females; about a quarter of them experienced both forms of arousal during the same year; and a similar number were sexually aroused by a female before they were ever sexually aroused by a male. About two thirds of the white homosexual females were sexually aroused by another female before they experienced heterosexual sexual arousal . . . a lengthy and detailed explanation of a person's self ratings on the Kinsey scale over the course of his or her lifetime can provide rich dividends. It enables both the clinician and the client to get a sense of the ebb and flow of homosexual versus heterosexual experience, to challenge the commonly held assumption that one is *either* homosexual or heterosexual, to consider and to compare the conditions under which homosexual and heterosexual arousal first occurred, to explore a person's reaction to such arousal as well as its behavioural consequences, and to delve into the nature of the client's masturbatory fantasies, cognitional rehearsals, romantic attachments and sexual dreams [Bell 1976b, pp. 8–9]

It should be noted that this continuum highlights the diversity at any moment in time *and* across the life cycle, and leads the authors to advocate the term 'homosexualities' rather than homosexuality.

The 'normalization' of homosexuality   One of the key forces in shaping a 'homosexual type' – discussed by Weeks and Marshall in this book – has been the process of medicalization. In declaring homosexuality a 'disease' and a 'sickness' – albeit in diverse ways – the psychiatrists and physicians effectively found a way of separating out and controlling homosexuality. It became a diagnostic category used to identify a species of person.

But all the time this massive medicalization process has been occurring, another subordinate one has been arguing the reverse. From Freud onwards, a great many psychiatrists, anthropologists, sociologists and psychologists have been arguing that homosexuality 'cannot be classified as an illness' (Freud

1951, p. 787; Crompton 1969; Freedman 1971; Green 1972), and indeed by 1973 this became the considered opinion of the American Psychiatric Association (Freedman *et al.* 1976). There are many good examples of early and recent social scientists trying to break down the idea of homosexuality as a clinical diagnosis and to pin-point the overlaps between homosexualities and heterosexualities. Indeed most recently leading practitioners from all scientific spheres have converged on the position that homosexuality is not a sickness. Thus alongside the recent work of the Kinsey Institute referred to above, the founding 'fathers' of sex therapy – Masters and Johnson – have also been studying homosexuality, both highlighting the functional equivalence of homosexuality and heterosexuality and stressing that 'therapists must realize homosexuality is not a disease' (Masters and Johnson 1979, p. 272).

A further, very lucid discussion is provided in the work of Robert Stoller, who crucially distinguishes between labels as social forces and psychiatric diagnoses, and then proceeds to consider whether homosexual categories are valid in the second sense. He suggests a psychiatric diagnosis should, at the least, specify a syndrome (a cluster of visible signs and symptoms), an underlying dynamic and a coherent aetiology from which this dynamic originates. Using such criteria he concludes that:

homosexuality is not a diagnosis; there is only a sexual preference, not a uniform constellation of signs and symptoms; different people with this sexual preference have different psychodynamics underlying their sexual behaviour; quite different life experiences can cause these dynamics and this behaviour [Stoller 1975, p. 199]

There remain many psychiatrists who would firmly reject the work of those like Masters and Johnson, Stoller or the Kinsey Institute and insist that homosexuality is a gross pathology; Socarides's updated text, for instance, does not even consider the possibility that it is anything other than a disease (1978). Nevertheless the lobby to demedicalize homosexuality is both highly visible and highly influential, and is increasingly becoming the dominant 'professional' mode of viewing homosexuality.[6]

The pluralization of identities   Much wider processes – nothing to do with homosexuality *per se* – can also be seen to contribute to this move to 'break down' the constructed homosexual role. At base it is suggested that since industrialization there has been a steady retreat from a public world to a private world of self, family, relationships. A split, which did not formerly exist, has occurred, and individuals who can no longer find support, sustenance or meaning from the public symbols 'retreat' to their own private worlds for 'life-enhancing meanings' (see Sennet 1974; Lasch 1979; Berger *et al.* 1973; Zaretsky 1976; Zijderveld 1971; Brittan 1977; Zurcher 1977). This complex argument – which takes many forms – suggests that in this transition our sense of identities become less stable and more negotiable; we are involved in a 'quest for identity' and part of that quest inevitably entails a view of the open-endedness of identity formation. In the past we were *given* our identities; now we *make* them ourselves (see Berger *et al.* 1973, p. 73).

Such a process takes us full circle for it would seem to hold contradictory implications for the homosexual experience. On the one hand, it suggests that people may experience homosexuality without it becoming a 'master-identity' since all identities are options; on the other, it implies that if individuals elect to call themselves 'homosexuals' in their private worlds, they could then erect this into a life-sustaining 'hero system' (see Becker 1973) around which to organize their lives. It is this peculiar tension which needs much more sustained analysis.

The origins of homosexual categories

The standard 'causal' question in the study of homosexuality has for a long time been: what makes people homosexual? The labelling perspective inverts this causal problem and asks: what makes people respond as they do to homosexuality? Partly the issue is why they should bother to invent a concern for homosexuality at all – why the experience should be recognized as an 'issue' and in our culture translated into a 'way of being'. But the bigger and more central question is why it should often be invested with so much fear, hostility and rage. It is this question that I wish to address here.

At root, there are two main approaches to understanding the origins of the fear of 'homosexuals'; one focuses upon individuals and seeks to explain 'homophobia', and the other focuses upon society and seeks to explain 'the homosexual taboo'. The concept of 'homophobia' – though far from new[7] –

was first explicitly discussed by George Weinberg in the early 1970s. In his book *Society and the Healthy Homosexual* (1973) he defined homophobia as a phobic disease whereby there is a 'dread of being in close quarters with homosexuals' and went on to identify the kind of panic reaction which this phobia can generate, usually in heterosexuals, but sometimes in oppressed homosexuals. Through the use of this concept it is the oppressors of homosexuals who come to be seen as sick, not the homosexuals themselves.[8]

Now as a tactical weapon in the gay movement I think the concept of homophobia contains a number of splendid ironies. At root it employs all the same pseudo-scientific weapons that are used to condemn homosexuality. Thus whereas once it was only the homosexual who was viewed as sick, it is now the heterosexual who is charged with pathology. Whereas once the homosexual was identified by a long series of character traits, it is now possible to identify the traits of the homophobe: authoritarian, cognitively restricted, with gender anxieties (MacDonald and Games 1974). Whereas once the diffuseness of homosexual experiences became channelled down into the idea of the homosexual person, it is now the homophobe who is seen as a special person. Whereas once the homosexual could be discovered by submitting him to a long battery of psychological tests, now the homophobe can be located by the use of homophobe scales – a social distance measure which asks respondents to write their agreement with such statements as 'if a homosexual sat next to me on a bus I would get nervous' and 'a homosexual could be a good president of the United States' (Lumby 1976). Further, whereas once it was the homosexual who got treated for his problem, it is now the sick homophobe who needs a therapist.

While the concept of homophobia may have a symbolic rallying value within the gay movement, as a social science concept it does raise a number of difficulties. Indeed its ironic twist – that is uses the same weapons which used to be employed in attacking homosexuality and applies them to heterosexuality – serves to reinforce much that current social science would now seek to reject. Most notably, four worries can be raised with the current use of the concept: that it reinforces the idea of mental illness, that it neglects women, that it directs attention away from sexual oppression in general and that it individualizes the entire problem.

First, then, it ratifies and strengthens the notion of mental illness. It is curious that in the same year as the American Psychiatric Association struck homosexuality off its sickness nomenclature classification, an American psychologist should create the new disease of homophobia (Weinberg 1973). Now whatever one may think about the current view propounded by the American psychiatrist Szasz[9] – that all mental illness is a myth – it is fair, I think, to say that *certain* problems are better viewed as problems in living rather than sickness. There may be some behavioural variations where notions of sickness are helpful. But the inability of some people to get along with homosexuals hardly seems one of these. If homosexuality is not inherently a sickness, and I obviously don't think it is, then homophobia should not be seen as one either.

A second problem flows from the misogyny frequently embedded in the term. 'Homophobia' is nearly always 'fear of *male* homosexuals', and it is frequently explained as having its origins in threats to masculinity (see Lehne 1976). Not much attention is given to either the 'lesbian threat' (Stanley 1976) or women's responses to gays, thereby reinforcing the persistent male bias of gay research (see Faraday, this volume).

Third, 'homophobia' directs attention to the attack on homosexuals to the detriment of other sexual minority groups, for homosexuals may actually be the least oppressed of all sexual minorities. Our wrath and anger become even greater when confronted with the paedophile, the incestuous father, the sado-masochist and the fetishist. Are we to produce a whole series of new words – 'sadophobia', 'paedophobia', 'fetophobia' – for each of these fears and hostilities, or could they all in some fashion be connected? To focus upon homophobia is to reveal one's own myopia and to do a disservice to the more general attitudes of sexual negativism in society.

Fourth, and most important, the notion of homophobia individualizes the entire problem of homosexual hostility, making it a problem of personalities rather than societies. The approach is reminiscent of that used to study the authoritarian, anti-Semitic, fascist personality by social scientists after the Second World War (Adorno *et al.* 1950). They too saw the problem of minority persecution as the outcome of thwarted personality types, rather than the social generation of a problem which subsequently gets justified through a learned ideology of racism.

While there are a number of difficulties with such a concept, it does highlight one critical feature of some homosexual hostility: its fear-based irrationality. To reduce public hostility to homosexuality cannot simply be seen as a matter of more education or more information, because much of the hostility appears to be a personal defence erected to conceal and keep at bay some terrifying fears and anxieties. How else can one account for some of its public manifestations – all the way from homosexual murder through queer-bashing to media mockery? These responses seem to be thinly veiled responses to fear (sometimes so terrifying that they traumatize the person to murder), and the research issue here is to get at the basis of it. Among the solutions suggested have been the fear of one's own homosexuality (Cory 1953), fear of one's own sex (Lehne 1976), fear of a loss of immortality (Weinberg 1973; Becker 1973) and fear of a loss of status (see Zurcher and Kirkpatrick 1976).

These notions of 'fear' and 'threat' also provide, I believe, a bridge into a wider social explanation – what I have referred to as 'The homosexual taboo' (Plummer 1976) – where the hostility is seen as a widespread social taboo (akin to the incest taboo) rather than as an individualistic phobia. Since few, if any, societies have accepted homosexuality as the major or dominant form of sexual experience, the problem cannot be reduced to the quirks of a few ill-informed or prejudiced individuals; it is more probable that the hostility is bound up with fears about widespread threats to social order, and this hostility becomes more intense under certain forms of social organization.

At the most general (and hence historically non-specific) level of social order, same sex experiences can come under attack because they act as a threat to a society's dominant set of symbols, which provides the overarching canopy of meaning for most of its members: the 'natural order'. People are born into a possibly meaningless universe with an enormous range of potentials and capacities; they could organize and experience the world in a vast assortment of different ways. They could change their identities, values, beliefs, friends, roles and perceptions of the world from day to day; nobody *has* to ritualize and routinize their worlds – everybody *could* do anything. But of course should everybody choose to, the world would become chaotic – a buzzing centre of booming confusion. Confronted with the possibility of new experiences at every minute of the waking day and the likelihood that nobody would know what to expect of anyone, the world would tumble away into chaos (see Scott 1972).

In our minds then we have to cast out these possibilities or else each day would be a Kafkaesque nightmare of unpredictability. To ward off this potential pandemonium, we come to believe that the world could not be otherwise – that it is 'natural' or 'God-given'. We thus make sense of our predicaments by imposing master schemes (symbols) of order upon the world; anything that arises outside of these symbols therefore comes to be seen as a threat to our own personal security and must be either explained away or expelled. We may explain them away by rendering them as anomalies or perversions of the system; calling homosexuals 'sick' serves to neutralize their threat. But when this fails, they need to be ejected from society (imprisoned, deported or killed).

Now in many societies, but notably ours, same sex experiences are one such threat; they shatter much common sense thinking and render the everyday world highly vulnerable. Thus many members of our society have learnt that it is natural 'to fall in love with a person of the opposite sex': 'homosexuals' imply that love need not be so narrowly channelled. Many members come to believe that the 'family is natural': 'homosexuals' imply that people do not have to make families and can live without them. Many members believe that the differences between men and women are instinctive: 'homosexuals' make gender much more ambiguous – men can be gentle and women can be assertive. Many members take it for granted that the lynchpin of morality is 'proper' sexual conduct: 'homosexuals' violate that assumed morality. Many members seek some meaning for their lives and find it in the idea of having children, providing a focus for one's life and a vicarious immortality: 'homosexuals' imply that life can be led without children.

On all these scores then, and others, 'homosexuals' are devastatingly threatening to the 'natural order'. They do not live in families, often cannot have children, muddle up the two gender system and stand in conflict to the assumed morality. 'Homosexuals' are hated because they violate the orderly 'natural world' that is taken for granted by many people.

Of course 'natural orders' are symbolic worlds which differ across cultures and – it can reasonably be argued – within

cultures once industrialization, bureaucratization and urban
diversity have set in. (Berger *et al.* 1973). So to say that
homosexuality constitutes a threat to the 'natural order' is not to
say it constitutes the same threat to all such orders. Indeed it is
likely that the more diffuse, complex, divergent and ambiguous
the symbolic order (in other words, the less simple and rigid),
the greater the potential for homosexual experiences to be more
acceptable.

The weakness of this view – and indeed all symbolic analyses
– is that it fails to explain *why* the existing order is as it is. It
looks at the consequences of existing arrangements; it rarely
looks at how the order emerged. It can therefore be
conservative rather than critical, descriptive rather than
explanatory, and concerned with the present rather than
unfolding changes from the past. Yet if homosexuals are
attacked because they do not fit into the prevailing familial,
gender and moral systems of today, we have to understand how
these systems came about, how they relate to the wider society,
whose interests – if any – they serve and what alternative
arrangements are possible. Questions like these need much
more examination in the future.

These questions demand a scrupulous search of historical and
anthropological materials; there are no easy answers. Some
studies have already been made of certain areas – Bailey, for
instance, examined in detail the impact of Judeo-Christian
culture on homosexual oppression and reached the somewhat
surprising conclusion that it did not play such a significant part
as is often imagined (Bailey 1955). As well as looking at religious
interests, historical studies should also consider the interests of
lawmakers, doctors and psychiatrists, moralists, pressure groups
and the like (see Spector 1977; Morrison and Tracey 1979).
The trouble with such materials is that they would still fail to
locate gay hostility in much wider contexts; they do not show
how hostility may be linked to increasing rationalization and
bureaucratization (Greenberg and Bystryn 1978), the Protestant
ethic (Rotenberg 1979) and the changing nature of family,
gender and class systems (Weeks 1977).

Once we start doing this another important possibility arises:
that gay oppression is not the *intended* outcome of specific
groups who hate gays for various reasons. Rather it is the
unintended price that has to be paid for organizing society in

certain ways. Thus attention should be directed not to why 'individuals suffer from homophobia' but rather to why we have societies built around strong families, clear gender roles, rigid class and status structures, and a belief system which equates morality with sexuality.

The conditions of categorization: homosexual careers and homosexual identities

A third set of research directions generated by the labelling perspective centres around the ways in which individuals come to be categorized as 'homosexuals'. This is by no means the same as asking why people become homosexuals – the standard aetiological problem – for this question prejudices the issue in assuming homosexuality to *be* a state or condition. It is perfectly possible – and from existing accounts, quite common – for people to have same sex fantasies, to engage in same sex behaviour or to have flirtations with the same sex and for these same people *not* to see themselves as 'homosexuals'. Likewise it is not at all unusual for people to spend large portions of their lives behaving and feeling 'heterosexually' only to adopt the label of 'homosexual' at a much later stage in their life.[10] Further, it is possible that some people apply the label 'homosexual' to themselves without ever meeting other homosexuals or having a same sex experience. There is, in short, no absolute 'fit' or congruency between doing, thinking or feeling, and there is no necessary fit between any of these and the act of labelling oneself as 'a homosexual'.[11] What is it then that prompts the adoption of the category for some people and not others?

The crudest answer to this question is to suggest that it is *imposed* by formal control agents – police, psychiatrists – on unsuspecting victims, 'more sinned against than sinning' (see Gouldner 1968). But this view is now recognized as wholly inadequate; *self-constructed, symbolic self-labelling* is a much more fundamental theoretical and empirical problem (see Warren 1974; Plummer 1975; Rotenberg 1979). We need to ask about the ways in which individuals come to categorize themselves as certain kinds of sexual (or non-sexual) beings, how they come to hook themselves on to both wider societal and narrower community definitions, and how such definitions are used in fashioning subsequent life styles.

There are two broad ways of approaching the problem of building a homosexual identity: the *sexual orientation model* and the *identity construct model*. The orientation model is found among geneticists, clinicians and behaviourists alike and suggests that a person's sexual orientation is firmly established by mid childhood.[12] For the geneticists it is there at birth; for the others it is shaped in early family experiences. Either way, our sexual attractions are firmly and irrevocably set up *before* we reach puberty. Money, for instance, argues that a core gender identity (the sense of being a man or a woman) is set up by the age of three and that sexual orientation is established in relationship to this a few years later:

Because the erotic preferences usually reveal themselves at puberty, it is often assumed that they were instilled by a first sexual experience at that time, or caught from exposure to erotic pictures, books or films, an assumption that is responsible for much of today's judicial panic about pornography. On the contrary, each person's turn-on has rather fixed boundaries which are set before puberty. Whether the boundaries are orthodox or unorthodox, conventional or unconventional, they were established in childhood as part of a differentiation of gender identity, by the coding of the schemers, and by any quirks or oddities that were incorporated into the schemers. Boundaries may first show themselves at puberty, but they are not set in puberty and they don't change much, at puberty or later. Their relative unchangability helps to explain such phenomena as why a second spouse so often resembles the first. Their persistence also explains why adult obligative homosexuals can be fond of and behave affectionately towards a member of the other sex, especially if the other is older, but can never fall in love with her or him. Tales of sex degenerates who go from one form of depravity to another, sampling everything, are only fiction; even so-called sex degenerates stick to their particular preferences. [Money and Tucker 1977, p. 123]

Side by side with this view of the development of sexual orientation is the idea that sexual identity emerges simultaneously. Thus either the identity emerges unproblematically, so that the child en route to becoming a heterosexual *being* also learns the heterosexual *identity*, or a disjunction may occur between the orientation (being) that is built up in childhood and the identity that developed. Thus, for

instance, in the category of the 'latent homosexual', the being –
that of 'a homosexual' – is set up in childhood, but the identity
that is acquired is inappropriate; the homosexual person comes
(falsely and maybe because of heterosexual coercion) to view
himself or herself as a 'heterosexual'. This model would assume
that the category of 'heterosexual identity' is inappropriate in
this case; the person's *actual* identity is that of a homosexual.

In sharp contrast to this 'orientation model', the
'identity-construct' view – favoured by symbolic interactionists[13]
– focuses upon the cognitive processes by which members of a
society interpret their sexual selves by scanning their past lives
(their bodies, group involvements, feelings and behaviours) and
connecting these to 'accounts' available in their contemporary
worlds (through friends, family, psychiatrists, media). The focus
here is not upon childhood determinations and permanent 'real'
orientations; rather it is upon the process of building identities
throughout life through significant encounters.

As Blumstein and Schwartz (1976) have noted, the issues I
have referred to here derive from the sociology of knowledge.
Basically the problem is to explain how the existing given social
categories – the heterosexual, the homosexual, the pederast, the
bisexual – come to be filled: how do individuals scan their life
history (at different moments) and identify themselves as certain
kinds of sexual people (at different moments)? The orientation
model answers this by saying that the individual experiences a
deep erotic attraction to members of the same sex, and thereby
comes to define himself or herself as homosexual. The
constructionist approach suggests that perhaps initially our
experiences are much more random, unstructured and
uncrystallized than we choose to believe, and that it is through
the definitional process that this randomness becomes
channelled into stable sexual identities.

At first sight these models seem mutually exclusive. One says
that identities are fixed by childhood; the other says they are
flexible and negotiated in adult life. One raises the spectre of
'latency', of having a true sexual identity of which one may be
unaware; the other denies such a 'realist' epistemology. The
immediate problem, however, of trying to decide which might
prove more valid is compounded by discovering that there is
certainly evidence available to support both models.

Thus most social surveys suggest that homosexual responses

are 'already determined and established very early in life' (Saghir and Robins 1973, p. 44). The Spada report (with its undoubtedly heavily biased sample) unequivocally reports that '35% of the respondents report their first homosexual attraction before the age of ten, and another 41% place it between the ages of ten and fourteen' (Spada 1979, p. 23). Further, Whitham, in his critique of the homosexual role, comments that:

Nearly half of the homosexual respondents reported feeling sexually attracted to males before they learned of the existence of such sexual relations in the adult world .... Respondents frequently reported knowing that they were or would become homosexuals without having heard the term homosexual or its equivalent and without knowing that such behaviour existed in the adult world. [Whitham 1977, p. 7]

It seems that for *some* homosexuals, an orientation – independent of social labelling – is firmly seen to be fixed in childhood.

But if this is true of some, there is certainly other evidence which shows the flux and sway of adult homosexual identity (and often this comes from the same survey). Many 'homosexuals' lead a heterosexual life style at some point in their history and do not construct a homosexual identity till later in life. Dank (1974), for instance, in his study of 377 self-identified male homosexuals, found the age at which they constructed a homosexual identity varied greatly. Thus 45 (or 12.2 per cent) of his sample saw themselves as gay before the age of 15; another 130 (35.3 per cent) saw themselves as gay before the age of 20; a further 113 (30.7 per cent) saw themsleves as homosexual by the time they were 25; and another 80 (21.8 per cent) saw themselves as gay once they were over the age of 25. Now this study is not talking about the emergence of homosexual behaviours or homosexual orientations, but rather the self-labelling as a homosexual. It may therefore be that there is a very real separation between the development of an *orientation* in a person and the development of an *identity* in a person. Likewise a small scale study by T. Weinberg (1978) distinguished between homosexual activities ('doing'), homosexual identities ('being') and suspicions of being a homosexual, and charted the order of their emergence in thirty male homosexuals. He found four patterns:

1 E → S → L Engaged in activity → suspected himself to be
             homosexual → labelled self as a homosexual

2 E → L   Engaged in activity → labelled a homosexual
3 S → E → L Suspicious of being homosexual → engaged in activity → labelled as a homosexual
4 S → L → E Suspicious, labelled, engaged

Of these thirty men, 'only four definitely thought of both their behaviour and themselves as homosexual at the time they were first engaging in sex with other males' (p. 151). Unless one regards this as a purely 'fluke' sample, the study must be taken to indicate the complexity of linking 'doing' with 'being'. There is no one pattern.

There is then evidence to support the orientation model, since it seems well established that for some individuals orientation is set up in early childhood; but there is also evidence to support the construct model, since people's identities do empirically shift and swap very much in adult life. Confronted with such evidence, the 'sexual orientation' theorists would say that although men and women may not become 'aware' of their identities till later in life, until that time they were 'latent', for their orientation was set up earlier. Likewise the 'identity construct' theorists would say that the significance of childhood experiences was a reconstructed 'vocabulary of motive' used as a legitimation of contemporary homosexuality.[14] Argument and counter-argument leave us undecided and in confusion.

For me, the problem is an important one demanding conceptual and empirical clarification. At present I believe a synthesis of the two views is required – a synthesis which acknowledges the importance of childhood experiences in the restricting of our sexual possibilities and the importance of adult experiences in moulding, further limiting and sometimes transcending this childhood base. Such a synthesis is often seen to be a contradictory nonsense: the irreconcilable cannot be reconciled. But empirically both *are* true; what is wrong is not the person's 'contradictory' lived experience but the social scientists' theoretical debates which fail to incorporate such lived confusions.

But such apparent confusions are in effect only confusions if we seek simple, uniform answers to questions of identity and orientation. *Orientations* are – in all likelihood – set up in childhood; but while some people develop restrictive and rigid orientations, others may be open and flexible, while still others may develop no 'orientations' at all. Further, underlying emotional predispositions are not cognitions, and many individuals may not – indeed may never throughout their life – be aware of them. If this is so, they are outside the participant's own world of meaning and should not therefore be given *too* much importance. Likewise *identities* are – in all likelihood – highly variable throughout social encounters; but while for some people this may mean drastic restructuring of self conceptions at critical turning points in life, others may develop relatively stable identities at early moments in life and use these as foci to orientate most future conduct. Even if such stable identities are out of harmony with underlying orientations, they have to be taken very seriously as how people define their situations.

The impact of labelling

This area is the one that sociologists have most frequently studied in the past, and hence only a little need be said here. The core idea highlights the negative consequences for homosexual experiences which flow from stigma. Elsewhere I have outlined how stigma may give rise to problems in at least three areas: in the process of becoming a homosexual, in the daily interactional problems and in the collective problems of the sub-culture. In the first area the situation of stigma gives rise to a series of engulfing problems – of guilt, identity and access to partners – for potential homosexuals as they move into the first stages of their homosexual career. In the second area the day-to-day life of homosexuals may become more problematic through such matters as concealment, passing, and the heightened self-awareness that at any moment one may slip from a discreditable into a discredited person (see Goffman 1963b). In the third area some of the characteristics of the gay sub-culture and the gay world flow from hostility. Hoffman (1968) has described many of the characteristics of the homosexual community and has tried to show how these characteristics flow out of the hostility of society. Others, such as Schur (1965) and Williams and Weinberg (1971), have dealt with the more objective consequences of negative sanctions – matters like blackmail, police harrassment, work discrimination and even sexual murder.

Now although I think these three areas constitute a major and important research programme in the sociology of homosexuality, they are not without their problems. One important problem has been voiced by Sagarin and Kelly (1976). They critically note an irony that runs through the work of many labelling theorists whereby two divergent strands of thought may be found. On the one hand, there is a strong statement in most labelling studies about the normality of deviants: deviants are not disturbed, sick or pathological. On the other hand, there is a strand in labelling theory that suggests that negative sanctions create stressful and difficult situations which in turn must lead to pathology, disturbance and even sickness. Now it is very clear in the labelling perspective on homosexuality that both these strands exist side by side, and as Sagarin and Kelly rightly comment *'pathology cannot be denied, and at the same time accounted for, in terms of social hostility'* (1976, p. 262). There is no doubt that the writings of Gagnon and Simon, Hooker and most notably Freedman suggest that 'homosexuals' are very frequently psychologically well-adjusted individuals. As Freedman says:

Homosexuality is compatible with positive psychological functioning. Studies demonstrate that most of the homosexually oriented individuals evaluated in the studies of adjustment function as well as comparable groups of heterosexually oriented individuals; that their functioning could be typically characterised as normal; and that in some cases, their functioning even approximates that of self-actualising people. Cumulatively these studies (reviewed by Freedman) dealt with more than six hundred homosexually oriented subjects, whereas the studies with negative or mixed results had only about a hundred and fifty homosexual oriented subjects in all. [1971, p. 87]

Likewise Gagnon and Simon, in their review of 550 Kinsey subjects, 'suggest that most homosexuals cope fairly well, and even particularly well when we consider the historical period involved and the stigmatized and, in fact, criminal nature of their sexual interests' (1973, p. 138).

However, while theorists do place a great deal of emphasis upon the psychologically normal functioning of many 'homosexuals', they acknowledge that disturbance, pathology and tragedy may be also found. Gagnon and Simon in fact comment:

We do not wish to say that homosexual life does not contain a great potential for demoralisation, despair and self-hatred. To the contrary, as in most unconventional careers there remains the potential for a significant escalation of individual psycho-pathology. [1973, p. 139]

The issue then may be simply put. Labellists seem to be saying that, on the one hand, homosexuals are normal – just like everybody else. On the other hand, they seem to be saying that stigmatization processes create the potential for pathology, despair and tragedy. The findings suggest that some homosexuals are well adjusted and that others are not. Sagarin and Kelly, however, seem to be producing a straw man in their criticism of labelling theory for *both* positions are tenable; there are both 'pathological' and 'non-pathological' homosexualities. The important variables to take into account are the *stage* of the homosexual career and the *nature* of the surrounding significant others. Thus in the early stages of the homosexual career, it is very likely that the stigmatizing context of the wider society will create an enormous potential for demoralization and despair. The problems of guilt, secrecy, access, identity and so forth may lead to a pivotally engulfing, depressive experience; and these experiences just may lead 'homosexuals' straight to the psychiatric couch. But as they work out solutions to these various problems, and in particular gain access to a supportive sub-culture ('gay', 'feminist' or just 'tolerant'), so the identity begins to change. Dank, for instance, has clearly demonstrated how access to other homosexuals serves to give one a more positive identity. Here then the 'labelling others' are those people who provide positive support rather than destructive and negative attack. Hence under these circumstances one would not predict a high potential for demoralization and despair, but indeed would predict a better psychologically functioning 'homosexual'. This is precisely what empirical work has so far found. Homosexuals in prisons and under psychiatric treatment tend to show more disturbed signs than homosexuals in the gay community at large (Schofield 1965).

While in the early stages of the homosexual career negative sanctions may lead to problems and pathology, and in the middle stages of the homosexual career the positive reference group of other homosexuals may lead to a positive identity, there comes perhaps a later stage for some homosexuals where, far from functioning poorly or just averagely, they actually begin to function better than many people in society. Freedman suggests that when male homosexuals learn to overcome the oppression and difficulties that confront them in a hostile society, they become more 'centred' people. They fight off the oppressive strait-jacketing of gender roles, the oppressive restrictions of emotional expression given to most men and rigid controls of monogamous sex. Through an active, self-conscious working out of one's personal problems, the person comes to be more sensitive, aware and creative, able to control and master life more adequately. This position of course is also compatible with labelling theory. Here it is no longer a simple matter of hostile society leading to problems, or supportive reference group giving stable identities, but now a self-defined positive evaluation which gives rise to higher levels of psychological functioning. Positive self-esteem leads to positive self-functioning.

The Sagarin and Kelly argument therefore seems to be misconceived. By taking into account the different stages of the career process of the homosexual and by allowing for the differential responses instead of the uniformly hostile responses that some theorists seem to suggest, differential modes of adjustment and response can be predicted. It is precisely of course this reason why the findings of Weinberg and Williams on homosexuals in New York, San Francisco, Copenhagen and Amsterdam, described in Chapter 1, seem to refute the labelling theory. In fact they do no such thing; they merely provide evidence for the argument that in tolerant, supportive cultures, homosexuals who are involved in the gay world will not show the signs of pathology and disturbance predicted by some of the propositions in labelling theory.

Conclusion

In this paper I have argued for the study of homosexual categorizations rather than for the study of homosexuals. The need is to grasp the ways in which specifiable, historically produced meanings shape – and often damage – human experiences. It is not an easy area for investigation, since while it raises some very broad worries (the four questions outlined on pages 53–4), it also raises a seemingly irresolvable question: does the 'category' mirror or construct the phenomena? We have had nearly a hundred years of assuming that 'categories' simply mirror; the sociologist's task now is to analyse the alternative 'constructionist' view.

4 Discourse, desire and sexual deviance: some problems in a history of homosexuality

Jeffrey Weeks

Introduction

The recent publication by the Kinsey Institute of the book *Homosexualities* underlines what is likely to become a truism in the next few years: that we can no longer speak of a single homosexual category as if it embraced the wide range of same sex experiences in our society (Bell and Weinberg 1978). But recognition of this, tardy as it has been, calls into question a much wider project: that of providing a universal theory and consequently a 'history' of homosexuality. The distinction originally made by sociologists (and slowly being taken up by historians) between homosexual behaviours, roles and identities, or between homosexual desire and 'homosexuality' as a social and psychological category (Hocquenghem 1978), is one that challenges fundamentally the coherence of the theme and poses major questions for the historian. This paper addresses some of these problems first, by examining approaches that have helped construct our concepts of homosexuality, second, by tracing the actual evolution of the category of homosexuality, third, by exploring some of the theoretical approaches which have attempted to explain its emergence and, finally, by charting some of the problems that confront the modern researcher studying 'homosexuality'.

Approaches

It has been widely recognized for almost a century that attitudes towards homosexual behaviour are culturally specific, and have varied enormously across different cultures and through various historical periods. Two closely related and virtually reinforcing sources for this awareness can be pinpointed: first, the pioneering work of sexologists such as Magnus Hirschfeld, Iwan

Bloch, Havelock Ellis and others, whose labelling, categorizing and taxonomic zeal led them, partially at least, outside their own culture, and, second, the work of anthropologists and ethnographers who attempted to chart the varieties of sexual behaviour and who supplied the data on which the sexologists relied. The actual interest and zeal in the pursuit of sex was, of course, a product of their own culture's preoccupations, and the resulting findings often displayed an acute 'ethnocentric bias' (Trumbach 1977, p. 1), particularly with regard to homosexuality; but this early work has had a long resonance. The three most influential English language cross-cultural studies – that of the traveller Sir Richard Burton in the 1880s (1888), the work of Edward Westermarck in the 1900s (1906), and the Human Area Files of Ford and Beach in the 1950s (1952) – have deeply affected perceptions of homosexuality in their respective generations. Unfortunately, awareness of different cultural patterns have been used to reinforce rather than confront our own culture-bound conceptions.

Three phases in the construction of a history of homosexuality are discernible. The first, manifested in the works of the early sexologists as well as the propagandists like Edward Carpenter (1914), attempted above all to demonstrate the trans-historical existence, and indeed value, of homosexuality as a distinct sexual experience. All the major works of writers such as Havelock Ellis (1920) had clear-cut historical sections; some, like Iwan Bloch's (1938), were substantive historical works. Writers during this phase were above all anxious to establish the parameters of homosexuality, what distinguished it from other forms of sexuality, what history suggested for its aetiology and social worth, the changing cultural values accorded to it, and the great figures – in politics, art, literature – one could associate with the experience. These efforts, taking the form of naturalistic recordings of what was seen as a relatively minor but significant social experience, were actually profoundly constructing of modern concepts of homosexuality. They provided a good deal of the data on which later writers depended even as they reworked them, and a hagiographical sub-school produced a multitude of texts on the great homosexuals of the past, 'great queens of history'; its most recent manifestation is found in the egregious essay of A. L. Rowse, *Homosexuals in History* (1977).

The second phase, most usefully associated with the reformist endeavours of the 1950s and 1960s, took as unproblematic the framework established by the pioneers. Homosexuality was a distinct social experience; the task was to detail it. The result was a new series of texts, some of which, such as H. Montgomery Hyde's various essays, synthesized in *The Other Love* in 1970, brought together a good deal of empirical material even as they failed to theorize its contradictions adequately.

As a major aspect of the revival of historical interest was the various campaigns to change the law and public attitudes, both in Europe and America, the historical studies inevitably concentrated on issues relevant to these. The assumed distinction, derived from nineteenth century sexological literature, between 'perversion' (a product of moral weakness) and 'inversion' (constitutional and hence unavoidable), which D. S. Bailey adumbrates in *Homosexuality and the Western Christian Tradition* (1955), was highly significant for debates in the churches. The influential essay on English legal attitudes by Francois Lafitte, 'Homosexuality and the law', was designed to indicate that laws which were so arbitrarily, indeed accidentally, imposed could as easily be removed (Lafitte 1958–9). Donald Webster Cory's various works of the 1950s, such as *The Homosexual Outlook* (1953), sought to underline the values of the homosexual experience. Employing the statistical information provided by Kinsey, the cross-cultural evidence of Ford and Beach, and the ethnographic studies of people like Evelyn Hooker, historians were directed towards the commonness of the homosexual experience in history and began to trace some of the forces that shaped public attitudes.

A third phase, overlapping with the second but more vocal in tone, can be seen as the direct product of the emergence of more radical gay movements in the late 1960s and 1970s in Europe and North America. Here the emphasis was on reasserting the values of a lost experience, stressing the positive value of homosexuality and locating the sources of its social oppression. A major early emphasis was on recovering the pre-history of the gay movement itself, particularly in Germany, the USA and Britain (Lauritsen and Thorstad 1974; Steakly 1975; Katz 1976). Stretching beyond this was a search for what one might term 'ethnicity', the lineaments and validation of a minority experience which history had denied. But the actual work of research posed new problems, which threatened to burst out of the bounds established within the previous half century. This is admirably demonstrated in Jonathan Katz's splendid documentary *Gay American History* (1976). But rather than exploring its virtues, I want to pick out two points which seem to me to pose fresh problems. The first concerns the title. It seems to me that to use a modern self-labelling term, 'gay', itself a product of contemporary political struggles, to define an ever-changing concept over a period of 400 years suggests a constant homosexual essence which the evidence presented in the book itself suggests is just not there. Katz in fact recognizes this very clearly. He makes the vital point that the 'concept of homosexuality must be historicized', and hopes that the book will revolutionize the traditional concept of homosexuality.

The problem of the historical researcher is thus to study and establish the character and meaning of each manifestation of same sex relations within a specific time and society . . . . All homosexuality is situational. [1976, pp. 6–7]

This is absolutely correct and is the measure of the break between this type of history and, say, A. L. Rowse's extravaganza. But to talk at the same time of *our* history as if homosexuals were a distinct, fixed minority suggests a slightly contradictory attitude. It poses a major theoretical problem on which the gay movement has had little to say until recently.

A second problem arises from this, concerning attitudes to lesbianism. Katz very commendably has, unlike most of his predecessors, attempted to give equal space to both male and female homosexuality, and although this is impossible in some sections, overall he succeeds. But this again suggests a problematic of a constant racial–sexual identity which Katz explicitly rejects theoretically. Lesbianism and male homosexuality in fact have quite different, if inevitably interconnected, social histories, related to the social evolution of distinct gender identities; there is a danger that this fundamental, if difficult, point will be obscured by discussing them as if they were part of the same experience. These points will be taken up later.

Certainly there has been a considerable extension of interest in the history of homosexuality over the past decade, and as well as the general works, a number of essays and monographs have appeared, most of which accept readily the cultural specificity of attitudes and concepts. Nevertheless considerable contradictions recur. A. D. Harvey in a study of buggery prosecutions at the beginning of the nineteenth century has noted that:

It is too commonly forgotten how far the incidence of homosexual behaviour varies from age to age and from culture to culture. .... In fact it is only very crudely true that there are homosexuals in every period and in every society. Societies which accept homosexual behaviour as normal almost certainly have a higher proportion of men who have experimented with homosexual activity than societies which regard homosexuality as abnormal but tolerate it, and societies which grudgingly tolerate homosexuality *probably* have a higher incidence of homosexual activity than societies where it is viciously persecuted. [1978, p. 944]

But Harvey, despite making this highly significant point, goes on to speak of 'homosexuals' as if they realized a trans-historical nature. He writes of the Home Secretary complaining in 1808 that Hyde Park and St James' Park were 'being used as a resort for homosexuals', apparently oblivious of the absence of such a term until the later part of the century. The actual term the Home Secretary used is extremely important in assessing his perception of the situation and the type of people involved, and the evidence suggests a problematic of public nuisance rather than a modern concept of the homosexual person.[1]

Similarly Randolph Trumbach, in what is a very valuable study of London 'sodomites' in the eighteenth century, despite a long and carefully argued discussion of different cross-cultural patterns, writes as if the homosexual sub-culture had a natural existence serving the eternal social needs (or at least eternal in the West) of a fixed minority of people (1977, p. 23). But there is plentiful evidence that the sub-culture changed considerably over time, partly at least dependent on factors such as urbanization, and can one really speak of the courtly or theatrical sub-cultures of the early seventeenth century as if they were the same as the modern sub-cultures of New York or San Francisco?

Implicit in Trumbach's essay is an alternative view which profoundly challenges such assumptions. He notes 'only one significant change' in attitudes during the Christian millennia:

'Beginning in the late 19th century it was no longer the act that was stigmatized, but the state of mind' (1978, p. 9). But this, I would argue, is *the* crucial change, indicating a massive shift in attitudes, giving rise to what is distinctively new in our culture: the categorization of homosexuality as a separate condition and the correlative emergence of a homosexual identity.

I would argue that we should employ cross-cultural and historical evidence not only to chart changing *attitudes* but to challenge the very concept of a single trans-historical notion of homosexuality. In different cultures (and at different historical moments or conjunctures within the same culture) very different meanings are given to same sex activity both by society at large and by the individual participants. The physical acts might be similar, but the social construction of meanings around them are profoundly different. The social integration of forms of pedagogic homosexual relations in ancient Greece have no continuity with contemporary notions of a homosexual identity (Dover 1978). To put it another way, the various possibilities of what Hocquenghem calls homosexual desire, or what more neutrally might be termed homosexual behaviours, which seem from historical evidence to be a permanent and ineradicable aspect of human sexual possibilities, are variously constructed in different cultures as an aspect of wider gender and sexual regulation. If this is the case, it is pointless discussing questions such as, what are the origins of homosexual oppression, or what is the nature of the homosexual taboo, as if there was a single, causative factor. The crucial question must be: what are the conditions for the emergence of this particular form of regulation of sexual behaviour in this particular society? Transferred to our own history, this must involve an exploration of what Mary McIntosh (1968) pin-pointed as the significant problem: the emergence of the notion that homosexuality is a condition peculiar to some people and not others.

An historical study of homosexuality over the past two centuries or so must therefore have as its focus three closely related questions: the social conditions for the emergence of the category of homosexuality and its construction as the unification of disparate experiences, the relation of this categorization to other socio-sexual categorizations, and the relationship of this categorization to those defined, not simply 'described' or labelled but created by it, in particular historical circumstances.

Evolution

The historical evidence points to the latter part of the nineteenth century as the crucial period in the conceptualization of homosexuality as the distinguishing characteristic of a particular type of person, the 'invert' or 'homosexual', and the corresponding development of a new awareness of self amongst some 'homosexuals' (Weeks 1977). From the mid nineteenth century there is a bubbling of debate, notation and classification, associated with names like Casper, Tardieu, Ulrichs, Westphal, Krafft-Ebing, Havelock Ellis, Magnus Hirschfeld, Moll, Freud, all of whom sought to define, and hence psychologically or medically to construct, new categorizations. Westphal's description of the 'contrary sexual instinct' in the 1870s may be taken as the crucial formative moment, for out of it grew the notion of 'sexual inversion', the dominant formulation until the 1950s.

The word 'homosexuality' itself was not invented until 1869 (by the Hungarian Benkert) and did not enter English usage until the 1880s and 1890s, and then largely as a result of the work of Havelock Ellis. I suggest that the widespread adoption of these neologisms during this period marks as crucial a turning point in attitudes to homosexuality as the adoption of 'gay' as a self-description of homosexuals in the 1970s. It indicated not just a changing usage but the emergence of a whole new set of assumptions. And in Britain (as also in Germany and elsewhere) the reconceptualization and categorization (at first medical and later social) coincided with the development of new legal and ideological sanctions, particularly against male homosexuality.

Until 1885 the only law dealing *directly* with homosexual behaviour in England was that relating to buggery, and legally, at least, little distinction was made between buggery between man and woman, man and beast and man and man, though the majority of prosecutions were directed at men for homosexual offences. This had been a capital crime from the 1530s, when the incorporation of traditional ecclesiastical sanctions into law had been part of the decisive assumption by the state of many of the powers of the medieval church. Prosecutions under this law had fluctuated, partly because of changing rules on evidence, partly through other social pressures. There seems, for instance, to have been a higher incidence of prosecutions (and executions) in times of war; penalties were particularly harsh in cases affecting the discipline of the armed services, particularly the navy (Radzinowicz 1968; Gilbert 1974, 1976, 1977). 'Sodomite' (denoting contact between men) became the typical epithet of abuse for the sexual deviant.

The legal classification and the epithet had, however, an uncertain status and was often used loosely to describe various forms of non-reproductive sex. There was therefore a crucial distinction between traditional concepts of buggery and modern concepts of homosexuality. The former was seen as a potentiality in all sinful nature, unless severely execrated and judicially punished; homosexuality, however, is seen as the characteristic of a particular type of person, a type whose specific characteristics (inability to whistle, penchant for the colour green, adoration of mother or father, age of sexual maturation, 'promiscuity', etc.) have been exhaustively and inconclusively detailed in many twentieth century textbooks. It became a major task of psychology in the present century to attempt to explain the aetiology of this homosexual 'condition' (McIntosh 1968). The early articles on homosexuality in the 1880s and 1890s treated the subject as if they were entering a strange continent. An eminent doctor, Sir George Savage, described in the *Journal of Mental Science* (October 1884) the homosexual case histories of a young man and woman and wondered if 'this perversion is as rare as it appears', while Havelock Ellis was to claim that he was the first to record any homosexual cases unconnected with prison or asylums. The sodomite, as Michel Foucault has put it (1979), was a temporary aberration; the homosexual belongs to a species, and social science during this century has made various – if by and large unsuccessful – efforts to explore this phenomenon.

These changing concepts do not mean, of course, that those who engaged in a predominantly homosexual life style did not regard themselves as somehow different until the late nineteenth century, and there is evidence for sub-cultural formation around certain monarchs and in the theatre for centuries. But there is much stronger evidence for the emergence of a distinctive male homosexual sub-culture in London and one or two other cities from the late seventeenth century, often characterized by transvestism and gender-role inversion; and by the early nineteenth century there was a recognition in the courts that homosexuality represented a condition different from the norm (McIntosh 1968; Trumbach 1977). By the mid nineteenth century, it seems the male homosexual sub-culture at least had characteristics not dissimilar to the modern, with recognized cruising places and homosexual haunts, ritualized sexual contact and a distinctive argot and 'style'. But there is also abundant evidence until late into the nineteenth century of practices which by modern standards would be regarded as highly sexually compromising. Lawrence Stone (1977) describes how Oxbridge male students often slept with male students with no sexual connotations until comparatively late in the eighteenth century, while Smith-Rosenberg (1975) has described the intimate – and seemingly non-sexualized – relations between women in the nineteenth century.

Nevertheless even as late as the 1870s there was considerable doubt in the minds of the police, the medical profession and the judiciary about the nature and extent of homosexual offences. When the transvestites Boulton and Park were brought to trial in 1871 for conspiracy to commit buggery, there was considerable police confusion about the nature of the alleged offences, the medical profession differed over the relevance of the evidence relating to anal intercourse, the counsel seemed never to have worked on similar cases before, the 'scientific' literature cited from British sources was nugatory, while the court was either ignorant of the French sources or ready to despise them. The Attorney General suggested that is was fortunate that there was 'very little learning or knowledge upon this subject in this country', while a defence counsel attacked 'the new found treasures of French literature upon the subject which thank God is still foreign to the libraries of British surgeons'.[2] Boulton and Park were eventually acquitted, despite an overwhelming mass of evidence, including correspondence, that today would be regarded as highly compromising.

The latter part of the nineteenth century, however, saw a variety of concerns which helped to focus awareness: the controversy about 'immorality' in public schools, various sexual scandals, a new legal situation, the beginnings of a 'scientific' discussion of homosexuality and the emergence of the 'medical model'. The subject, as Edward Carpenter put it at the time, 'has great actuality and is pressing upon us from all sides' (1908, p. 9). It appears likely that it was in this developing context that some of those with homosexual inclinations began to perceive themselves as 'inverts', 'homosexuals', 'Uranians', a crucial stage in the prolonged and uneven process whereby homosexuality began to take on a recognizably modern configuration. And although the evidence cited here has been largely British, this development was widespread throughout Western Europe and America.

The changing legal and ideological situations were crucial markers in this development. The 1861 Offences Against the Person Act removed the death penalty for buggery (which had not been used since the 1830s), replacing it by sentences of between ten years and life. But in 1885 the famous Labouchere Amendment to the Criminal Law Amendment Act made all male homosexual activities (acts of 'gross indecency') illegal, punishable by up to two years hard labour. And in 1898 the laws on importuning for 'immoral purposes' were tightened up and effectively applied to male homosexuals (this was clarified by the Criminal Law Amendment Act of 1912 with respect to England and Wales – Scotland has different provisions). Both were significant extensions of the legal controls on male homosexuality, whatever their origins or intentions (Weeks 1977, p. 28; Smith 1976; Bristow 1977). Though formally less severe than capital punishments for sodomy, the new legal situation is likely to have ground harder on a much wider circle of people, particularly as it was dramatized in a series of sensational scandals, culminating in the trials of Oscar Wilde, which had the function of drawing a sharp dividing line between permissible and tabooed forms of behaviour. The Wilde scandal in particular was a vital moment in the creation of a male homosexual identity (Ellis 1936, p. 392). It must be noted however, that the new legal situation did not apply to women, and the attempt in 1921 to extend the 1885 provisions to women failed, in part at least on the grounds that publicity would only serve to make more women aware of homosexuality (Weeks 1977, p. 107). But the different legal situation alone does not explain the different social resonances of male and female homosexuality. Much more likely, this must be related to the complexly developing social structuring of male and female sexualities.

The emergence of a psychological and medical model of homosexuality was intimately connected with the legal situation.

The most commonly quoted European writers on homosexuality in the mid nineteenth century were Casper and Tardieu, the leading medico-legal experts of Germany and France respectively. Both, as Arno Karlen has put it, were 'chiefly concerned with whether the disgusting breed of perverts could be physically identified for courts, and whether they should be held legally responsible for their acts' (1971, p. 185). The same problem was apparent in Britain. According to Magnus Hirschfeld, most of the 1000 or so works on homosexuality that appeared between 1898 and 1908 were directed, in part at least, at the legal profession. Even J. A. Symond's privately printed pamphlet, *A Problem in Modern Ethics*, declared itself to be addressed 'especially to Medical psychologists and jurists', while Havelock Ellis's *Sexual Inversion* was attacked for not being published by a medical press and for being too popular in tone. The medicalization of homosexuality – a transition from notions of sin to concepts of sickness or mental illness – was a vitally significant move, even though its application was uneven. Around it the poles of scientific discourse ranged for decades: was homosexuality congenital or acquired, ineradicable or susceptible to cure, to be quietly if unenthusiastically accepted as unavoidable (even the liberal Havelock Ellis felt it necessary to warn his invert reader not to 'set himself in violent opposition' to his society) or to be resisted with all the force of one's Christian will? In the discussions of the 1950s and 1960s these were crucial issues: was it right, it was sometimes wondered, to lock an alcoholic up in a brewery; should those who suffered from an incurable (or at best unfortunate) condition be punished? Old notions of the immorality or sinfulness of homosexuality did not die in the nineteenth century; they still survive, unfortunately, in many dark corners. But from the nineteenth century they were inextricably entangled with 'scientific' theories which formed the boundaries within which homosexuals had to begin to define themselves.

The challenge to essentialism

Clearly the emergence of the homosexual category was not arbitrary or accidental. The scientific and medical speculation can be seen in one sense as a product of the characteristic nineteenth century process whereby the traditionally execrated (and monolithic) crimes against nature – linking up, for instance, homosexuality with masturbation and mechanical birth control (Bullough and Voght 1973) – are differentiated into discrete deviations whose aetiologies are mapped out in late nineteenth and early twentieth century works (Krafft-Ebing, Havelock Ellis, Hirschfeld, Moll). In another series of relationships the emergence of the concept of the homosexual can be seen as corresponding to and complexly linked with the classification and articulation of a variety of social categories: the redefinitions of childhood and adolescence, the hysterical woman, the congenitally inclined prostitute (or indeed, in the work of Ellis and others, the congenital criminal as well) and linked to the contemporaneous debate and ideological definition of the role of housewife and mother.[3] On the other hand, the categorization was never simply an imposition of a new definition; it was the result of various pressures and forces, in which new concepts merged into older definitions.

It is striking that the social purity campaigners of the 1880s saw both prostitution and male homosexuality as products of undifferentiated male lust (Weeks 1977, p. 17), and equally significant, if generally unremarked, that the major enactments affecting male homosexuality from the 1880s (the Labouchere Amendment, the 1898 Vagrancy Act) were primarily concerned with female prostitution. Indeed as late as the 1950s it was still seen as logical to set up a single government committee – the Wolfenden Committe – to study both prostitution and male homosexuality. It is clear, however, that the emergence of the homosexual category and the changing focus of the definition of homosexual behaviour are intimately related to wider changes. The problem is to find means of explaining and theorizing these changes without falling into the twin traps of a naive empiricism or a reductive materialism. The former would assume that what was happening was simply a discovery of pre-existing phenomena, a problematic which, as we have suggested, has little historical validity; the latter poses the danger of seeing the restrictive definitions of homosexual behaviours as a necessary effect of a pre-existing causative complex (usually 'capitalism'). Given the absence in orthodox Marxism of any theorization of sexuality and gender which is able to cope with the actual historical phenomena, the tendency has been to graft a form of functionalism on to historical materialism which, while it suggests useful connections which might be worth exploring, simultaneously produces historical descriptions which are often difficult to fit with more empirical substantiation.

Most attempts to explain this more closely have relied on variations of role theory. Male homosexuality has been seen as a threat to the ensemble of assumptions about male sexuality and a perceived challenge to the male heterosexual role within capitalism.

> In Britain sexual intercourse has been contained within marriage which has been presented as the ultimate form of sexual maturity ... the heterosexual nuclear family assists a system like capitalism because it produces and socialises the young in certain values ... the maintenance of the nuclear family with its role-specific behaviour creates an apparent consensus concerning sexual normalcy. [Brake 1976, p. 178]

So that:

> Any ambiguity such as transvestism, hermaphrodism, transsexuality, or homosexuality is moulded into 'normal' appropriate gender behaviour or is relegated to the categories of sick, dangerous, or pathological. The actor is forced to slot into patterns of behaviour appropriate to heterosexual gender roles. [Brake 1976, p. 176]

The result is the emergence of a specific male 'homosexual role', a specialized, despised and punished role which 'keeps the bulk of society pure in rather the same way that the similar treatment of some kinds of criminal helps keep the rest of society law abiding' (McIntosh 1968, p. 184). Such a role has two effects: first, it helps to provide a clear-cut threshold between permissible and impermissible behaviour, and, second, it helps to segregate those labelled as deviant from others, and thus contains and limits their behaviour patterns. In the same way, a homosexual sub-culture, which is the correlative of the development of a specialized role, provides both access to the socially outlawed need (sex) and contains the deviant. Male homosexuals can thus be conceptualized as those excluded from the sexual family, and as potential scapegoats whose oppression can keep the family members in line.

The notion of a homosexual role in this posing of it has certain difficulties. It is, for example, a negative role, not one that is socially sustained. It also assumes a unilinear fit between the socially created role and the identity that it delineates, whereas all the evidence indicates that this is problematical. It also suggests an intentionality in the creation of the role that again is historically dubious. But beyond this are other related problems in the functionalist model. It apparently assumes that the family acts as a unilinear funnel for the channelling of socially necessary sexual identities and responds automatically to the needs of society (or in the Marxist functionalist model, capitalism). It assumes, in other words, that the family can be simply defined as a unitary form (the 'nuclear family') which acts in a determined way on society's members, and at the same time it takes for granted a sexual essence which can be organized through this institution.[4] Neither is true.

Mark Poster has recently suggested that 'historians and social scientists in general have gone astray by viewing the family as a unitary phenomenon which has undergone some type of linear transformation' (1978, p. xvii). He argues instead that the history of the family is discontinuous, evolving several distinct family structures, each with its own emotional pattern. What this points to is the *construction* of different family forms in different historical periods and with different class effects. A functionalist model which sees the family as an essential and necessary agent of social control and with the role of ensuring efficient reproduction ignores both the constant ineffectiveness of the family in doing so and the immense class variations in family forms.

But even more problematic are the assumptions classically made about the nature of sexuality, assumptions current both in traditionalist and in Left thought (and particularly evident in the writings of the Freudian Left: Reich, Fromm, Marcuse). They also have the undoubted strength of the appearance of common sense: in this view sex is conceived of as an overpowering, instinctive force, whose characteristics are built into the biology of the human animal, which shapes human institutions and whose will must express itself, either in the form of direct sexual expression or, if blocked, in the form of perversion or neurosis. Krafft-Ebing expressed an orthodox view in the late nineteenth century when he described sex as a 'natural instinct' which 'with all conquering force and might demands fulfilment' (1965, p. 1). The clear presupposition here is that the sex drive is basically male in character, with the female conceived of as a passive receptacle. More sophisticated versions of what Gagnon and Simon have termed the 'drive reduction' model (1974) recur in twentieth century thought. It is ambiguously there in parts of Freud's work, though the careful distinction he draws between 'instinct' and 'drive' has often been lost, both by commentators and translators. But it is unambiguously present in the writings of his epigones. Thus Rattray Taylor in his neo-Freudian interpretation of *Sex in History*:

> The history of civilisation is the history of a long warfare between the dangerous and powerful forces of the id, and the various systems of taboos and inhibitions which man has erected to control them.   [1965b]

Here we have a clear notion of a 'basic biological mandate' that presses on, and so must be firmly controlled by the cultural and social matrix (Gagnon and Simon 1973, p. 11). What is peculiar about this model is that it has been adopted both by Marxists, who in other regards have firmly rejected the notion of 'natural man', and by taxonomists, such as Kinsey, whose findings have revealed a wide variety of sexual experiences. With regard to homosexuality, the instinctual model has seen it either as a more or less pathological deviation, a failure of social necessary repression, as the effect of the morally restrictive organization of sexual morality, or, more romantically but no less ahistorically, as the 'great refusal' (Marcuse 1969) of sexual normality in the capitalist organization of sexuality.[5]

Against this, Gagnon and Simon have argued that sexuality is subject to 'socio-cultural moulding to a degree surpassed by few other forms of human behaviour' (1973, p. 26), and in so arguing they are building both on a century of sex research and on a century of 'decentring' natural man. Marx's formulation of historical materialism and Freud's discovery of the unconscious have been the major contributions to what over the past few decades, in structuralism, anthropology, psychoanalysis and Marxism, has been a major theoretical effort to challenge the unitary subject in social theory. 'Sexuality' has in many ways been most resistant to this challenge, precisely because its power seems to derive from our natural being, but there have recently been three sustained challenges to sexual essentialism from three quite different theoretical approaches: the interactionist (associated with the work of Gagnon and Simon), the psychoanalytic (associated with the re-interpretation of Freud initiated by Jacques Lacan) and the discursive, taking as its starting point the work of Michel Foucault. They have quite different epistemological starting points and different objects of study – the social sources of human conduct, the unconscious and power – but between them they have posed formidable challenges to our received notions of sexuality, challenges which have already been reflected in the presentation of this paper.[6]

Despite their different approaches and in the end different aims, their work converges on several important issues. First, they all reject sex as an autonomous realm, a natural force with specific effects, a rebellious energy which the 'social' controls. In the work of Gagnon and Simon, it seems to be suggested that nothing is intrinsically sexual, or rather that anything can be sexualized (though what creates the notion of 'sexuality' is itself never answered). In Lacan's 'recovery' of Freud, it is the law of the father, the castration fear and the pained entry into the symbolic order – the order of language – at the Oedipal moment which instigates desire (cf. Mitchell 1974). It is the expression of a fundamental absence, which can never be fulfilled, the desire to be the other, the father, which is both alienated and insatiable: alienated because the child can only express its desire by means of language which itself constitutes its submission to the father, and insatiable because it is desire for a symbolic position which is itself arbiter of the possibilities for the expression of desire. The law of the father therefore constitutes both desire and the lack on which it is predicated.

In Foucault's work 'sexuality' is seen as a historical apparatus, and 'sex' is a 'complex idea that was formed within the deployment of sexuality'.

Sexuality must not be thought of as a kind of natural given which power tries to hold in check, or as an obscure domain which knowledge gradually tries to uncover. It is the name that can be given to a historical construct: not a furtive reality that is difficult to grasp, but a great surface network in which the stimulation of bodies, the intensification of pleasures, the incitement to discourse, the formation of special knowledges, the strengthening of controls and resistances, are linked to one another, in accordance with a few major strategies of knowledge and power. [Foucault 1979, pp. 105–6]

It is not fully clear what are the elements on which these social constructs of sexuality play. In the neo-psychoanalytic school there is certainly rejection of the concept of a pool of natural instincts which are distorted by society, but nevertheless there seems to be an acceptance of permanent drives; and the situation is complicated by what must be termed an essentialist and trans-historical reading of Oedipus, which seems to be essential for any culture, or in Juliet Mitchell's version, 'patriarchal' culture.[7] Gagnon and Simon and Plummer (1975) seem to accept the existence of a pool of possibilities on which 'sexuality' draws, and in this they do not seem far removed from Foucault's version that 'sexuality' plays upon 'bodies, organs, somatic localisations, functions, anatamo-physiological systems, sensations, and pleasures', which have no intrinsic unity or 'laws' of their own (Foucault 1979, p. 153).

Second, then, what links the anti-essentialist critique is a recognition of the social sources of sexual definitions. In the feminist appropriation of Lacan this can be seen as a result of patriarchal structures and the differential entry into the symbolic of the human male and female. But this poses massive theoretical problems, particularly in the attempt at a materialist position. The problem here is that the trans-historical perception of the Oedipal crisis and the consequent focusing of sex and gender already presuppose the existence of a unified notion of sexuality which we are suggesting is historically specific. Both the interactionists and Foucault make this clear. Gagnon and Simon suggest that:

It is possible that, given the historical nature of human societies we are victim to the needs of earlier social orders. To earlier societies it may not have been a need to constrain severely the powerful sexual impulse in order to maintain social stability or limit inherently anti-social force, *but rather a matter of having to invent an importance for sexuality*. This would not only assure a high level of reproductive activity but also provide socially available rewards unlimited by natural resources, rewards that promote conforming behaviour in sectors of social life far more important than the sexual. [1973, p. 17, my italics]

Foucault makes much clearer a historical specification and locates the rise of the sexuality apparatus in the eighteenth century, linked with specific historical processes. As a consequence of this, a third point of contact lies in the rejection, both by the interactionists and Foucault, of the notion that the history of sexuality can fruitfully be seen in terms of 'repression'. Foucault, as Zinner has put it:

offers four major arguments against the repression hypothesis. (1) it is based on an outmoded model of power; (2) it leads to a narrow construction of the family's function; (3) it is class specific and applies historically to bourgeois sexuality; and (4) it often results in a one-sided conception of how authority interacts with sexuality – a negative rather than a positive conception. [1978, pp. 215–16]

Again Gagnon and Simon have been less historically specific, but both interactionists and Foucault tend to the view that sexuality is organized not by repression but through definition and regulation. More specifically, regulation is organized through the creation of sexual categories – homosexual, paedophile, transvestite and so on. In the case of Gagnon and Simon and those influenced by them (for example, Plummer) the theoretical framework derives both from Meadean social psychology, which sees the individual as having a developing personality which is created in an interaction with others, and from labelling theories of deviance (cf. Plummer, in this volume). In the case of Foucault it derives from his belief that it is through discourse that our relation to reality is organized – or rather, language structures the real – and in particular Foucault analyses discourse 'as an act of violence imposed upon things' (Zinner 1978, p. 219).

Fourth, however, in all three tendencies there is a curious relationship to history. Symbolic interactionism, by stressing the subjective and the impact of particular labelling events, has almost invariably displayed an ahistorical bias. The psychoanalytical school, almost by definition, has based itself on supra-historical assumptions which have been almost valueless in conjunctural analyses. Foucault stresses that his work is basically aimed at constructing a 'genealogy', the locating of the 'traces' of the present; it is basically a history of the present. So while the interactionist adherent by and large has stressed the contingent and personalist, the tendency in the others is towards a form of structuralism in which 'history cannot be a study of man but only of determinate structures of social relations of which men and women are "bearers" ' (History Workshop 1978).[8]

It is this ambiguous relationship of the critique of essentialism to traditional historical work which has made it seem difficult to absorb unproblematically any one of the particular approaches. Nevertheless, each in quite different ways ultimately poses problems which any historical approach to homosexuality must confront, particularly in the difficult relationship of historical structuration to individualized meanings. A close examination of the historical implications of the various approaches will illustrate this.

Constructing the homosexual

The dominant theoretical framework in Britain and the USA has derived from 'symbolic interactionism'. Here ideas are not treated in terms of their historical roots or practical effectiveness, but are seen as forming the background to every social process so that social processes are treated essentially in terms of ideas, and it is through ideas that we construct social reality itself. Most of the important work that has informed the theoretical study of homosexuality in Britain has derived from symbolic interactionism (for example, Kenneth Plummer's *Sexual Stigma*, which is the major British study of how homosexual meanings are acquired). In this theory sexual meanings are constructed in social interaction: a homosexual identity is not inherent, but is socially created. This has had a vitally important clarifying influence, and has, as we have seen, broken with lay ideas of sex as a goal-directed instinct. Linked to labelling theories of deviance, it has been a valuable tool for exploring the effects of public stigmatizations and their impact on sub-cultural formation.

But interactionism has been unable fully to theorize the sexual variations that it can so ably describe; nor has it conceptualized the relations between possible sexual patterns and other social variables. Although it recognizes the disparities of power between various groups and the importance of the power to label, it has often had difficulties in theorizing questions of structural power and authority. Nor has it been willing, in the field of sexuality, to investigate the question of determination. It is unable to theorize why, despite the endless possibilities of sexualization it suggests, the genitals continue to be the focus of sexual imagination, nor why there are, at various times, shifts in the location of the sexual taboos. And there is a political consequence too, for if meanings are entirely developed in social interaction, an act of collective will can transform them; this leads, as Mary McIntosh has suggested, to a politics of 'collective voluntarism'. Both in theory and practice it has ignored the historical location of sexual taboos. Interactionism therefore stops precisely at the point where theorization seems essential: at the point of historical determination and ideological structuring in the creation of subjectivity.

It is for this reason that recently, particularly amongst feminists, interest has begun to switch to a reassessment of Freud and psychoanalysis with a view to employing it as a tool for developing a theoretical understanding of patriarchy. It is becoming apparent that if the emergence of a distinct homosexual identity is linked to the evolution of the family, then within this it is the role of the male – theorized in terms of the symbolic role of the phallus and the law of the father – that is of central significance. This, it is suggested, will allow the space to begin to understand the relationship between gender and sex (for it is in the family that the anatomical differences between the sexes acquire their social significance) and also to begin to uncover the specific history of female sexuality, within which the social history of lesbianism must ultimately be located. The focal point for most of the preliminary discussion has been Juliet Mitchell's *Psychoanalysis and Feminism* (1974), which takes as its starting point the work of Lacan, Althusser and Levi-Strauss and which, as it was recently put by a sympathetic critic:

opens the way to a re-evaluation of psychoanalysis as a theory which can provide scientific knowledge of the way in which patriarchal ideology is maintained through the foundation of psychological 'masculinity' and 'femininity'. [Albury 1976, p. 7]

But though the question of sexuality (and its role in the creation of sexed and gendered subjects) has now been strategically linked to the whole problematic of patriarchy, there has been no effort to theorize the question of sexual variation.

The tendency of thought that Juliet Mitchell represents can be criticized on a number of grounds. Politically she seems to accept that separation of the struggle against patriarchy from the struggle against capitalism which most socialist feminist work has in theory attempted to overcome. Historically she appears to accept the universality of the Oedipal experience. A historical materialist when analyzing capitalist social relations, she readily accepts idealist notions of the primal father when discussing the origins of patriarchy. Theoretically in her universalizing of the Oedipal processes she comes close to accepting drive as autonomous, pre-individual and again trans-historical and trans-cultural. It is a peculiar feature of recent radical thought that while stressing the conjunctural forces which partly at least shape the political, social and ideological, and while stressing the historical construction of subjectivity, it has nevertheless at the same time implicitly fallen back on a form of psychic determinism which it nominally rejects.

It is this which gives a particular interest to the recent appearance in English translation of Guy Hocquenghem's *Homosexual Desire* (first published in France as *Le Désir Homosexual* in 1972). The essay is located in the general area generated by the Lacanian reinterpretation of Freud, linguistic theory and the question of ideology, but its specific debt is to Gilles Deleuze and Felix Guattari, their work *L'Anti Oedipe*, their critique of Freudian (and Lacanian) categories and their subsequent theory of 'desire' and their espousal of schizoanalysis (Deleuze and Guattari 1977). As in our argument, Hocquenghem recognizes the culturally specific function of the concept of 'the homosexual'; Hocquenghem makes references to Foucault and he points to what he calls the 'growing imperialism' of society, which seeks to attribute a social status to everything, even the unclassified. The result has been that homosexuality has been ever more closely defined (see Weeks 1978).

Hocquenghem argues that 'homosexual desire', indeed like heterosexual, is an arbitrary division of the flux of desire, which in itself is polyvocal and undifferentiated, so that the notion of exclusive homosexuality is a 'fallacy of the imaginary', a misrecognition and ideological misperception.[9] But despite this, homosexuality has a vivid social presence, and this is because it expresses an aspect of desire which appears nowhere else. For the direct manifestation of homosexual desire opposes the relations of roles and identities necessarily imposed by the Oedipus complex in order to ensure the reproduction of society. Capitalism, in its necessary employment of Oedipalization to control the tendency to decoding, manufactures 'homosexuals' just as it produces proletarians, and what is manufactured is a psychologically repressive category. He argues that the principal ideological means of thinking about homosexuality are ultimately, though not mechanically, connected with the advance of Western capitalism. They amount to a perverse 're-territorialization', a massive effort to regain social control, in a world tending toward disorder and decoding. As a result the establishment of homosexuality as a separate category goes hand in hand with its repression. On the one hand, we have the creation of a minority of 'homosexuals', on the other, the transformation in the majority of the repressed homosexual elements of desire into the desire to repress. Hence sublimated homosexuality is the basis of the paranoia about homosexuality which pervades social behaviour, which in turn is a guarantee of the survival of the Oedipal relations, the victory of the law of the father. Hocquenghem argues that only one organ is allowed in the Oedipal triangle, what Deleuze and Guattari call the 'despotic signifier', the phallus. And as money is the true universal reference point for capitalism, so the phallus is the reference point for heterosexism. The phallus determines, whether by absence or presence, the girl's penis envy, the boy's castration anxiety; it draws on libidinal energy in the same way as money draws on labour. And as this comment underlines, this Oedipalization is itself a product of capitalism and not, as the Lacanian school might argue, a law of culture or of all patriarchal societies.

Without going into further details several difficulties emerge. The first relates to the whole question of homosexual paranoia – reminiscent in many ways of the recent discussion of homophobia in Britain and the USA (Weinberg 1973). The idea that repression of homosexuality in modern society is a product of suppressed homosexuality comes at times very close to a hydraulic theory of sexuality, which both symbolic interactionism and Lacanian interpretations of Freud have ostensibly rejected. It is not a sufficient explanatory principle simply to reverse the idea that homosexuality is a paranoia, peddled by the medical profession in the present century, into the idea that hostile attitudes to homosexuality are themselves paranoid. Nor does the theory help explain the real, if limited, liberalization of attitudes that has taken place in some Western countries or the range of attitudes that are empirically known to exist in different countries and even in different families.

Second, following from this, there is the still unanswered problem of why some individuals become 'homosexual' and others do not. The use of the concept of Oedipalization restores some notion of social determinancy that symbolic interactionism lacks, but, by corollary, its use loses any sense of the relevance of the specific family pressures, the educational and labelling processes, the media images that reinforce the identity and the individual shaping of meaning. Third, there is the ambiguous relationship of capitalism to patriarchy. If Mitchell can be rightly criticized for creating two separate areas for political struggle, the economic (against capitalism) and the ideological (against patriarchy), then Hocquenghem can be criticized for collapsing them together.

Finally, there is Hocquenghem's failure to explore the different modalities of lesbianism. It is important to note that what Hocquenghem is discussing is essentially male homosexuality, for in Hocquenghem's view, although the law of the father dominates both the male and the female, it is to the authority of the father in reproduction (both of the species and of Oedipalization itself) that homosexuality poses the major challenge; as Deleuze and Guattari note, male homosexuality, far from being a product of the Oedipus complex, as some Freudians imply, itself constitues a totally different mode of social relationships, no longer vertical, but horizontal. Lesbianism, by implication, assumes its significance as a challenge to the secondary position accorded to female sexuality in capitalist society. It is not so much lesbianism as female sexuality which society denies. But Hocquenghem quite fails to pursue the point, which is central if we are to grasp the formation of sexual meanings. Despite these objections, however, Hocquenghem's essay raises important questions, some of which will be taken up below.

Whereas Hocquenghem, following Deleuze and Guattari, is intent on developing a philosophy of desire, Foucault, though much influenced by and having influence on this tendency, is more concerned in his later works with delineating a theory of power and the complex interplay between power and discourses. Foucault's work marks a break with conventional views of power. Power is not unitary, it does not reside in the state, it is not a thing to hold.

By power, I do not mean 'Power' as a group of institutions and mechanisms that ensure the subservience of the citizens of a given state. By power, I do not mean, either, a mode of subjugation which, in contrast to violence, has the form of the rule. Finally, I do not have in mind a general system of domination exerted by one group over another ... these are only the terminal forms power takes. It seems to me that power must be understood in the first instance as the multiplicity of force relations, immanent in the sphere in which they operate and which constitute their own organisation; as the process which, through ceaseless struggles and confrontations transforms, strengthens, or reverses them; as the support which these force relations find in one another, thus forming a chain or a system, or on the contrary, the disfunctions and contradictions which isolate them from one another; and lastly, as the strategies in which they take effect, whose general design or institutional crystallization is embodied in the state apparatus, in the formulation of the law, in the various social hegemonies. [Foucault 1979, pp. 92–3]

The problem with this theory of power is that by breaking with a reductive or negative view, power 'remains almost as a process, without specification within different instances' (Coward 1978, p. 20). And although he is unwilling to specify in advance any privileged source of power, there nevertheless underlies his work what might be termed a 'philosophical monism' (Zinner 1978, p. 220), a conception of a will to power (and hence his complex linkage with Nietzsche) forever expanding and bursting forth in the form of the will to know. It is the complexes of power/knowledge that Foucault explores in his essay on *The History of Sexuality*; the original French version of its 'Introduction' has the title 'La volonté de savoir', 'The will to knowledge', which makes his concerns transparent:

Things are accorded the weight of creation, while the human subject becomes a mere appendage – the speaker, the knower, the listener, the transmitter – and above all the spectator of the passage of discourse. (Zinner 1978, p. 220)

It is through discourse that the complex of power/knowledge is realized. Foucault is not interested in the history of mind but in the history of discourse:

The question which I ask is not of codes but of events: the law of existence of the statements, that which has rendered them possible – these and none other in their place: the conditions of their singular emergence; their correlations with other previous or simultaneous events, discursive or not. The question, however, I try to answer without referring to the consciousness, obscure or explicit, of speaking subjects; without relating the facts of discourse to the will – perhaps involuntary – of their authors. [Foucault 1978b, p. 14]

What he is suggesting is that the relationship between symbol and symbolized is not only referential but productive. The order of language produces its own material forms and desires as much as the physical possibilities. But there is no single hidden hand of history, no complex causative complex, no pre-ordained goal, no final truth of human history. Discourses produce their own truths as the possibilities of seeing the world in fresh ways emerge.

The history of sexuality therefore becomes a history of our discourses about sexuality. And the Western experience of sex, he argues, is not the inhibition of discourse but a constant, and historically changing, deployment of discourses on sex, and this ever-expanding discursive explosion is part of a complex growth of control over individuals, partly through the apparatus of sexuality. Power is articulated through discourse: it invests, creates, produces. 'Power as a form of productivity forms the subject rather than simply imposing itself; power is desiring rather than constraining' (D'Amico 1978, p. 179).

But behind the vast explosion of discourses on sexuality since the eighteenth century, there is no single unifying strategy valid for the whole of society. And in particular, breaking with an orthodox Marxist problematic, he denies that it can be simply interpreted in terms of problems of 'reproduction'. In the 'Introduction' to *The History of Sexuality* (which is a methodological excursus, rather than a complete 'history') Foucault suggests four strategic unities, linking together a host of practices and techniques, which formed specific mechanics of knowledge and power centering on sex: a hysterization of women's bodies, a pedagogization of children's sex, a socialization of procreative behaviour, a psychiatrization of perverse pleasures. And four figures emerged from these preoccupations, four objects of knowledge, four subjects subjected, targets of and anchorages for the categories which were being simultaneously investigated and regulated: the hysterical woman, the masturbating child, the Malthusian couple and the perversive adult. The thrust of these discursive creations is control, control not through denial or prohibition, but through production, through imposing a grid of definition on the possibilities of the body.

The deployment of sexuality has its reasons for being, not in reproducing itself, but in proliferating, innovating, annexing, creating, and penetrating bodies in an increasingly detailed way, and in controlling populations in an increasingly comprehensive way. [Foucault 1979, p. 107]

This is obviously related to Foucault's analysis of the genealogy of the disciplinary society, a society of surveillance and control, in *Discipline and Punish* (Foucault 1977a) and to his argument that power proceeds not in the traditional model of sovereignty but through administering and fostering life.

The old power of death that symbolised sovereign power was now carefully supplanted by the administration of bodies and the calculated management of life. [Foucault 1979, pp. 139–40]

The obvious question is why. Foucault's 'radical nominalism' rejects the question of causation, but he quite clearly perceives the significance of extra-discursive references. In *I, Pierre Riviere*, the French revolution is perceived as having profound resonances (Foucault 1978a). In *The History of Sexuality*, as in *Discipline and Punish*, he refers to the profound changes of the eighteenth century:

What occurred in the eighteenth century in some western countries, an event bound up with the development of capitalism, was. . . nothing less than the entry of life into history. [Foucault 1979, p. 141]

And in the emergence of 'bio-power', Foucault's characteristic term for 'modern' social forms, sexuality becomes a key element. For sex, argues Foucault, is the pivot of two axes along which the whole technology of life developed; it was the point of entry to the body, to the harnessing, identification and distribution of forces over the body, and it was the entry to control and regulation of populations. 'Sex was a means of access both to the life of the body and the life of the species' (Foucault 1979, p. 146). As a result, sex becomes a crucial target of power organized around the management of life, rather than the sovereign threat of death which organizes 'pre-modern' societies.

Foucault stresses not the historical cause of events but the conditions for the emergence of discourses and practices. Nevertheless there appears to be a strong functionalist tendency in his work. 'Social control' is no longer a product of a materially motivated ruling class but the concept of subjection within discourse seems as ultimately enveloping a concept.

'Where there is power, there is resistance', he argues, but nevertheless, and *because* of this, 'resistance is never in a position of exteriority in relation to power' (1979, p. 95). Indeed the very existence of power relies on a multiplicity of points of resistance, which play the role of 'adversary, target, support, or handle in power relations'. Foucault apparently envisages the power of social explosions in forcing new ways of seeing: the great social changes (industrial capitalism?) of the eighteenth and nineteenth centuries, the French Revolution, the possibilities opened up by the 'evenements' of 1968. But one reading of his work would suggest that without such explosions, techniques of discipline and surveillance, strategies of power/knowledge leave us always, already, trapped.

But an alternative reading is possible. First of all there is the possibility of struggles over definition. This can be seen both in struggles over definitions of female sexuality and over the various and subtle forms of control of homosexuality.

There is no question that the appearance in nineteenth century psychiatry, jurisprudence, and literature of a whole series of discourses on the species and subspecies of homosexuality, inversion, pederasty, and 'psychic hermaphrodism' made possible a strong advance of social controls into this area of 'perversity'; but it also made possible the formation of a 'reverse' discourse: homosexuality began to speak on its own behalf, to demand that its legitimacy or 'naturality' be acknowledged, often in the same vocabulary, using the same categories by which it was radically disqualified. [Foucault 1979, p. 101]

This reverse affirmation is the sub-text of the history of the homosexual rights movement; it points to the significance of the definitional struggle *and* to its limitations. Hence Foucault's comment:

I believe that the movements labelled 'sexual liberation' ought to be understood as movements of affirmation starting with sexuality. Which means two things: they are movements that start with sexuality, with the apparatus of sexuality in the midst of which we're caught, and which make it function to the limit; but, at the same time, they are in motion relative to it, disengaging themselves and surmounting it. [1977b, p. 155]

The ramifications of this 'surmounting' are not clear, but it is apparent that both the evolution of homosexual meanings and identities is not complete or 'scientifically' established and that homosexuals are, possibly for the first time, self-consciously participating as a group in that evolution.

The other point of high importance in Foucault's work is the emphasis on the genesis of particular institutions: of prisons, the clinic, medical and psychiatric practices which both produce and regulate the objects of knowledge. Appreciation of this emphasis will draw us away from such questions as: what is the relationship between the mode of production and this form of sexuality? Instead we can concentrate on the practices which actually constitute social and sexual categories and ensure their controlling impact. But, in turn, to do this we need to recognize that discourses do not arbitrarily emerge from the flux of possibilities, nor are discourses our only contact with the real: they have their conditions of existence and their effects in concrete, historical, social, economic, and ideological situations.

Perspectives and projects

We are now in a sounder position to indicate more effective lines of historical research, or rather to pose the questions to which the historians of sexuality need to address themselves. They are effectively in two parts. First, what were the conditions for the emergence of the homosexual category (or indeed other sexual categories), the complex of factors which fixed the possibilities of homosexual behaviours into a system of defining concepts? Second, what were and are the factors which define the individual acceptance or rejection of categorizations? This is a question that many might regard as invalid but which seems to us of critical importance in determining the impact of control and regulation.

Conditions

Foucault and others have stressed the growing importance of the 'norm' since the eighteenth century.

Another consequence of this development of bio-power was the growing importance assumed by the action of the norm at the expense of the juridical system of the law. [Foucault 1979, p. 149]

A power whose task is to take charge of life needs continuous regulatory and corrective mechanisms. It has to qualify, measure, appraise and hierarchize: 'it affects distributions around the norms'. This is not far removed from a more commonplace observation that the development of liberal ('individualistic') society in the nineteenth century led to an increase of conventionality, or to dicussions of ideological 'interpellations' in the construction of hegemonic forms (Laclau 1977); but the examination of the 'norm' does point effectively to the centrality since the nineteenth century of the norm of the monogamous, heterosexual family. The uncertain status of sodomy points to the fact that before the nineteenth century, the codes governing sexual practices – canonical, pastoral, civil – all centred on non-reproductive relations. Sodomy was part of a continuum of non-procreative practices, often more serious than rape precisely because it was barren. But these regulations were not extra-marital; they entered the marriage bed, were directly about non-reproductive sex in conjugality, whatever the effectiveness of enforcement. From the nineteenth century the regulations are increasingly of non-conjugal relations: from incest and childhood sex to homosexuality. As sexuality is increasingly privatized, seen as the characteristic of the personal sphere, as its public manifestations are challenged (in terms that speak all the time of sex while denying it), so deviant forms of sex become subject to more closely defined *public* regulation. The family norm is strengthened by a series of extra-marital regulations, which refer back all the time to its normality and morality. This is, of course, underlined by a whole series of other developments, from the enforcement of the Poor Laws and the Factory Acts to the Welfare State support of particular household models in the twentieth century. To repeat a point made earlier, the specification, and hence greater regulation, of homosexual behaviour is closely interconnected with the revaluation and construction of the bourgeois family, not necessarily as a conscious effort to support or sustain the family but because, as Plummer has put it:

The family as a social institution does not of itself condemn homosexuality, but through its mere existence it implicitly provides a model that renders the homosexual experience invalid. [1975, p. 210]

But if we accept this outline as a fruitful guideline for research we need, second, to stress its class specificities. For if 'sexuality' and its derivative sexual categorizations are social constructs, then they are constructions within specific class milieux, whatever the impact of their 'diffusion' or re-appropriation. We need to explore, in much greater depth than before, the class application of the homosexual categorizations. The common interest among many early twentieth-century middle-class, self-defined homosexuals with the male working class, conceived of as relatively indifferent to homosexual behaviour, is a highly significant element in the homosexual sub-culture.

There was in fact a notable predominance of upper middle class values. Perhaps on one level only middle-class men had a sufficient sense of a 'personal life' through which to develop a homosexual identity (Zaretsky 1976). The stress that is evident among male homosexual writers on cross-class liaisons and on youth (typically the representative idealized relationship is between an upper middle-class man and a working-class youth) is striking, and not dissimilar, it may be noted in passing, to certain middle-class heterosexual patterns of the nineteenth century and earlier. See for example, the anonymous author, usually known as Walter, of the nineteenth century sexual chronicle, *My Secret Life* (Anon. c. 1880). The impossibility of same-class liaisons is a constant theme of homosexual literature, demonstrating the strong elements of guilt (class and sexual) that pervade the male identity. But it also illustrates a pattern of what can be called 'sexual colonialism', which saw the working-class youth or soldier as a source of 'trade', often coinciding uneasily with an idealization of the reconciling effect of cross-class liaisons.

But if the idealization of working-class youth was one major theme, the attitude of these working-class men themselves is less easy to trace. They appear in all the major scandals (for example, the Wilde trial, the Cleveland Street scandal) but their self-conceptions are almost impossible to disinter. We may hypothesize that the spread of a homosexual consciousness was much less strong among working-class men than middle class – for obvious family and social factors – even though the law in Britain (on, for example, importuning) probably affected more working-class than middle-class men. We can also note the evidence regarding the patterns of male prostitution as, for example, in the Brigade of Guards, a European-wide phenomenon. Most of the so far sparse evidence on male prostitution suggests a reluctance on the part of the 'prostitute' to define himself as homosexual (Weeks 1980).

A third point relates to this, concerning the gender specificity of homosexual behaviour. The lesbian sense of self has been much less pronounced than that of the male homosexual and the sub-cultural development exiguous. If the Wilde trial was a major labelling event for men, the comparable event for lesbianism, the trial of Radclyffe Hall's lesbian novel, *The Well of Loneliness*, was much less devastating in its impact, and a generation later. Even science, so anxious to detail the characteristics of male homosexuals, largely ignored lesbianism.

These factors underline the fact that what is needed is not so much a monist explanation for the emergence of a 'homosexual identity' as a differential social history of male homosexuality and lesbianism. But this in turn demands an awareness of the construction of specific gender definitions, and their relationship to sexual identities. Gagnon and Simon have noted that:

the patterns of overt sexual behaviour on the part of homosexual females tend to resemble those of heterosexual females and to differ radically from the sexual patterns of both heterosexual and homosexual males. [1973, p. 180]

The impact on lesbianism of, for example, the discourses on (basically male) homosexuality has never been explored (but see Faraday in this volume).

Fourth, this underscores again the need to explore the various practices which create the terrain or space in which behaviour is constructed. There is a long historical tradition, as we have seen, of exploring legal regulation, but its impact in constructing categories has never been considered. The role of the medicalization of sexual deviance has also been tentatively explored, but it is only now that its complexly differentiated impact is being traced. Equally important are the various forms of ideological representations of homosexual behaviour, whether through the press or through the dramatizing effects of major rituals of public condemnation, such as the Oscar Wilde trial in the 1890s.

Fifth, there is an absence of any study of the political appropriation of concepts of sexual perversity, although there is a great deal of empirical evidence from the nineteenth century to the present that sexual deviance had a significant place in sexual–political discourse. This indicates the need for a close attention to specific conjunctures of sexual politics and to the social forces at work in constructing political alliances around crimes of morality. The role of sexual respectability in helping to cement the dominant power bloc in the nineteenth century and the relevance of sexual liberalism in constructing the social democratic hegemony of the 1960s in Britain and elsewhere are examples in point (Gray 1977; Hall *et al*. 1978).

What this schematic sketch suggests is the importance of locating sexual categorization within a complex of discourses and practices, but also at the same time it is important to reject descriptions which ignore the importance of external referents. The agitation for legal regulation, the impact of medicalization and the stereotyping of media representation all have sources in perceptions of the world and in complex power situations. One may mention, for example, the network of fears over moral decay, imperial decline and public vice behind the 1885 Criminal Law Amendment Act or the Cold War fears that form the background to the establishment of the Wolfenden Committee in 1954. Or, with regard to the growth of a medical model, we cannot disregard the significance of the growing professionalization of medicine in the nineteenth century, its ideological and material links with upper middle class male society and its consequent role in defining sexuality as well as 'sexual perversions'. So although it would be wrong to see the regulation of homosexual behaviour as a simple effect of capitalist development, it is intricately linked to wider changes within the growth of a highly industrialized, bourgeois society.

Identities

All ideologies, Althusser has argued, work by interpellating ('hailing') particular subjects, and the ideological discourses that establish the categories of sexual perversity address particular types of persons. They also, as Foucault suggest, create the possibility of reversals within the discourses: where there is power, there is resistance. Foucault is here offering a space for the self-creation of a homosexual identity, but what is absent is any interest in why some are able to respond or recognize themselves in the interpellation and others are not (Johnson 1979, p. 75).

There are major problems in this area for which our guidelines are tentative. There is abundant evidence that individual, self-defined homosexuals see their sexuality as deeply rooted, and often manifest at a very early age. This would, on the surface at least, seem to deny that interaction with significant others creates the desire (as opposed to the identity), hence undermining a purely voluntarist position. On the other hand, the notion of a deeply structured homosexual component is equally questionable, if for no other reason than that all the evidence of historical variations contradicts it. Labelling theory has been quite able to accept the distinctions we are making, for example, between primary and secondary deviation.

Primary deviation, as contrasted with secondary, is polygenetic, arising out of a variety of social, cultural, psychological, and adventitious or recurring combinations . . . secondary deviance refers to a special class of socially defined responses which people make to problems created by the societal reaction to their deviance . . . . The secondary deviant, as opposed to his actions, is a person whose life and identity are organised around the facts of deviance. [Lemert 1967, p. 40]

This is a valuable distinction stressing the real (and hitherto ignored) importance of social labelling, but it ignores precisely those historical (and hence variable) factors which structure the differences. To put it another way, if the homosexual component is not a factor present only in a fixed minority of people, but on the contrary an aspect of the body's sexual possibilities, what social and cultural forces are at work which ensure its dominance in some people, whereas in others the heterosexual element is apparently as strong and determined? Social labelling is obviously central in making the divide between 'normal' and 'deviant', but what shapes the components at the level of the human animal?

This must lead us again to ask whether we can rescue any lessons from psychoanalytical speculations. A recent attempt to reinterpret Freud's analysis of Little Hans throws some light on this question. Mia Campioni and Liz Gross appear to accept the arguments of Deleuze and Guattari (and Foucault) that Freud's work was simultaneously a recognition of, and another form of control over, the organization of desire under capitalism (Campioni and Gross 1978). The function of Oedipus is thus to organize sexuality into properly different gender roles to accord both with patriarchal norms *and* a society which privileges sexuality.

The purpose of concentrating on the case of Little Hans is to reveal the precise mechanisms whereby a system of representation (ideology), correlative with existing social structures, is inscribed upon the child within the constraints of relations specified by the family ... the process by which Hans is inserted into his patriarchal heritage gives us an indication of this process's mechanisms – at least in the case of male socialisation .... Moreover, the case allows us to clarify the strategies by which the child is inscribed into the power relations that stratify society, and to discover that this occurs by means of the sexualisation of privileged erogeneous zones. It is by the privileging of sexual zones, desires and objects, and by their social control through psychical defence mechanisms, in particular repression, that class and patriarchal social values are instilled in the child which are constructive of his or her very identity. Sexualisation is the means both of the production and the limitation of desire, and therefore is also the locus of the control of desire. Sexual desire provides the socio-political structure with a specific site for power relations (relations of domination and subordination in general) to be exercised. [Campioni and Gross 1978, p. 103]

At the beginning of Hans' case what is most apparent are the overwhelming number of objects and aims of his eroticism. Over the two years of the analysis this sexuality is channelled into the forms of masculine sexuality demanded by familial ideology, and in this we can see, dramatically at work in Freud's analysis and the father's work as agent, the actual imposition of the Oedipal network by the psychoanalytical institution, a paradigm of its controlling role in the twentieth century.

Several points come out of this which are worth underlining. First, this re-analysis does not assume the family is a natural, biological entity with single effects. On the contrary, it is seen as historically constituted and a consequent intersection of various developments, including the development of childhood and the social differentiation of women and men. Second, the analysis does not assume the naturalness of heterosexuality. Instead it relates its privileging precisely to the construction of masculinity and femininity within the monogamous (and socially constituted) family. Third, it does not see the Oedipus complex as in any way universal. Not only is it historically specific, but it is also class specific. Fourth, the analysis suggests that the child's development is neither natural nor internal to the family unit. The young human animal, with all his or her potentialities, is structured within a family, which all the time is a combination of social processes, and by constant reference to the social other.

It is within this context that psychological masculinity and femininity are structured at the level of the emotions. It seems likely that the possibilities of heterosexuality and homosexuality as socially structured limitations on the flux of potentialities are developed in this nexus in the process of emotional socialization. The emotion thus draws on sexuality rather than being created by it.

But what is created, this would suggest, is not an identity but a propensity (see Dannecker 1977, p. 52). It is the whole series of social interactions, encounters with peers, educational processes, rituals of exclusion, labelling events, chance encounters, political identifications and so on which structure the sexual identities. They are not pre-given in nature; probably like the propensities themselves they are social creations, though at different levels in the formation of psychological individuality. This again suggests a rich field for historical explorations: the conditions for the growth of sub-cultural formations (urbanization, response to social pressure, etc.), the degree of sub-cultural participation, the role of sub-cultural involvement in the fixing of sexual identities, the impact of legal and ideological regulation, the political responses to the sub-culture, both from within the homosexual community and without, and the possibilities for transformations.

Conclusion

What has been offered here is neither a prescription for correct research procedures nor a collection of dogmatic answers, but a posing of important and fundamentally *historical* questions which the historians of sexuality have generally ignored. Earlier in the paper, the problem was posed on two levels: the level of the *social* categorization and the level of the *individual*, subjective construction of meaning. Until very recently, as Mary McIntosh pointed out, the latter level was exclusively concentrated on, to the extent that the question of aetiology dominated. Since then, particularly with the rise of deviancy studies, the social has rightly been emphasized. What I am now tentatively suggesting is that we must see both as aspects of the same process, which is above all a historical process. Social processes construct subjectivities not just as 'categories' but at the level of individual desires. This perception, rather than the search for epistemological purity, should be the starting point for future social and historical studies of 'homosexuality' and indeed of 'sexuality' in general.

5 Liberating lesbian research

Annabel Faraday

The greatest threat to men is solidarity among women and 'lesbianism' epitomizes that solidarity.

SIDNEY ABBOTT and BARBARA LOVE

It is perhaps tokenistic, and certainly ironic, that a collection of papers concerned with researching 'homosexuality' should include one contribution concerned with 'lesbians', a situation which would appear to reflect and reproduce the nature of the entire field of sociological and clinical research into 'homosexuality', which has been overwhelmingly concerned with men. Any attentions to women have tended to be, at best, attempts to constrict them within male models, thus duplicating on a smaller scale the kinds of work done on gay men, or, at worst, footnoting or appendixing mention of women in studies concerned only with men. What I wish to stress throughout this paper, however, is that while research on lesbians is less extensive, itself a reflection of the neglect or denial of women in the broader field of sociology, the task is not to 'redress the balance' or to put lesbians 'on the map' alongside male homosexuals as if they could be discussed within the same conceptual frameworks. Emotional relationships between women, *whether or not they have involved overt physical expression*, have tended to remain invisible and insignificant to historians and sociologists alike; it is essential that notions of 'the lesbian' are reconceptualized within the context of her oppressed social position as woman and not as 'female homosexual'. Any discussion of lesbian women can do and does great harm and injustice to lesbians, indeed to all women, if it fails to examine the power differentials between the sexes, the implications of those power differentials for relationships between women and between male researchers and female research 'objects', or if it presents a definition of 'lesbian' in sexual terms without examining the socially constructed and male-defined nature of 'sexual' meanings.

In short, this paper (a) calls for a radical re-examination of the patronizing, paternalistic and patriarchal assumptions which underlie contemporary sociological definitions of lesbianism, (b) questions the aims of sociological research based on those definitions, and (c) suggests possible orientations for feminist research which start from an awareness of and commitment to the interests of women, whether or not they define themselves, or are defined as, lesbian.[1]

Lesbian definitions

Within sociological research, lesbians are widely referred to as 'female counterparts' of male homosexuals, either explicitly (see, for example, Saghir and Robins 1973; Tripp 1977; Bell and Weinberg 1978) or by implication where studies on homosexuality contain a section on men followed by a shorter section on women (the discussion of lesbians in McIntosh 1968 is a prime example). Historically lesbian women and gay men have been co-categorized as perverts, inverts, homophiles, queers, homosexuals and gays, both in 'scientific' literature and popular language. Such co-categorization is based on behaviouristic understandings of the nature of 'same-sex' relationships; it has been widely assumed that lesbians and gay men, by virtue of the fact that they relate on an intimate level with members of the same sex, must share certain characteristics which place them well within the same category. What is *not* recognized is that while both lesbians and gay men are not 'heterosexual', heterosexuality itself is a power relationship of men over women; what gay men and lesbians are rejecting[2] are essentially polar experiences.[3]

Working on this assumption of common ground, many researchers have deliberated at length as to why more attention has been given to men than to women within 'scientific' literature on 'homosexuality'. Gagnon and Simon do appear to be deploring the fact when they state that 'the scientific literature on the lesbian is extremely sparse' (1973, p. 176) and refer to 'the limited body of research on the area'. Likewise Donna Tanner states, 'In contrast to the time, money and attention paid to male homosexuality, relatively little is known about female homosexuality' (1978, p. 2). In her psychoanalytic study Charlotte Wolff declared that 'lesbianism has been neglected, even in scientific enquiry', before going on to present her own work in terms of an 'authoritative book wholly devoted to the subject' (1971, p. 6). Finally E. M. Ettore asks 'why has there consistently been more concern for homosexual men than lesbians?', describing 'homosexuality' as 'the practice of an alternative sexuality for either men or women' (1980).

This perceived neglect in contrast to research on male homosexuality has tended to result in studies which claim to present definitive portraits of 'the lesbian', almost as some newly discovered species or sub-category of 'woman', and which are defined initially or centrally in terms of sexual behaviour. What I wish to explore in this section are the male assumptions about 'sexuality' which underlie behavioural definitions of lesbians, and to show how the use of those definitions has enabled researchers to draw justificatory conclusions about the 'invisibility' of women.

Suggested reasons for the interest paid to gay men tend to centre on their greater 'visibility', through their involvement in public and impersonal sex, and the consequent problems which this poses for them (Tanner 1978); the fact that their greater visibility makes them easier to recruit for research purposes (Bell and Weinberg 1978); that research funding bodies tend to be more interested in the 'problem' of gay men (Bell and Weinberg 1978); and that until recently most social scientists were men, for whom the idea of two women in an erotic embrace – an image often conjured up by men when thinking about lesbians – is a source of sexual arousal rather than a problematic research field (Gagnon and Simon 1973).

It has been suggested that gay men are more visible because of their stronger 'sex drive':

The promiscuity of most uninhibited males rests partly on biological traditions – a high sex-drive, an easily triggered responsiveness, and perhaps a kind of species history of the sexual chase .... Their situation is in sharp contrast to that of most women who are neither so 'driven' nor so visual; ... in homosexuality the difference between the sexes is sharply drawn, not only by the ease of male–male contacts but by the near total lack of promiscuity among lesbians. [Tripp 1977, p. 154]

In addition it is argued that lesbians are less visible because fewer women than men engage in 'homosexual behaviour' (Kinsey *et al.* 1953; McIntosh 1968). It has even been asserted that lesbians' 'invisibility' is a direct result of the physiology of their genitals:

> Biologically sex between women would be 'impractical' under other than the bedroom situation. Thus, while the life of the homosexual man is often public and complicated, the life of *his female counterpart* can be kept private and that is often what it is. [Saghir and Robins 1973, p. 305; emphasis mine]

Gay men's visibility is discussed by Mary McIntosh in terms of their having a more 'well-developed role' than lesbians. This difference is seen as a direct result of mechanisms of social control over sexual behaviour. Using data from Kinsey it is argued that:

> Fewer women than men engage in homosexual behaviour. By the time they are 45, 26% of women have had *some* homosexual experience, whereas about 50% of men have. But this is probably a cause rather than an effect of the difference in the extent to which the homosexual role is crystallized, for women engage in less non-marital activity of any kind than men. [McIntosh 1968, p. 191]

The concepts which need to be questioned here are those of social control and sexual behaviour; within a society where all women are socially controlled through the enforcement of 'femininity' and defined in terms of the psychological, emotional and physical dependency on men through the very internalization and enactment of the 'feminine' role with all its attendant attributes, it remains unnecessary to control and divide women by more formal methods. I shall examine later how the concept of 'sexual' is widely used within these debates.

Continually, then, comparisons are drawn in social science between women's and men's same sex relationships using models of male sexuality from which to look at lesbians. From the bulk of sociological research studies conducted since 1968,[4] over half define lesbians on the basis of 'sexual' activity with other women, the remainder avoiding definitional problems by seeing lesbians as women who belong to lesbian organizations or communities. For example, a lesbian, when defined, is seen as:

(a) a woman who has chosen to have sex with a member of the same gender, has undergone a period of transformation which is termed in the gay community, 'coming out', and whose identity now encompasses among other elements, the attributes which this woman associates with the label 'lesbian'. These attributes will include actual sexual behaviour between two females (or more) and the ability and the desire to eroticize other women as opposed to men. [Tanner 1978, p. 7]

(b) a female who focusses her sexual attentions, fantasies and activities upon members of her own sex . . . [Hedblom 1973, p. 333]

(c) a woman who interacts sexually with a same sex partner . . . [Masters and Johnson 1979, p. ix]

or who has:

(d) a history of repetitive homosexual activity . . . [Saghir and Robins 1973]

In short, no sociological research on lesbians to date would appear to challenge the view that lesbian relationships are based on, defined by and necessarily involve 'sexual behaviour'.[5] In its most explicit form, this position is succinctly stated by Saghir and Robins when discussing gender differences in 'homosexual' behaviour; both lesbians and gay men are viewed within male models whereby the desire for 'sex' is the raison d'etre of any woman who defines herself as lesbian:

In her search for sex, the homosexual woman looks first for a relationship and usually establishes a relationship prior to any sexual activity. [1973, p. 313; emphasis mine]

A distinction is made then between 'sexual activity' and 'lesbian relationships'; the latter is somehow presumed to be endured for the sake of the former – the area of the 'sexual' becomes that which defines relationships with women. What is meant by 'sexual' in these definitions? To begin to answer this, it helps to look at some of the ways in which women's sexuality has been defined in post-Kinsey sexual behaviourism.

Sexology and male heterosexism

Since their studies first appeared, Kinsey and his team have left a legacy of popular myth-conceptions concerning the 'nature' of sexuality, not the least being their deterministic hydraulic model of sexual 'need' or 'outlet' (Kinsey *et al.* 1948, 1953). Kinsey *et al.* acknowledged problems in defining the 'sexual' area only in so far as their interest was in 'stimulus' and 'response'; their major achievement appears to have been in wrenching and reinforcing a distinction between the 'social', the 'socio-sexual' and 'definitely sexual', whereby the only unambiguously sexual situation is that which results in orgasm, or what they preferred to call 'sexual outlet'.[6] Using this orgasm definition of 'sexual', the Kinsey studies posited the same models of 'sexual response' for men and women, the difference in them being only in terms of frequency and regularity. Women, it was declared, are less sensitive than men to psychological stimuli and require more direct arousal to achieve the same 'end'. The studies even went as far as to suggest that these differences in 'sensitivity' are directly related to differences in male and female brain structure.[7] But whatever their suggested 'explanation', the Kinsey 'observations', that sex equals orgasm equals basic physiological need to which men are more subject than women, is a male supremacist construct par excellence; wrench the area of the 'sexual' from that of the 'social', observe that men are more 'sexual' than women, and the seeds are sown for a male-defined 'science' of sexology.

The early works of Masters and Johnson (1966, 1970) in many ways complemented that of Kinsey's team. While the latter were concerned with varieties of behaviour leading to orgasm, the former forced the concept of 'sexual' even further away from the area of the 'social', to examining the nature of physiological arousal. What Masters and Johnson stressed above all else was (a) the irrelevance of the vagina and the centrality of the clitoris to women's attainment of orgasm, (b) women's multi-orgasmic potential, and (c) the essential similarity of men's and women's 'sexual response' patterns in masturbation.

These 'findings' have been taken up by sexologists in more recent years as evidence that there is no 'basic' difference between male and female sexuality; the *base line* from which comparison is made is the male definition of sex equalling orgasm. As Masters and Johnson stated, historically male orgasm has been seen as more significant and important than female orgasm, and they suggest that this is primarily for reproductive reasons – women do not need to have an orgasm in order to reproduce. However, they present the female orgasm as having an *equally* important role in reproduction and a central role in men's sexual arousal – by suggesting that if a woman is genuinely aroused in coitus (as opposed to faking orgasms or simply not 'responding'), men's sexual arousal will be even greater. The onus is on the woman to ensure her own arousal in order to arouse the man further: •

With the need for [orgasmic] pretence removed, a sexually responding woman can stimulate effectively the interaction upon which both the man's and the woman's psychosocial requirements are culturally so dependent for orgasmic facility. [Masters and Johnson 1966, p. 138]

Since Masters and Johnson's work, there has been a growing body of literature on the orgasm. Much sexology and sexual theorizing of recent years can be seen as a reaction to Kinsey's notion of women's 'sexual inferiority' by attempting to prove that women can out-do men on their own ground, that is, in terms of orgasmic 'achievement'. Most notably Sherfey (1973), drawing on the 'multi-orgasmic potential' finding, suggested that women possess a biologically determined high sexual drive which, by necessity of 'civilization' and the 'requirements' of family life, has been and must continute to be suppressed. Observing the behaviour of women in the late 1960s, Sherfey commented:

Just within the very recent past, a decided lifting of the ancient social injunctions against the free expression of female sexuality has occurred . . . it is hard to predict what will happen should this trend continue; if women's sexual drive has not abated and they prove incapable of controlling it, thereby jeopardizing family life and child care, a return to the rigid, enforced suppression will be inevitable and mandatory. [1973, p. 140]

Here women have come to be seen as 'dangerous' rather than 'inferior' in the sexual realm; either way they lose out.

Other 'sexological' attempts to bring women into line have included research into women's emotional and physiological responses to pornography. Laboratory results have shown that women report 'excitement' when exposed to such material (Sigusch *et al.* 1970), and this has led to the conclusion that 'the actual facts do not support notions about women's *sexual deficiencies*' (Fisher 1973, p. 157, emphasis mine). There has been no research to date on the meaning which that form of women's 'excitement' takes in response to pornography. As Brownmiller has observed, heterosexual pornography consists of degrading images of women:

(Women) whose bodies are being stripped, exposed and contorted for the purpose of ridicule to bolster that 'masculine esteem' which gets its kick and sense of power from viewing females as anonymous, panting playthings, adult toys, dehumanized objects to be used, abused, broken and discarded .... There can be no 'equality' in porn, no female equivalent, no turning of the tables in the name of bawdy fun. Pornography, like rape, is a male invention, designed to dehumanize women, to reduce the female to an object of sexual access, not to free sensuality from moralistic or parental inhibition. [1976, p. 394]

Given then the essentially degrading nature of pornographic depictions of women, it seems logical to assume that such 'excitement' which women report would be more akin to that experienced through sexual assault than to any autonomous and self-affirming sexual pleasure. Moreover physiological research into women's arousal response to pornography (Wincze *et al.* 1977) suggests that reports of 'excitement' are not necessarily congruent with genital arousal, demonstrating that this type of research cannot account for the meanings which women attribute to such 'excitement'.[8]

Sexology has ascertained then that the clitoris and the penis are not biologically dissimilar in terms of arousal potential; but to make the leap from recognizing physiological potential to asserting that 'sex' is essentially the same phenomenon for men and women[9] – which is what happens when social meaning, social context and power relations are ignored – is an act of gross misrepresentation which serves to constrict and confine women within male definitions. An alternative approach to 'sexuality' which does purport to examine context and meaning is that arising from the symbolic interactionist perspective. How are lesbians defined from this approach?

Women as non-men – the deviance perspective and lesbians

Recent sociological research about lesbians has been dominated by the 'deviance' approach and is characterized by the work of John Gagnon and William Simon. Broadly speaking, this perspective presents an attack on 'positivist' notions of deviance by stressing that individuals come to be defined as deviant as a result of rule breaking, via formal and informal labelling processes. Rather than concentrating on causes and characteristics with the implicit aim of reform or prevention, proponents of this essentially liberal perspective claim to undertake an initial commitment to those defined as deviant, by focusing on the ways in which members of 'deviant' worlds interpret and fashion meaning in response to stigma.

In contrast to essentialist notions of sexual 'instinct' or biological drive, the symbolic interactionist approach to sexuality and sexual deviance posits sex drive as social construct. In taking this position, Gagnon and Simon assert that sexual 'deviance', rather than resulting from biological factors, is an identity which arises out of a process of labelling and stigmatization of 'unconventional' *behaviour*. They stress that sexual behaviour is 'scripted', a script appearing to refer to a set of symbolic constructs which define a situation as 'sexual'. What is conspicuously absent from their analysis, however, is any suggestion of how and why scripts come to be defined as 'conventional' or 'normal'.

In their brief discussion of 'the lesbian', Gagnon and Simon define 'her' as a woman who 'differs from other women in the gender of the object that engages her sexuality' (1973, p. 176). That is, lesbian women are not seen as choosers or definers but rather as women whose 'sexuality' happens to latch on to other women, described here as 'objects'. While admitting that there may be *some* element of significance in this difference, they suggest that most research concerning lesbians overemphasizes this significance, since it is carried out by male researchers who allow the idea of the sexually aroused woman to consume their interest. However, Gagnon and Simon appear to accept as given and unproblematic the assertion that 'society [whoever that may be] seems less interested in the repression of homosexuality among females than among males', implying some reified notion of 'society' which just happens to invest certain kinds of interest in some areas of behaviour rather than others. Moreover, they claim that as a result of 'society's' differential interests, 'there is less pressure to conceive of [lesbian] behaviour as narrowly, nor is there much need to protect the self [presumably male] against the fantasies generated by thinking about the behaviour' (1973, p. 177).

As a reaction against this perceived overemphasis on sexual life, Gagnon and Simon stress that lesbians share the same 'sex-role learning' with all women:

The female homosexual follows conventional feminine patterns in developing her commitment to sexuality and in conducting not only her sexual career but her non-sexual career as well. This should not be particularly surprising considering that despite the specific experiences that influenced her sexual object choice, *which are still obscure*, the lesbian is exposed to the numerous and diffuse, subtle and unsubtle experiences and relationships that generally serve to promote conventional gender role identification in the society. [1973, p. 178; emphasis mine]

For Gagnon and Simon, then, lesbians act 'just like women'; they are explained away in terms of their 'femininity', although the authors still betray a certain positivistic concern with 'sexual object choice'. Their functionalism is made explicit by their view of society as a 'single model system of producing women' in conformity with male 'needs', whereby 'female sexuality is designed to conform to a relatively wide range of male sexual performance without major upset or anxiety' (Gagnon and Simon 1973, p. 179f).

Their focus is largely devoted to detailing how lesbians conform to 'the conventional world' of women in Western society through the patterns of their sexual behaviour, which is seen as having an essentially feminine quality with some masculine aspects (ibid., p. 199), while leaving unquestioned the categories of 'masculine' and 'feminine'. There are, however, more than vague hints that they consider those categories to be biologically determined; they state that 'what we conventionally describe as sexual behaviour is rooted in biological capacities and processes' (ibid., p. 15). We are left to believe, then, that male sexual 'needs' in contrast to 'women's conformity to the needs of the male' are unchanging and unchangeable.[10]

Implicit throughout Gagnon and Simon's work is the notion that only men can be deviant.[11] They describe 'the lesbian' in terms of 'a conformity greater than deviance' because of her 'essential' femininity; their earlier work set out to document 'femininity in the lesbian community' (1967b). Even the relationship of the prostitute to the pimp is 'best understood in terms of her deprived emotional relationship with other males' (1973, p. 231). There is reference throughout their work to the problems of 'our hero' in deciding whether or not a situation is 'sexual'. Herein lies the crux of their perspective: only men can and do define situations; women only 'act like women':

> For the female, sexual activity does not occur for its own sake but for the sake of children, family and love. Thus sexuality for the female has less autonomy than it has for the male, and the body (either of the self or of others) is not seen by women as an instrument of self pleasure. This vision of sexuality as a form of service is continuous with the rest of female socialization. [ibid., p. 182]

This discussion of Gagnon and Simon's work is presented for two reasons; first, because the bulk of sociological research on lesbians over the last decade has been heavily influenced by an uncritical acceptance of their perspective and, second, because their stress on the socially constructed nature of 'sexuality' suggests a revolutionary alternative to essentialist and drive reduction models. However, by neglecting any analysis of the ways in which men and women negotiate or fail to negotiate sexual meaning, they substitute one reductionist explanation for another – that of 'gender' for that of 'drive'. Moreover, while stressing that the very concept of 'sexual' should be radically questioned, they focus on forms of behaviour which are socially defined as 'sexual', thus reinforcing rather than radically questioning those definitions – definitions which they concede originate with men and not women.

Recent research trends

Since Gagnon and Simon made their 'definitive' statements about lesbians in the late 1960s, there has been a spate of empirical research within the 'deviance' tradition, aimed either at developing their perspective or simply at exemplifying some of their assertions.

Few researchers have chosen to take up the query of 'sexual object choice'. Hedblom touches on the 'problem', but after eliminating the possibility of heterosexual 'frigidity' as an explanation – what he calls the 'inability to have satisfactory sexual relations with men', which again is defined in terms of 'achieving orgasm' – he concludes, in a somewhat tautological way, that 'the choice of sex partner . . . is a preference based on psychosexual identity' (1973, p. 34). Within a rather more novel vein, McCaghy and Skipper have attempted to isolate structural conditions which give rise to 'sexual' contact between women, otherwise known as 'lesbian behaviour', by focusing on the world of the stripper. Their concern is with understanding 'rates of deviant behaviour' in much the same way as an epidemiologist might study diseases, and they conclude that, in this specific case, such behaviour is an 'adaptation' to an intolerable occupation. They make direct links with the prison setting – drawing on previous research done in this area (for example, Giallombardo 1966) – which they feel 'not only curtails avenues of heterosexual release, but deprives inmates of meaningful affective relationships they would otherwise have' (1969, p. 263). McCaghy and Skipper were refused interviews by women whom they 'suspected' of maintaining relatively stable 'homosexual' relationships; this is not altogether insignificant. In equating lesbians with object choice and deprivation, and without acknowledging the positive meanings which women have for their own lives,[12] McCaghy and Skipper's study leads one to conclude that, given the right 'conditions', the 'object which engages her sexuality' could vary anywhere from a corned beef sandwich to an articulated lorry, depending on the type of job, level of job dissatisfaction, etc., which a woman experiences.

By and large, most recent 'deviancy' research on lesbians has taken advantage of the growing visibility of lesbian organizations and communities and has not had to rely on captive research samples or covert methods. In contrast to more simplistic behavioural research, the emphasis has increasingly been on following Gagnon and Simon's maxim of linking patterns of homosexual behaviour to non-deviant behaviour and roles. Much of this work (most explicitly Tanner 1978 and Wolf 1979) has also been influenced by the directives of Del Martin and Phylis Lyon, two women who were active in 'homophile' movements of the late 1960s and early 1970s and who called for more research on lesbian life styles with the aim of relieving 'homophobia'. Their view of themselves as lesbians was essentially libertarian and harked back to Kinsey's continuum model:

Lesbianism is, and must be accepted as one facet on the continuum scale of human sexual expression .... A lesbian relationship is, and must be accepted as a viable life style. [Martin and Lyon 1972, p. 198]

This recent body of writing has tended to emphasize the 'feminine' aspect of lesbians and the problems which a 'homosexual life style' is presumed to dictate, and to document 'faithfully', within the ethnographic tradition, the negotiation of day-to-day life in couples or in the community. Following again in the wake of research on gay men, and imposing the same definitions, this perspective has increasingly seen lesbians as an oppressed minority group by virtue of their 'object choice' and the stigma attached to this choice, placing them in effect alongside not only 'sexual deviants' such as sado-masochists and foot fetishists, but also oppressed handicapped groups such as epileptics and the blind. The emphasis, however, on lesbians as 'women first and homosexuals second' (Hedblom 1973, p. 333) or as a 'special class of woman' by virtue of not being married (Tanner 1978, p. 12) has begun to create an image of 'doubly stigmatized' and hence, labelling theory would suggest, 'doubly deviant' women.[13] There remains, however, a tradition of research which, while observing that lesbians differ from male homosexuals in so far as they are interested in women and not men, pays only lip-service to this pivotal difference and continues to conceptualize lesbians within the male framework.[14] Thus lesbians continue to be viewed as pseudo-male, as 'more passive' and 'more inhibited':

The texture of lesbian courtship differs in tempo from heterosexual patterns. Though women may make love with each other fairly soon in the relationship, the intitial advances may take longer. And, since lesbians early learn in the role expected of women in our culture, they tend to be more passive and more inhibited by possible rejection in making advances to another woman than men might be. [Wolf 1979, p. 92]

Rather than concentrating on what might lead women to choose other women in preference to men, 'deviance' research tends to assume that preference as given, and instead highlights the problems or adaptations which women may face and which are presumed to flow from that choice. The result has tended to be a reversion to the 'condition' view of lesbians whereby women are believed to 'stumble' upon their 'homosexuality'; there is constant reference in recent 'deviancy' lesbian research to the 'process of discovering that one is gay' (Tanner 1978), of women 'gradually realising that they are lesbian' (Wolf 1979), and having to 'contend with the prospect of rejection on the basis of [their] condition' (Hedblom 1973).

The other major result of this approach has been to present lesbians as necessarily problem ridden, albeit as a result of 'stigma' or 'societal demands' rather than arising from any inherent or genetic factors. Some researchers have concentrated solely on the 'lesbian as a cripple'; as Siegrid Schafer in her study 'The sexual and social problems of lesbians' claims:

No woman in our society can be lesbian without problems. And as individual as these problems may appear in any given case, they still have the same collective cause; the discrepancy between societally demanded behaviour – and the internalized heterosexual moral concepts deriving from this – on the one hand and one's own homosexual needs on the other. [1976, p. 60]

In a rather more sociological vein, some researchers have stressed that it is the 'need' for secrecy, resulting from stigma, which is the root of all lesbians' problems. Barbara Ponse claims that 'secrecy is an inextricable part of lesbian life' (1977, p. 53), and she devotes an entire study to the ways in which 'secrecy affects relationships between gay groups and the members of the larger heterosexual society' (ibid., p. 55), again avoiding any distinction between 'gay' men and women. Similarly Jack Hedblom, concentrating on 'Dimensions of lesbian sexual experience', claims that lesbians *necessarily* identify themselves as 'homosexual' and that 'homosexuality' is stigmatized social adjustment which affects (read 'cripples') lesbians' lives at a most basic level:

The simple fact of being homosexual creates innumerable difficulties in playing basic social roles. Being homosexual affects associations, entertainment patterns and occupational roles as well as delimiting the possibility of certain types of social mobility. [1973, p. 333]

Finally Delos Kelly states that 'most would agree that lesbianism is associated with both actual and potential costs' (1979, p. 593). Such sentiments, arising as they do out of supposedly non-judgemental observations, have given even greater force to the belief that only more and more 'faithful' portraits of lesbian life can help to change 'societal attitudes' and hence relieve the 'stigma' associated with lesbianism. Kelly elaborates:

Instead of tolerating the lesbian, some have suggested that we need to do away with negative or deviant labels. Given the present structure and prevailing attitudes of American society, this proposition is most unrealistic. On a more practical level, if people could gain more knowledge – and were willing to do so – then many of the stereotypes and misconceptions surrounding the lesbian and her life style could perhaps be dispelled .... Obviously the task of demythologizing and educating will involve a long and arduous process. Nonetheless, it is a task that many feel needs to be accomplished rapidly and successfully. [ibid., p. 601]

Generally, then, the task of liberal social science with regard to lesbians has been one of normalization through humanization with a touch of feminization thrown in for good luck. The composite image of lesbians constructed in the interests of 'education' has generally been one of noble suffering in secrecy. While this image may have reflected the experiences of a proportion of women in the lesbian community, it is crucial to reflect on their possible motivation for colluding in such image building through participation in deviancy research. Researchers have tended to objectify the experiences of women forced into isolation through their refusal to be male-identified, and have added insult to injury by feedback mechanisms, constructing negative images of 'the lesbian' which serve to divide and isolate woman further.[15] I am not arguing that lesbians as a group and as individuals are not oppressed; there are ubiquitous examples of the ways lesbians are *terrorized* by patriarchy – the International Tribunal on Crimes Against Women has provided introductory documentation (Russell and Van de Ven 1976). What I wish to emphasize is that social science, by the very nature of its constructs, has played a central role in contributing to lesbian oppression. By defining lesbians in 'sexual' terms, each trek into the field is sure to result in yet another moral warning on the price to be extracted for not meeting men's (so-called) 'sexual needs'.

One recent exception to the lesbian-as-cripple construct in social science may be found in the work of Deborah Goleman Wolf (1979), and it arises, not surprisingly, from participant observation amongst lesbian feminists. Within this ethnography, lesbians are portrayed as women who initiate and build communities, rather than getting sucked into them, who have chosen a life style rather than it choosing them, and who embody strength and celebration rather than secrecy and suffering. Tragically, Wolf's position is one of anthropologist-cum-deviancy-theorist, and her study betrays a voyeuristic concern with 'ritual' as well as a faithful adherence to a biologically deterministic model of 'sexuality'.[16] Rather than being feminist research, Wolf's study portrays lesbians *as* deviants. It is an interesting example of the way traditional deviancy research cannot cope with feminism as anything other than an 'oppressed minority' position, despite the fact that the women's liberation movement is international. Wolf's concern is with studying 'the sources of women's strength in contemporary America', and her desire to 'control as many variables as possible' functions to contain and confine the applicability of her work to other 'minority groups' rather than to the overall position of women in American society, let alone elsewhere in the world.

I have tried to demonstrate the political significance of lesbian definitions within social science, to examine the ways in which those definitions serve as a control mechanism to divide and isolate women, either by reinforcing concepts of 'femininity' or by delineating categories of 'woman' presumed to possess or exhibit varying peculiar characteristics. This is not to deny the validity or reality of lesbian identities as they are embraced by women themselves; this is neither desirable nor possible. What I do wish to suggest, however, is that researchers who are genuinely concerned with the area of 'lesbianism' sensitize themselves to the power of naming and of category creation.

One of the earliest statements of lesbian-feminism was provided in 1970 by a group of women calling themselves the Radicalesbians; this still remains an invaluable starting point for conceptualization. In contrast to earlier, non-feminist writing linking lesbians with femininity (for example Gagnon and Simon), this statement presented the lesbian identity not only as a positive choice but also as a level of consciousness which challenges the essentially oppressive and restricting nature of male-defined and male-enforced 'femininity'. Their statement encapsulated how the primarily sexual definition of 'lesbian' is continuous with the sexual definition of 'woman'; both demonstrate contempt for women in general and give primacy to men and male sexuality:

A lesbian is not considered a 'real woman'. And yet in popular thinking, there is really only one essential difference between a lesbian and other women; that of sexual orientation – which is to say, when you strip off all the packaging, you must realize that the essence of being a 'woman' is to get fucked by men. [Radicalesbians 1970, p. 173]

The Radicalesbians defined the lesbian not in terms of her 'sexual' behaviour, but in terms of her total identity – as a 'woman-identified woman'; they went on to show the political significance of putting women first in a society which demands that women structure their lives around men. The use of the label 'lesbian' has historically been a mechanism of control which radically affects *all* women; if lesbians are women who, via whatever initial experiences, come to reject not only the male servicing role but also images of themselves as sexual objects – self-images upon which patriarchy is built – they must be portrayed negatively:

'Lesbian' is one of the sexual categories by which men have divided up humanity . . . . Affixing the label lesbian not only to a woman who aspires to be a person but also to any situation of real love, real solidarity, real primacy among women is a primary form of divisiveness among women; it is the condition which keeps women within the confines of the feminine role, and it is the debunking scare term that keeps women from forming any primary attachments, groups or associations among ourselves. [ibid., p. 174]

Since that statement appeared, lesbian-feminism as a life style and as a political orientation has provided a springboard for analysing the control of women through the politics of sexuality under male supremacy.[17] The perspective throws into question one of the main tenets of the 'deviancy' approach – namely, the 'taken for granted' nature of labels and their stigmatizing effect – by focusing on the origins and functions of 'lesbian' labels and definitions and by emphasizing the positive and political nature of lesbian identities. The former focus can be found in recent etymological research on lesbian labels (Roberts 1979) and in analysis of the 'lesbian threat' (Stanley 1976) – which can be seen in sharp contradistinction to the 'homosexual taboo' (Plummer 1976) and is a concept essentially concerned with *women* in a phallocentric culture. The latter can be found widely in feminist writings of the last decade (Birkby *et al.* 1973; Myron and Bunch 1975; Galana and Covina 1977). Overall the perspective suggests that research interests would be most usefully directed away from focus on 'the lesbian' and towards examination of the multiple methods of male control over women's relationships with each other, through the ideology and practice of male sexuality.

With the growth in size and strength of the women's liberation movement, women have increasingly redefined what it can mean to identify oneself as lesbian, as well as distinguished and exposed what it implies to be labelled lesbian in a patriarchal society. Future research into the history and sociology of 'lesbianism' which claims to be in the primary interests of women, rather than of some abstract notion of 'science' or 'society', must make that distinction clear.

Part Three

The Making of the Modern Male Homosexual: Explorations in Research

6 Pansies, perverts and macho men: changing conceptions of male homosexuality

John Marshall

'You're a homosexual,' she said quite kindly. 'Am I?' I said, really surprised. How was I to tell? . . . The word was not in general use, as it is now. Then it was still a technical term, the implications of which I was not entirely aware of; it implied, if anything, 'cissiness'. Cissy I certainly wasn't. Wasn't I on the contrary if not a tough, at least a masculine athlete? [Worsley 1967, p. 26]

I was over thirty before, for the first time, I heard somebody say that he did not think of himself as masculine or feminine but merely as a person attracted to other persons with male sexual organs. [Crisp 1969, p. 61]

Taken together, the above quotations indicate a profound shift in modern conceptions of the homosexual person. The first illustrates the extent to which, in the 1930s, it was difficult or impossible for many people with homosexual feelings to conceptualize themselves as being 'homosexual'. It further suggests that at that time the homosexual category referred not to the nature or direction of one's sexual preferences but to the character of one's gender identity. In popular stereotypes this was reflected in the image of the feminine man and the masculine woman (or more crudely, the 'pansy' and the 'dyke'), and it was also reflected in various theories which attempted to define the essence of the species. As we shall see, most theorists from the end of the nineteenth century were concerned with the problem of human 'intersexuality', and the homosexual person was constantly defined in these terms.

In sharp conceptual contrast, the comment from Quentin Crisp, referring to roughly the same period, suggests the gradual emergence of a newer and quite different conception based not upon gender ideas but upon the notion of 'sexual object choice' or 'sexual orientation' which came to be defined independently of gender identity. It is probably fair to say that this conception is now firmly established in our own culture, and it is the purpose of this chapter to trace some of the main features of this major conceptual shift. In the process, I will try to indicate the lack of any clear concept of the homosexual person (in the contemporary sense) during the late nineteenth century, and I will suggest that the modern conception is far newer than has usually been supposed.

Models of sexual identity: an analytic detour

In order to clarify the differences between the older and newer conceptions, it is worthwhile considering, in a purely abstract way, the various assumptions about sexuality and gender which give rise to both 'normal' and 'deviant' identities. For this purpose, I have distinguished between five basic components of sexual identity which are listed and defined below.[1]

1   *Biological sex* refers to those physical attributes by which we usually distinguish between the male and female of a species.
2   *Gender identity* refers to the basic self knowledge and conviction that one is either a man or a woman.
3   *Gender role* refers more specifically to the behaviour, personality traits and general societal expectations usually associated with the masculine or feminine role.
4   *Sexual behaviour* refers to patterns of sexual activity with partners of a particular sort.
5   *Sexual meaning* refers to the way in which sexual activity and identity are interpreted and experienced by actors.

Now it is quite clear that even in the present day these components are often assumed to be logically linked. Gender divisions are based, in the first instance, upon the labelling of biological sex, and it is expected that this labelling will give rise to a consistent sense of gender identity, a willingness to adopt the prescribed gender role and a desire to behave and interpret sexuality in the 'appropriate' gender terms. It is this pattern of expectations which produces a particular definition of the norm. This norm is shown in Table 1 as models A and B. Only against these models can we begin to consider the possibilities of conceptualizing discrepant sexual identities.

Perhaps the most important characteristic of these initial models is the centrality of gender in defining sexual identity. Gender is

Table 1

	Model A	Model B
Biological sex	male	female
Gender identity	man	woman
Gender role	masculine	feminine
Sexual behaviour	heterosexual	heterosexual
Sexual meaning	heterosexual	heterosexual
Sexual/gender identity	Heterosexual man	Heterosexual woman

clearly a 'master determining status' (Hughes 1945) since, in this case, gender concepts contain all of the necessary presuppositions for defining biological sex, on the one hand, and sexual orientation, on the other. In this sense, the models seem to preclude the possibility of conceptualizing 'the homosexual man' or 'the homosexual woman' since the terms 'man' and 'woman' are themselves defined in heterosexual terms. The concept of a homosexual man or woman could only be rendered meaningful if there was a conscious distinction between gender identity and sexual orientation. Without this distinction, any deviations or ambiguities are likely to be regarded as gender anomalies rather than sexual anomalies since gender is the all-inclusive concept.

Now given the stress on gender ambiguity and intersexuality which seem to have dominated the traditional conception of 'the invert', it would appear that during the nineteenth century and for much of the present century, the distinction between gender identity and sexual orientation had not been clearly made. It was for this reason that persons with same-sex sexual interests might reconceptualize themselves in the appropriate gender terms. Biological males, for example, might think of themselves as possessing a 'feminine temperament' and would thereby rationalize their emotional and sexual feelings. Theorists of sexuality evidently employed the same logic, producing a conception of the 'sexual invert' as shown in Table 2 as model C.

The curious result of such gender inversion, however, was that it effectively eliminated the need for a homosexual concept. For as long as the person in question could be conceptualized as a

Table 2

	Model C	Model D
Biological sex	male	male
Gender identity	man/woman	man
Gender role	feminine	masculine
Sexual behaviour	homosexual	homosexual
Sexual meaning	'heterosexual'	heterosexual
Sexual/gender identity	Male gender invert	Heterosexual man

'non-man', his 'real' sexual identity could be interpreted as 'female heterosexual' (in a male body) rather than 'homosexual male'.

This is not to say, however, that all homosexual behaviour was necessarily rationalized in this way. Men with a strong sense of their male gender identity and their masculine gender role could easily enter same sex sexual relations without challenging their heterosexual sense of self. Numerous strategies exist to accommodate or neutralize ostensibly homosexual acts by processes of definition.[2] For example, an elderly homosexual respondent recalled that in his youth:

Opinion generally was that homosexuality consisted of older men taking younger boys as female substitutes. When a man seduced a youth I don't think people regarded it as a homosexual act. It was a homosexual situation satisfying a heterosexual need.

Here gender ideas remain intact by denying or avoiding a homosexual interpretation. Indeed given the strength of gender concepts (as implied by models A and B) it was often impossible, as we saw with Worsley, even to contemplate a homosexual definition. A great deal of homosexual behaviour was therefore likely to have been conceptualized in this manner and this is portrayed in Table 2 as model D.

The central argument of this chapter will be that until comparatively recently the major responses to homosexual behaviour can be characterized conceptually by either models C or D. That is, the specialized identity has predominantly involved a gender invert role, whilst homosexual behaviour as such has been relatively free of a homosexual category. Homosexual behaviour, in the latter sense, was much more likely to have been conceptualized in moralistic terms as 'gross indecency' or 'perversion' rather than 'true' sexual inversion. Not until a clear distinction was made between gender identity and sexual orientation was it possible to include all forms of homosexual behaviour within the scope of the homosexual category. This new conception is illustrated in Table 3 as models E and F.

Table 3

	Model E	Model F
Biological sex	male	female
Gender identity	man	woman
Gender role	masculine	feminine
Sexual behaviour	homosexual	homosexual
Sexual meaning	homosexual	homosexual
Sexual/gender identity	Homosexual man	Homosexual woman

Nineteenth-century interpretations of homosexuality

It has been argued quite strongly that the late nineteenth century was the crucial period in the conceptualization of homosexuality as the distinguishing characteristic of a particular type of person (see Weeks 1977). Such a claim is supported by evidence relating to the changing legal situation, the social purity campaigns, changing definitions of sexuality and marriage, various sexual scandals, the medicalization of homosexuality and the emergence of new theoretical definitions of a distinct sexual type (variously referred to as 'inverts', 'homosexuals' and 'Uranians'). While such evidence is certainly persuasive it can easily be overstated, and it is with this in mind that I wish to review the late nineteenth century situation. In particular I will want to emphasize the uncertainty and ambiguity in responses to homosexuality, and I will also wish to draw attention to the continuing distinction between homosexual behaviour and gender role inversion.

Perhaps the most striking characteristic of the late nineteenth century was the consolidation of ideals relating to domesticity, femininity, marriage and the family. Central to this was a belief in the necessary link between sexuality and marriage. It was within this context that an attack was launched on the double standard of morality which had conspired to allow a moral ideal of spiritual purity to go hand in hand with a self-indulgent display of male lust directed at what were seen as animalistic working class prostitutes. Since the family by this time was seen as the central symbol of a stable society, it was particularly important in the eyes of the social purity campaigners that male lust be regulated and harmonized in accordance with the highest moral ideals. Such a demand was reinforced in the 1880s by the evident concern over imperialism and national decline. This decline tended to be viewed in moral terms, and it encouraged a new concern with the health and welfare of the working class, since the restoration of the nation depended upon the production of healthy workers and soldiers. This again led to an emphasis upon the strengthening of the family, and this was reflected in the social security legislation after the turn of the century (Pearce and Roberts 1973).

This concern with marriage, the family and the regulation of male lust meant that homosexuality was a central target for the social purity campaigners, and it is no surprise to find that legislation dealing with prostitution was so closely linked to changes in the law relating to homosexuality. The Criminal Law Amendment Act of 1885, for example, which outlawed all male homosexual acts, was originally drafted to 'make further provision for the protection of women and girls, the suppression of brothels and other purposes', (Parliamentary Debates 1885a) and the Vagrancy Act of 1898 was concerned in a general way to control importuning for immoral purposes, although it included clauses against homosexual soliciting.

This link between homosexuality, prostitution and sexual decadence was dramatically reinforced by a series of public scandals in the early 1880s, including the case in 1884 involving high officials in Dublin Castle and culminating eventually with the trials of Oscar Wilde in 1895 (Hyde 1948, 1970; Weeks 1977). There was also a concern over various sexual scandals which arose in the single sex public schools, and this led to a particular emphasis upon the moral health of children. Within a context in which childhood innocence was increasingly emphasized (the 1885 Act had raised the age of consent for girls from 13 to 16), there was a particular concern to guard against the corruption of youth, and this fear was stimulated by the role played by working class boys in the major homosexual scandals at the end of the century.

Now from the point of view of my argument, it is particularly noteworthy to consider the way in which this historical background provides no indication of a developing homosexual category. The emphasis throughout (and the reason for the link between homosexuality and prostitution) is upon the regulation of male lust and the channelling of sexuality into an institutionalized pattern of 'normal' heterosexual monogamy.

However, certain of these events have nevertheless been seen as indicators of a growing awareness of 'the homosexual' category. Central to this view is the alleged significance of the Criminal Law Amendment Act of 1885, which is sometimes thought to be the point at which the concept of the homosexual was first recognized in law. This is an understandable but extremely misleading assumption. It is certainly true that the long term consequences of the strengthened legal situation was an important factor in creating the later concept of the homosexual person, and, viewed in retrospect, the law did seem to contain a tacit view of the homosexually inclined man. However, it we examine the motives behind the introduction of the anti-homosexual amendment, we will see that the law was consistent with the general drive against sexual decadence and did not presuppose the existence of a special type of person.

Judging from the written records (Parliamentary Debates 1885b), Henry Labouchere, who introduced the amendment, was concerned essentially with indecent assaults involving males, which at that time had to be committed on persons under 13 years of age to be punishable. His clause was designed to make any assault of this kind punishable whatever the age of the assailant. However, the actual amendment referred rather vaguely to 'acts of gross indecency', and it was this undefined offence that was to be so widely interpreted in the years that followed. Apparently Labouchere did not intend his clause to penalize 'grossly indecent' acts which involved the consent of both parties (see Winter 1978)

It is understood that Labouchere later admitted that he had taken the new clause from the French penal code, and as Montgomery Hyde has pointed out, this is

an admission which suggests that he must have had in mind primarily the corruption of youth, since the French code did not penalize homosexual acts between consenting adults in private ... but it did protect children and juveniles against sexual interference [1970, p. 135]

Although it has often been suggested that the Labouchere Amendment was a confused and casually passed part of the Act (Lord Fitzgerald felt that 'some of the amendments by the Commons were beyond the scope of the preamble' [Parliamentary Debates 1885c]), it seems that, given the emphasis upon sexual decadence, public decency and the protection of youth, the Amendment was actually consistent with the overall aims of the Act. However, its implications were to be far reaching and probably unintended. Even so, at this stage it is important to remember that legal hostility was still being directed towards homosexual behaviour rather than a category of 'homosexuals'.

One immediate consequence of the new legislation was to bring about some widely acclaimed public scandals, the most famous of which were the three trials of Oscar Wilde in 1895. Whilst the Act of 1885 may not have contained even an implicit notion of the homosexual person, it has been argued (Weeks 1977) that the real significance of the Labouchere Amendment was that it allowed such scandals to occur. These scandals, or so it is argued, were significant in creating a public image of 'the homosexual':

The Wilde trials were not only the most dramatic, but also the most significant events, for they created a public image for the homosexual, and a terrifying moral tale of the dangers that trailed closely behind deviant behaviour. They were labelling processes of the most explicit kind, drawing an impassable border between acceptable and abhorrent behaviour. [Weeks 1977, p. 21]

This claim is certainly not without merit, although there is considerable need for caution. It is clearly true that the Wilde trials highlighted the distinction between acceptable and unacceptable behaviour, but it is less clear that they created a 'public image for the homosexual'. Was Wilde being stigmatized as a special and exclusive sexual type (that is, a homosexual), or was he being attacked, in moralistic terms, for his outrageous behaviour? The editorial comment in the London *Evening News* (25 May 1895) certainly suggests the latter:

Never has the lesson of a wasted life come home to us more dramatically and opportunely. England has tolerated the man Wilde and others of his kind for too long. Before he broke the law of this country and outraged human decency he was a social pest, a centre of intellectual corruption. He was one of the high priests of a school which attacks all the wholesome, manly, simple ideals of English life, and sets up false gods of decadent culture and intellectual debauchery.

If there is an image here, it is that of the intellectual Bohemian. The homosexual behaviour was seen as part of his general moral decadence, and this was typical of the traditional conception of unnatural sexual behaviour. We should also note that a major element of the social reaction to Wilde revolved around the perceived corruption of youth. As previously mentioned, this concern over youth had been a prominent theme at this time, especially in the expanding public schools which had produced a number of sexual scandals. Such concern was reflected in the preoccupation with masturbation and schoolboy immorality (Bullough 1976; Hare 1962). The fact that Wilde had directed his attention to youths and boys merely aggravated these fears, and it is no surprise to find that the newspapers echoed this emphasis. Following Wilde's conviction, the *Daily Telegraph* (26 May 1895) saw fit to issue a warning to those, including 'young men at the universities', who might follow Wilde's example. The London *Evening News* (25 May 1895) showed similar concern with this comment:

We venture to hope that the conviction of Wilde for these abominable vices, which were the natural outcome of his diseased intellectual condition, will be a salutary warning to the unhealthy boys who posed as sharers of his culture.

It therefore seems that the public image being presented here was not one of 'homosexual man' but a much more generalized account of moral decline, unregulated male lust and contagious social disease. A clear concept of the 'homosexual man' (model E) would have minimally required an emphasis upon exclusivity, but this appears to be absent. Indeed Wilde was a married man so it seems all the more likely that his behaviour would have been conceptualized, however vaguely, in terms of model D.

However, this is not to say that no sense of identity was emerging for some 'homosexuals'. A self-defined identity is clearly encouraged as a direct result of strengthening prohibitions against homosexual behaviour, since those who were inclined towards such behaviour might easily come to regard themselves as odd, abnormal or, at the very least, different. This is the sense in which we can understand the reaction of Ellis to the Wilde trials when he said that it 'appears to have generally contributed to give definiteness and self consciousness to the manifestations of homosexuality' (1936, p. 352). But this sense of identity was by no means a necessary corollary of homosexual inclination, and the developing self-conceptions were far from clear at this stage. Since the major public articulation of an identity concept was related in various ways to gender ambiguity,[3] the idea of the homosexual man or woman (models E and F) was extremely difficult to contemplate.

In order to expand and strengthen the general theme of this argument, I now wish to turn to the explicit theories being developed during this period. Although we cannot assume that such theories necessarily had a strong impact in shaping popular conceptions, the theories nevertheless provide an indication of the ways in which sexuality and gender were likely to have been regarded. At the very least, the various theories of sexual deviance which began to appear during the second part of the nineteenth century reflected the increasing preoccupation throughout Europe with what were perceived as undesirable forms of sexual conduct. In the process, homosexuality emerged as a central theme, and Germany a focal point for theorists. Indeed it was in response to German anti-homosexual legislation that Benkert developed his ideas, coining the term 'homosexuality' in 1869 to describe what he defined as an 'inborn, and therefore irrepressible, drive' (Lauritsen and Thorstad 1974, p. 8).

In terms of initial ideas, however, the key figure seems to have been Karl Heinrich Ulrichs, who was also a German and a prolific writer on the subject from the 1860s to the 1890s. Ulrichs argued that homosexuality was congenital, resulting from an anomalous combination of male and female characteristics in a single biological body. The human embryo, he believed, is at first neither male nor female but develops these characteristics only after the first few months of life. In the male homosexual the genitals become male, but the same differentiation fails to occur in that part of the brain that determines the sex drive. The result is a 'feminine soul enclosed in a male body'. Ulrichs coined the term 'Urning' (or 'Uranian') to describe the homosexual, and he also elaborated a complex classification of homosexual types. He distinguished, for example, between the *Mannling*, who is thoroughly masculine in appearance and character, the *Weibling*, who is effeminate, and the *Zwischen-urning*, who is an intermediate type.

These ideas did not achieve a very wide circulation at the time, but their significance lies in the fact that they set the tone of much of the work that followed. The major text of the period, *Psychopathia Sexualis: A Medico-Forensic Study* by Richard von Krafft-Ebing (1965), had initially described homosexuality as the product of hereditary degeneration of the central nervous system, but by later editions many of Ulrichs's ideas had been incorporated (see Karlen 1971). He seemed to accept the idea of an initially undifferentiated embryo, and he produced a typology of homosexuals which stressed, like Ulrichs, the mental feminization of men and the masculinization of women.

Such ideas were to form part of a strong German tradition, but they also influenced a number of theorists in Britain. John Addington Symonds, for example, was intrigued by the theories of Ulrichs. Although keen to dispute the idea that male homosexuals were necessarily effeminate, Symonds found much to admire in Ulrichs's basic approach and was particularly impressed by the avoidance of disease concepts (which stood in sharp contrast to the earlier writings of Krafft-Ebing). Symonds in fact was the first to introduce many of the new German ideas into England in his essay, '*A problem in modern ethics*', which he produced in 1890 (see Symonds 1964). Unfortunately, however, the essay was limited to private circulation.

Nevertheless these ideas undoubtedly had some impact, and they were to find a wider audience through the writings of Edward Carpenter. In 1895 Carpenter produced a concise essay on the subject 'The intermediate sex', which was largely indebted to Ulrichs (see Carpenter 1952). In the essay Carpenter admitted that Ulrichs's theory was at certain points 'somewhat vague and indefinite', but it is quite clear that he accepted the main theme. In later works Carpenter was to repeat and expand the argument, eventually suggesting that the combination of male and female characteristics represents a 'higher type of humanity' (Carpenter 1924, p. 14). Indeed he went so far as to suggest that such androgynous traits are present in all individuals and that the recognition of their value might one day transform society. However, despite this drift in his thought, Carpenter was never to question his fundamental belief in the biological basis of gender, and he accepted 'masculinity' and 'femininity' as intrinsic characteristics. He also assumed that the direction of sexual preference, or 'love sentiment', was inherently connected to these inborn gender traits. To this extent his potential radicalism was locked in a vicious circle.

A similar commitment to biological determinism was even more pronounced in the theories of Havelock Ellis. Ellis, who was the most influential English theorist of the period, had made his major statement on homosexuality in *Sexual Inversion*, which later formed the second volume of his *Studies in the Psychology of Sex* (1936). Although Ellis had apparently rejected the notion of an 'intermediate sex', his ultimate arguments amounted to a similar conception. He was sure that the division between the sexes had deep biological roots, and the discovery of hormones at the beginning of this century provided him with a convenient explanation of homosexuality.

In Germany meanwhile Magnus Hirschfeld was emerging as the leading authority on the subject. He too was deeply indebted to Ulrichs (his first major work in 1903 was entitled *The Uranian*), and he was to conceptualize homosexuals as a 'third sex' – a species which combined not only the mental qualities but also the physiological features of men and women. He also stressed the importance of sex glands in determining sexual characteristics and in this he influenced Ellis (see Hirschfeld 1946).

Hirschfeld's contribution, however, went far beyond the mere articulation of 'scientific' theory. Through his involvement in the Scientific Humanitarian Committee (which he formed in 1897), Hirschfeld had popularized many of his ideas and had encouraged a widespread campaign against anti-homosexual laws. A similar situation did not exist in Britain. Harsh obscenity laws had restricted the capacity of English theorists to be equally outspoken, and this was to remain the case for the first fifty years of this century. As we have noted, John Addington Symonds was reluctant to publish material, and even his collaboration with Havelock Ellis on the latter's *Sexual Inversion* was kept a closely guarded secret. Ellis himself was less inclined towards self-censorship, but when his book appeared in 1897 the official censors immediately intervened. The secretary of the Legitimation League, a society pressing for changes in the law relating to illegitimacy, was brought to trial because he:

unlawfully, wickedly, maliciously, scandalously did publish, sell and utter, a certain lewd, bawdy, scandalous and obscene libel, in the form of a book entitled 'Studies in the Psychology of Sex', Volume 1, 'Sexual Inversion' by Havelock Ellis [Pearce and Roberts 1973, p. 60]

However, despite these problems an attempt was made in 1914 to establish a wider audience, when Carpenter and Ellis were instrumental in forming the British Society for the Study of Sex Psychology. Even so, the society's approach to homosexuality was always marked with caution, and their major statement on the subject was merely a version of an earlier German pamphlet which summarized third sex ideas (BSSP 1915).

This constant stress on congenital factors and in particular on the notion of an 'intermediate sex' was important primarily as a means of overcoming the traditional emphasis on sin, criminality and perversion. However, it also had an awkward twist. For if homosexuality was to be defined as the distinguishing characteristic of the 'invert', how could the theory explain the homosexual behaviour of apparently 'normal' men? In approaching this problem Ellis was eventually to make an explicit distinction between homosexual behaviour *per se* and 'true' congenital inversion (Ellis 1936). However, this merely revived the old concern with perversion and simultaneously reinforced the popular conception of the invert as an ambiguous *gender* type. It also gave rise to the curious distinction between the 'invert' and the 'pervert' which was to play a significant part in debates during the 1950s.[4]

Into the twentieth century

In the previous section I have attempted to highlight the extent to which the notion of a specialized homosexual identity has traditionally revolved around gender ideas rather than alternative types of sexual orientation. In so doing, I have also tried to indicate the extent to which homosexual behaviour was often open to different interpretations which avoided an identity label. The main emphasis of the discussion has been upon the situation in the late nineteenth century. However, it seems probable that many of the old ideas continued to dominate well into the present century. Indeed in a series of interviews recently carried out among elderly homosexual men, this impression was repeatedly confirmed. There seems to have been a tacit yet sharp distinction between the homosexual person (defined as a cross-gender species) and homosexual behaviour (defined in traditional terms of vice and perversity). One man, for example, gave the following account:

Effeminacy in men and masculinity in women were recognised. The name for a butch woman, 'collar and tie', came from my childhood and I remember two women who, before 1920, regularly dressed so. These people were thought of as mistakes of nature.

There was also a somewhat older man, an old boy of my school, who was openly known as Pansy 'X', and this for obvious reasons. At the same time I remember an Ashley 'Y', whom I was told wore women's clothes. Both were certainly effeminate-looking.

There was certainly no appreciation of the fact that (to use a modern term) there could be 'straight-looking gays'.

The link between 'true' homosexuality, effeminacy in men and cross-dressing, which this account implies, suggests that the distinction between homosexuality and transvestism had not yet been clearly articulated. Theoretically the distinction had been made by Hirschfeld as early as 1910 (see King, this volume) and it was later taken up by Ellis. However, in terms of popular conceptions, it seems to have had little influence during the first part of this century and this, in fact, was encouraged by 'third sex' theories.

For those who believed themselves to be homosexual, these ideas were to have a strong impact. It was not unusual, for example, for homosexual men to distinguish quite clearly between 'homosexuals' and 'men'. Indeed it was sometimes their proud boast that their most frequent encounters were with 'men' rather than with 'homosexuals' (Weeks 1979). In his famous autobiography Quentin Crisp made a similar distinction when he mentioned what he regarded as the basic dilemma of all homosexual men:

. . . they set out to win the love of a 'real' man. If they succeed, they fail. A man who 'goes with' other men is not what they would call a real man. [1968, p. 62]

The same type of distinction was often implicit in the sharp dichotomy between 'active' and 'passive' male homosexuals, which was particularly common during the first part of this century. This again involved the interpretation of sexual behaviour entirely in terms of rigid ideas of 'masculinity' and 'femininity', and it also reinforced the distinction between 'true' (feminine) and 'pseudo' (masculine) homosexuality. As D. J. West put it in 1955:

Some psychiatrists believe . . . that male homosexuals fall into two contrasting categories known respectively as *active* and *passive*. The active type is forceful and masculine in his love-making, while the passive is gentle, yielding, coy and liking to be chased. If sodomy occurs, it is the active partner who penetrates the passive. The active type tends to display his masculinity, to cultivate athletic pursuits and to reject all feminine traits. The passive type is more likely to adopt pseudo-feminine mannerisms. The use in homosexual circles of such slang expressions as 'bull' and 'butch' or 'cow' and 'queen' shows that some at least must conform to type.

According to some theorists causes operate to produce these two types. The passive type, often regarded as the 'true' invert, is thought more likely to possess feminine physique or to have some glandular disturbance, whereas the active type is merely looking for a substitute for a woman. [1955, p. 25]

This distinction had actually been challenged much earlier by Havelock Ellis, but the image was to have a long career and a deep impact upon many homosexual men. Moreover the strict adoption of an active role in sodomy allowed many men to engage in homosexual behaviour without coming to regard themselves as 'really' homosexual. This was reflected in the distinction between 'men' and 'homosexuals' already cited, and it was also evident in the views of my elderly interviewees. One man, for example, mentioned the reluctance of any of his partners to act in any way which could be interpreted as 'girlish' or 'effeminate', since this would render them 'queer'.[5]

Despite the strength of these ideas, however, it is quite clear that many men *did* come to regard themselves as homosexual, regardless of public stereotypes. As one of my respondents said:

I knew that the old fashioned choice of effeminate men and masculine women as the only homosexuals was wrong. I looked ordinary enough but I knew I was homosexual. This did not worry me. I just knew that popular opinion was wrong.

However, for men without access to the homosexual world, this sense of identity was often vague. A number of the elderly men I interviewed had never heard the term 'homosexual' until the 1950s.

I had a friendship with someone, George. We both joined the Territorial Army at the same time and formed an association from that point on. That carried on for about four or five years after the war. We were together all through the war; slept together and everything. [Q: Did you think of that as a homosexual relationship?] Well to tell you the truth, the word homosexual didn't strike me; the word didn't mean anything to me until, oh, some years after the war. Because you'd never heard of it. We heard about experiences between boys and that, but we didn't talk about it. We didn't use the word homosexual. I don't think that arose until about twenty years ago. [Q: And when the word arose, did you then start to think of yourself as homosexual?] Well yes, I think I did.

Another man, when asked if the term 'homosexual' was used during the 1920s and 1930s had this to say:

I don't think that expression was ever used. I think that only came out with, well, with some of the psychologists, Freud or somebody, used that term as a medical term. I don't think it was in general use at all. If somebody got into trouble with the law they would just call it improper conduct or gross indecency.

The significance of these comments is not simply that they indicate the absence of a particular word. More important, they imply the lack of a clear *concept* of homosexuality. As another respondent put it:

Forty years ago homosexuality was so little recognized that there was little discussion over it; it was a 'hole in the corner' affair, restricted to homosexuals.

A similar point was made by D. J. West in the preface to his comprehensive review of the subject in 1977:

A generation ago the word homosexuality was best avoided in polite conversation, or referred to in muted terms appropriate to a dreaded and scarcely mentionable disease. Even some well-educated people were hazy about exactly what it meant. [p. vii]

This absence of a clear public conception inevitably meant that many persons with homosexual feelings were prevented from identifying themselves as being 'homosexual'. Indeed the very idea of a homosexual relationship was often difficult to contemplate, even for those who were later to adopt a homosexual identity. As one elderly man reported to me:

When I was a young man I got married because it seemed the natural thing to do. I had friendships, close friendships, with other men but nothing ever came of it. Loving other men and especially having sexual relations with them was almost unthinkable. I realize now that I had deep desires in that direction but it was always something I fought. I didn't have the words to think it out, much less the courage to act upon it.

It was not until the 1950s that the general taboo on discussion, which all of these accounts imply, rapidly began to fade. But even then what emerged was not a questioning of old ideas but a repetition of the connection between homosexuality and gender inversion. In 1952, for example, the *Sunday Pictorial* (25 May) published the following comment:

Most people know there are such things – 'pansies' – mincing effeminate, young men who call themselves queers. But simple, decent folk regard them as freaks and rarities.

A similar image was echoed in a number of reports during the 1950s and 1960s (Pearce 1973). As late as 1968 a reporter on *The People* (24 March) posed the question 'Do we need pubs like this?' when claiming that he:

watched effeminate-looking men disappear into the 'ladies' to titivate their appearance and tidy their waved, dyed hair before going into the back room to dance and cuddle with their 'boyfriends'.

However, the additional idea that anyone is capable of homosexual behaviour was also presented, usually in terms of moral corruption. References were made to youths being led into perverted practices, men who were not homosexual being 'tainted' by their contacts in prison, and non-homosexual customers at a gay bar 'going bent' (Pearce 1973). This assumption that 'normal' *heterosexual* men can be led into such behaviour clearly implies a sharp distinction between 'real' homosexuality (or 'inversion') and 'pseudo' homosexuality (or 'perversion').

The same distinction was also found in the debates encouraged by the movement for law reform. This is illustrated by various comments made during the passage of the Sexual Offences Bill in 1966. Adopting a popular theory, Leo Abse, on the occasion of the First Reading, told the Commons:

A lad without a father, lacking a male figure with whom to identify, is sometimes left with a curse, for such it must be, of a male body encasing a feminine soul. [Parliamentary Debates 1966–7a]

His concern, he added, was to reduce the number of homosexuals by making more adequate provision for boys to learn the masculine role. However, there was also a concern about the potential spread of homosexual behaviour among otherwise 'normal' adults. Captain Walter Elliot, for example, is reported to have said:

I sincerely believe that if the Bill is passed it will increase homosexual practices and not reduce them. It will not cleanse the national bloodstream; it will corrupt and poison it. It will not bring more happiness; it will bring greater misery. For these reasons I hope that the House will reject it. [Parliamentary Debates 1966–7b]

It was this belief which informed the successful attempt to exclude the merchant navy and armed forces from the provisions of the Act. In the words of Simon Mahon:

The normal distractions of shore life do not exist on board a ship. Men live and work together for long periods and in such circumstances overt forms of homosexuality could be a very corrupting influence. [Parliamentary Debates 1966–7c]

Now this conception of homosexuality as a potentially contagious disease takes us back once again to traditional ideas. It implies that homosexuality is a vice born of man's inherent lust rather than the distinguishing characteristic of a particular type of person. And it also suggests the familiar distinction between homosexual behaviour and homosexual identity. 'The homosexual' tended to be viewed as the 'gender freak' – characterized by a lack of fit between biological sex and gender identity – whilst homosexual behaviour was seen as a much more widespread potential. Tacitly, at least, this echoes yet again the distinction between 'true' and 'pseudo' homosexuality.

One difficulty in transcending the theme of gender inversion as the basis of the specialized identity was the rather late historical development of more precise conceptions of 'components' of sexual identiy.[6] The subject of transvestism and, in particular, transsexualism was still a relatively new area (see King, this volume). However, the fact that transsexualism was increasingly discussed during the 1950s suggests that important changes were beginning to appear in conceptions of homosexuality.

Theoretically the major foundation for the newer definitions had been laid by Freud at the beginning of the century. In his early writings on sexuality (see Freud 1977) he had made the first tentative break with older 'third sex' tradition, and a number of contributions from other writers encouraged this trend (Fenichel 1934; Ferenczi 1963).[7] By the 1950s many Freudian ideas had entered popular usage (Berger 1965; North 1972), and the specific theories on homosexuality had also found popular expression (Allen 1949, 1958; Westwood 1952; West 1955).

Stimulating this movement was the general growth of psychology and the simultaneous tendency to medicalize behavioural 'problems'. A report by East and Hubert (1939) on the *Psychological Treatment of Crime* had indicated the first positive steps in that direction, but by the late 1940s and early 1950s the trend was increasingly apparent. In the process, homosexuality received an ample share of attention, and various medical journals in Britain began to devote more generous space to the subject.[8] Although many of the theories at this stage were still somewhat muddled, it is quite clear that the overall effect of this interest was to replace the older conception of 'the invert' with a medicalized account of 'the pervert'. In short, it was now increasingly 'discrepant sexual behaviour', rather than gender anomalies, which formed the basis of the homosexual category.

This radical shift in emphasis was largely brought about by the general moral panic which revolved around the whole subject of homosexual behaviour throughout the 1950s (see Hall 1980). A dramatic rise in the number of prosecutions, plus the impact of several major scandals, had forced both public and 'expert' attention upon 'the problem of homosexuality'. It was within this context that the Wolfenden Committee was set up in 1954 to consider the laws relating to homosexual offences and prostitution. This link between homosexuality and prostitution again shows the influence of traditional ideas, but the conclusions of the report were eventually to break that bond. The inquiry in fact acted as a major stimulus in clarifying the views of the medical and psychiatric professions,[9] and the final report offers a good indication of the changing perspectives. It is significant, for example, that the report explicitly rejected the older distinction between 'inverts' and 'perverts', remarking that:

> We have not found this distinction very useful. It suggests that it is possible to distinguish between two men who commit the same offence, the one as a result of his constitution, the other from a perverse and deliberate choice, with the further suggestion that the former is in some sense less culpable than the latter. To make this distinction as a matter of definition seems to prejudge a very difficult question. [HMSO 1957, pp. 16–17]

We have already seen, however, that traditional views were still significant and they were to remain so for years to come. Indeed the reluctance to act upon the recommendations of Wolfenden was put down largely to the pervasive force of old ideas and their impact on 'public opinion'. But the increased publicity and the influence of newer perspectives (including the refinement of disease models) did at least encourage new initiatives to be taken. In 1958, for example, the Homosexual Law Reform Society was founded, and although its aims were rather circumscribed, its mere existence symbolized important changes. Among these changes were the newer emphasis upon sexual pleasure, new definitions of personal relationships, gradual changes in the position of women, the re-emergence of the women's movement, and counter-cultural challenges – particularly in the 1960s – to the style and content of the male role.[10]

It was within this changing climate that more people eventually felt able to identify themselves as homosexual and, especially among the newer generation, to commit themselves to a gay liberation movement. It seems quite clear that this movement, starting in the United States but rapidly spreading to Britain, had an enormous impact upon the consciousness of modern homosexuals (see Altman 1971; Humphreys 1972; Teal 1971; Weeks 1977). Its style, rhetoric and visibility presented a new image at last for homosexual men and women. And perhaps more important, it presented a positive identity concept to those who, in other circumstances, might never have come to regard themselves as being 'homosexual'. Indeed it is remarkable that in recent years the shift away from images of gender inversion has been so great that there is now a positive identification amongst many male homosexuals (especially in the United States) with masculine style and demeanour (see Blachford, this volume). This cult of machismo has arrived, interestingly, at the same time as the further relaxation of traditional masculine style within the young heterosexual male population. As one observer commented to me:

At the straight disco the boys were rather pretty. They danced together, though not intimately. Some of them wore earings and most of them had styled, blow-dried hair cuts. They wore tight cords or denims with bright shirts or T-shirts. But at one gay bar I visited in London I found that it was all black leather boots and jackets, muscles and moustaches, cropped hair and hardness – that sort of thing.

Summary and conclusion

In this chapter I have suggested a re-evaluation of the historical evidence relating to the emergence of the male homosexual category. Taking note of various components of sexual identity and the assumed strength and direction of the relationships between such components, I have argued that the special role has traditionally been based not upon deviant sexual behaviour but upon transgressions of social sex role and gender identity. That is, 'the homosexual', as a category, has been employed to describe various patterns of gender inversion in which the individual so labelled has been characterized as a congenital anomaly. The taboo informing this notion has been on effeminacy in men and masculinity in women rather than mere homosexual behaviour. Homosexual behaviour as such has not been a sufficient condition for the employment of the label since other accounts have existed to explain such 'aberrations'. Such accounts have been based upon a general belief that homosexual behaviour is the product of sexual vice which exists as a potential in all 'normal' men. However, the link between gender inversion and homosexuality has been used as an important device to control homosexual behaviour and, in particular, to maintain appropriate definitions of masculine and feminine roles. As Lehne once put it:

Homophobia is only incidentally directed against homosexuals – its more common use is against the 49% of the population which is male.

This explains why homophobia is closely related to beliefs about sex-role rigidity, but not to personal experience with homosexuals or any realistic assessment of homosexuality itself. Homophobia is a threat used by homosexist individuals to enforce social conformity in the male role, and maintain social control. The taunt 'What are you, a fag?' is used in many ways to encourage certain types of male behaviour and to define the limits of 'acceptable' masculinity. [1976, p. 78]

The partial relaxation of gender roles in the post-war period, together with more liberal attitudes towards sexual pleasure, have contributed to changing processes of social control, changing directions of stigma and changing conceptions of homosexual identities. However, the emergence of 'macho men' within the contemporary gay world illustrates, in an ironic way, the extent to which definitions of male homosexuality continue to be pervaded by the tyranny of gender divisions.

7 Gender confusions: psychological and psychiatric conceptions of transvestism and transsexualism

Dave King

In the preceding paper Marshall argues that until very recently the homosexual role has been conceived principally in terms of gender and social sex-role deviance, and yet from the late nineteenth century onwards, there emerged a separate conception of gender role deviance developing into the clinical categories of transvestism and also (later) transsexualism. Whilst the medical, psychological and lay approaches to homosexuality have predominantly been characterized by notions of gender inversion (despite many protestations at the confusion from at least the late nineteenth century onwards), in the literature on transvestism and transsexualism a conception of gender deviance has emerged comparatively free of confusion with homosexuality. Wider public conceptions, however, probably concur with the view of some psychoanalytic writers that transvestism and transsexualism are manifestations of latent homosexuality, despite the fact that public reaction towards transvestites and transsexuals seems to be more tolerant than that towards homosexuals, which suggests that a distinction *is* somehow made.[1]

Many accounts exist to testify to the existence, in our own past and in different societies, of individuals who to varying degrees have identified themselves with, dressed as or have attempted to be socially accepted as members of the sex opposite to their own, anatomical one.[2] Here are three such accounts. The first is of members of the Mollies Club in seventeenth century London.

When they are met together their usual practice is to mimick a female gossiping and fall into all the impertinent tittle tattle that a merry society of good wives can be subject to. Not long since they had cushioned up one of their brethren or rather sisters, according to female dialect, disguising him in a woman's night-gown, sarsonet hood and night-rail who, when the company were men, was to mimick a woman, produce a jointed baby they had provided, which wooden offspring was to be afterwards christened . . . .

And for the further promotion of their unbecoming mirth, everyone was to talk of their husbands and children, one extolling the virtues of her husband, another the genius and wit of their children; whilst a third would express himself sorrowfully under the character of a widow. [Ward 1896, p. 28]

The second account is of the 'nadl E' in the Navaho Indian culture. Nadl E is a term used for both the hermaphrodite and the transvestite, although the Navaho did distinguish between the two.

The outlook of the Navaho society toward the Nadl E is very favourable. They are believed to have been given charge of the wealth in the beginning and control it to the present day. The family which counted a transvestite among its members or had a hermaphrodite child born to them was considered by themselves and everyone else as very fortunate. The success and wealth of such a family was believed to be assured. Special care was taken in the raising of such children and they were afforded favouritism not shown to other children of the family . . . . The economic role of the Nadl E is dual, their activities overlapping both those of men and women. They quite generally act as head of the family and are given the control and disposal of all the property . . . . Sodomy with a Nadl E is countenanced by the culture and the insanity believed to follow such an act with a normal person does not occur if the relation is with a Nadl E. [Hill 1935, pp. 274–6]

And finally the following is an extract from a letter published in the *Bulletin* of the Beaumont Society (vol. 11, no. 3), a contemporary British organization for transvestites:

Ever since I can remember, I have always wanted to wear the same clothes as my neighbour's girls. Of course, I never had a chance, but had to hide behind doors, sometimes trying on mother's clothes, which were far too big and uncolourful. Until I married, I never came across the word 'transvestism'. Nor did I know that there are in existence many people who have the same habit. I was ashamed of myself, stressful, had feelings of guilt and with tremendous pressure and conflict. Since marriage four years ago and starting work, I began to feel more pressure on myself, as I do love my wife and the children . . . my wife does not understand why (nor do I) I want to wear women's clothes. She has never approved of my wearing them although she has not actively prevented me from doing so. I have no idea how to explain this need to myself and to her. I have tried many times to stop doing it; each time I failed. The urge is there!

In this paper I begin to attempt to look at how such phenomena are conceptualized in terms of transvestism and transsexualism in contemporary (mainly British and American) society. Instead of assuming that we have discovered the existence of transvestism and transsexualism (and transvestites and transsexuals) and scouring historical and anthropological sources for further examples of these 'conditions',[3] I start with the assumption that transvestism and transsexualism are contemporary conceptualizations which can be linked to their historical and cultural context and which have consequences for the phenomena to which they refer.

The emergence of these terms points to the changed meaning of gender reversal so that sociologically one is dealing with a new phenomenon; thus being a transvestite or a transsexual is likely to be very different depending on whether the society provides a legitimate (perhaps relatively esteemed) place for persons so labelled or whether they are regarded as sick individuals and the best they can hope for is to slip quietly over into the ranks of the opposite sex with the knowledge of as few people as possible. Indeed the whole idea of *being* a transsexual or a transvestite becomes problematic since the nature of being itself (as self and social identity) is different in these two situations. The point is not simply that tolerance for a particular (constant) form of behaviour varies from culture to culture; rather it is to put the stress on meanings – meanings which are not simply given in objects themselves, but which are socially constructed and negotiated and which are creatively used in acting in the world. Action, experience and identity are formed, channelled, shaped and transformed in relation to the use an actor makes of cultural meanings. 'Mediating between people and the contents of their experience are the forms of interpretations which define situations' (Rock 1979, p. 55).

The three accounts quoted above are all of behaviour to which the label transvestite has been applied. The term is actually used in the last two accounts, and the first account is used by McIntosh (this volume) as evidence that the early homosexual sub-culture was characterized by transvestism. Yet apart from the fact that cross-dressing in some form is involved, these three accounts seem to differ in all other respects, in the more detailed aspects of the behaviour, in the way in which that behaviour is understood and in the feelings towards it on the part of participants and non-participants. Although the term transsexualism appeared around 1950, it was not until the early or mid 1960s that it became fairly clearly differentiated from transvestism as a clinical category. Taking an absolutist stance and seeing transvestism and transsexualism as eternal conditions, some of the cases and comments described under the heading of transvestism would be conceptualized as really concerned with transsexualism and probably *vice versa*. But given the contrary view outlined earlier, I have used the author's own terms in order to categorize the material, although that on 'sex changes' which is not described (at the time) as either transvestism or transsexualism is included in the section on the latter area.

It is difficult in this area to avoid taking some absolutist or behavioural standard of the phenomena as a yardstick when analysing changing conceptions. For how can one compare conceptions of homosexuality or transvestism without some notion of a constant form of behaviour or being which is common to the societies or periods under study? Labelling theory rightly stresses the independence of label and behaviour (at least in the sense that a label is simply a name for behaviour or a 'type' of person), and focuses on the creation and changing nature of labels and their impact on the social world. But to do this, must it implicitly assume criteria by which non-labelled deviants can be identified – those who steal but are not labelled thieves, those men who suck other men's penises but are not labelled homosexual, those men who dress in women's clothes but are not labelled transvestites and so on? It seems probable that some people are able to cross-dress and even 'change' sex without being labelled as suffering from some psychopathological condition, sin or whatever. Occasion, frequency, perceived motive and presentation of self during cross-dressing, together with general societal attitudes towards such behaviour, all probably influence the likelihood of a person being labelled a transvestite. Prior to the widespread dissemination of the notion of transsexualism, it appears likely that some biologically normal individuals were able to change sex and be seen as hermaphrodites of some kind or avoid any definite label at all. But making these claims requires me to have some constant standard of behaviour or whatever against which the conditions and nature of labelling vary. Simply separating out behaviour and label is perhaps at best only a partial solution. As labelling theory itself recognizes, at least in its more sophisticated versions, label and behaviour do not fit in some naturally given way, but rather influence each other continually in various complex ways. This aside, however, has been mentioned only to indicate a hazy recognition of such problems rather than to offer a resolution.

In terms of the four problems of labelling theory outlined by Plummer (Chapter 3), this paper seeks to examine one aspect of the nature of the labels transvestite and transsexual – namely, psychiatric and psychological conceptions. It does not examine closely the social conditions under which these labels emerged, the conditions of their use or their impact upon those so labelled. The 'what' (happened, is *happening*) and the 'why' questions are closely interrelated; available possible answers to the why questions may affect the answers to the what question (for example, the significance given to various events), and perhaps more obviously, our knowledge of what happened and is happening in the field of transsexualism and transvestism is so scanty (as will become increasingly obvious to the reader) that work directed towards the 'what' seems more urgent than that concerned with 'why'.

The following chronology lists the main events in the history of the construction of transvestism and transsexualism, hopefully clarifying the sequence of the events and processes discussed in the following sections. The periods used are of course only rough guides.

1870–1920

Much reporting and discussion of cases of men and women who cross-dress and/or wish to (or actually do) adopt the role ascribed to those of the opposite sex. Coining of a number of new terms to refer to this.
Westphal 'contrary sexual feeling' 1876.
Laurent 'psychic hermaphroditism' 1896 (in Ellis 1928).
Krafft-Ebing 'metamorphosis sexualis paranoica' 1890 (quoted by Ellis 1928).
Hirschfeld 'Transvestism' 1910.

Ellis 'sexo aesthetic inversion' and 'eonism' 1913, cited by Ellis 1928.

Anthropological accounts of cross-dressing and sex role change in primitive societies. See for example the material in Carpenter 1914.

1920–50

Something more of a dark age.

Further reporting of cases, but compared with the previous period the volume of publications seems to have been not so great.

The terms transvestism and eonism become the accepted ones in the literature.

Psychoanalytical material is published, for example, Stekel 1934; Fenichel 1954, first published 1930.

The development of endocrinological knowledge and techniques of plastic surgery.

Some attempts at 'changing sex' by surgical means (see Hirschfeld 1938), most notably the case of Lili Elbe (Hoyer 1933).

1950–65

Term transsexual first used (Cauldwell 1950b).

Benjamin begins to promote the term in 1953, but its use not widespread until the early 1960s.

Christine Jorgensen operation and publicity (1951–2); paper on this (Hamburger *et al.* 1953).

Roberta Cowell, operation (1951–2) and publicity (1954).

Work on hermaphrodites at John Hopkins University.

Discovery of methods of determining chromosomal sex.

Sex change stories became a regular feature in particular newspapers. Operations usually performed in Casablanca or Scandinavia.

Entry of gender terminology into the literature (Stoller 1964).

FPE founded in 1960 (see page 179). Up to about 1960 sex change reported in literature in terms of transvestism.

1965–79

Rise of gender identity clinics and legitimated 'sex change surgery', especially 1965–70. Publications on transsexualism increase. Much less interest in transvestism.

Beaumont Society founded 1967.

Increased sub-cultural activity and visibility. Beaumont Society Conferences 1974 and 1975. Rise and fall of several transsexual organizations.

Entry of transvestite/transsexual theme into more respectable media, especially since 1974.

Criticism of transvestites/transsexuals from gays and women.

Further breakdown and proliferation of term 'gender dysphoria' (Meyer and Hoopes 1974), primary and secondary transsexualism (Person and Ovesey 1974a and b).

The transvestite

At the end of the nineteenth century homosexuality was seen, as Foucault aptly describes it, as 'a kind of interior androgyny, a hermaphroditism of the soul' (1979, p. 43) a conception now incorporated into the image of the transvestite and transsexual so that the term 'homosexual' now refers to the direction of sexual preference rather than the characteristics of a gender type (see Marshall, this volume). The beginning of this process of separation can be seen in the coining in the late nineteenth century of new terms for and new categories of 'gender deviance'. This was part of a larger process of categorizing activity. Thus 'there emerged a world of perversion ... a setting apart of the unnatural as a specific dimension in the field of sexuality ... an entire sub-race race was born' (Foucault 1979, pp. 39–40).

In the setting apart of transvestism and transsexualism, foremost in this activity were Havelock Ellis and Magnus Hirschfeld. Havelock Ellis is portrayed (by Weeks 1977 and Robinson 1976, among others) as one of several writers who in the late nineteenth and early twentieth centuries were seeking to normalize homosexuality. 'Ellis was striving to emphasize that "inverts" were essentially ordinary people in all but their sexual behaviour' (Weeks 1977, p. 63). In part this involved a rejection of the view that a preference for sexual relations with members of the same sex is necessarily associated with the adoption of the dress, mannerisms and so on of the opposite sex. Likewise he wrote that it is possible for a person 'to feel like a person of the opposite sex and to adopt, so far as possible, the tastes, habits and dress of the opposite sex while the direction of the sexual impulse remains normal' (Ellis 1920, pp. 1–2). Ellis originally used the term 'sexo-aesthetic inversion' to refer to this because he saw its essence as:

the impulse to project themselves by sympathetic feeling into the object to which they are attracted or the impulse of inner imitation [which] is precisely the tendency which various recent philosophers of aesthetic feeling have regarded as the essence of all aesthetic feeling. [1928, p. 28]

This term was later rejected because Ellis saw it as 'too apt to arouse suggestions of homosexuality', and he argued that just as 'a large proportion perhaps the majority of sexual inverts have no strongly pronounced feminine traits' so, 'the majority of sexo-aesthetic inverts . . . are not only without any tendency to sexual inversion but they feel a profound repugnance to that anomaly' (ibid., pp. 102–3). Ellis preferred his term 'eonism' coined from the name of a famous 'transvestite', the Chevalier d'Eon (Cox 1966), and designed as a parallel to masochism and sadism. This was the only alternative term to transvestism to enjoy any currency and has survived in some writings, being used to refer to the transsexual (Hamburger *et al.* 1953; Meyer and Hooper 1974). Ellis stated that there were two main types of eonist:

One, the most common kind in which the inversion is mainly confined to the sphere of clothing and another less common *but more complete* in which cross-dressing is regarded with comparative indifference but the subject so identifies himself with those of his physical and psychic traits which recall the opposite sex that he feels really to belong to that sex although has no delusion regarding his anatomical conformation [1928, p. 36, my emphasis]

The distinction comes very close to the contemporary one between transvestism and transsexualism. Ellis seems, however, to regard this 'less common but more complete' type as embodying the essence of eonism, and he objected to the term transvestism because it focused attention solely on the element of cross-dressing. Ellis was mainly attracted by a biological theory of the aetiology of eonism, although he was rather vague as to the specific mechanisms involved. 'Early environmental influences assist but can scarcely originate Eonism. The normal child soon reacts powerfully against them. We must in the end seek a deeper organic foundation for Eonism as for every other aberration of the sexual impulse.' He surmised that the 'real physical basis' of eonism was 'some unusual balance in the endocrine system' (ibid., p. 110).

The terms transvestism (more rarely transvestitism) and transvestite are traced back to Magnus Hirschfeld and his book *Die Transvestiten* first published in 1910.[5] Carpenter[6] seems to have been the earliest writer to employ the term cross-dressing as a translation of Hirschfeld's term. In 1918 Hirschfeld defined transvestism as 'the impulse to assume the external garb of a sex which is not apparently that of the subject as indicated by the sexual organs'.[7] Transvestism, with the translation/synonym cross-dressing, became the accepted term although, Hirschfeld admitted that the term indicated only the most obvious aspect of this phenomenon. Like Ellis, Hirschfeld distinguished transvestism from homosexuality. He criticized Krafft-Ebing who he said remained ignorant of the true nature of the phenomenon. 'He saw in it like most authors before him and after him nothing but a variant of homosexuality whereas today we are in a position to say that transvestism is a condition that occurs independently and must be considered separately from any other sexual anomaly' (Hirschfeld 1938, pp. 188–9). According to Ellis (1928) in Hirschfeld's view 'we may fit this anomaly [transvestism] into the frame of intermediate or transitional forms of the sexual disposition, and regard it as a form of feminism; though why the feminine strain should so operate,' he remarks, 'that in one case hermaphroditism should appear, in a second gynacomasty, in a third inversion and in a fourth transvestism, at present escapes our knowledge'.

Of these 'intermediate forms of the sexual disposition' Hirschfeld (1938) distinguished between:
1 Hermaphroditism proper. Modification in the primary sex characteristics, that is, genital organs towards the structure that is typical in the genitals of the opposite sex.
2 Androgyny, the mixing of secondary sex characteristics.
3 Transvestism, the mixing of psychological sexual differences (hermaphroditismus psychius)

4   Homosexuality, a masculine sexual impulse in woman and a feminine sexual impulse in men.

When writing of actual cases, however, these categories often become combined. In a chapter on androgyny, he notes that there are 'notably among transvestites, men with a completely feminine mentality but without any corresponding physical characteristics as well as psychologically masculine women without physical masculine characteristics'. Thus 'the so called androgynous urge (the strong desire to possess on one's own body characteristics of the opposite sex) often accompanies actual physical androgyny but occurs not infrequently without this in transvestites and homosexuals. The mind becomes instinctively dissatisfied with the unsuitable body and endeavours to correct it' (Hirschfeld 1938, pp. 177–8). He goes on to cite cases of persons who have tried to alter their body to conform to that of the opposite sex. In the chapter on transvestism he cites cases of 'persons in whom transvestism is combined with androgyny and homosexuality'. The first writes, 'as long as I can remember I have always felt a girl or woman and have considered my masculine existence only a disguise', a sentiment which would not be out of place in the autobiography of a modern transsexual. Although Ellis and Hirschfeld saw transvestism and homosexuality (or inversion) as 'intermediate forms of the sexual disposition', along with androgyny and hermaphroditism, both were concerned to emphasize the separateness of these phenomena – a preference for sexual relations with members of the same sex did not necessarily mean a preference for dressing like or taking on the social role of the opposite sex and *vice versa*.

Nevertheless there persisted and still persists a view among some psychoanalytically inclined writers and others that transvestism is merely a mask for latent homosexuality (Allen 1969; Sim 1974). Thus Stekel (1934) took issue with Hirschfeld and wrote, 'I fail to understand the need of setting up besides the hetero and homosexuals, a third group, the so-called transvestites' (p. 69), and 'it was nothing less than doing violence to facts to attempt to distinguish the transvestites from the homosexuals' (pp. 70–1). However, Lukianowicz was probably correct when he wrote in 1959 that 'Hirschfeld's view has been generally accepted and nowadays almost all writers regard transvestism as an independent sexual deviation'.

By the Second World War transvestism seems to have become an established 'perversion', at least in the psychiatric field. As with other 'perversions' the question of aetiology was of paramount importance, and probably the most sophisticated attempts in this area were the psychoanalytic ones, the others being mainly elaborate ad hoc statements of common sense ideas rather than being derived from any coherent theoretical framework. For example, transvestism was seen as resulting from the parental wish for a child of the opposite sex or from dressing a child in the clothing of the opposite sex as a punishment (see examples in Lukianowicz 1959). Curiously few reports of attempts at therapy were published in this period, the literature consisting mainly of additional case material. Often papers would consist simply of detailed case histories with a few comments.[8] No one up to the early 1950s, with the exceptions of Ellis and Hirschfeld, seems to have seen large numbers of transvestites. So although transvestism was a known 'condition' or 'perversion', there were still few if any generally agreed notions of its more detailed nature apart from cross-dressing and probably its separateness from homosexuality. The term was used widely enough to encompass those wishing to change sex through to the 'automonosexual' fetishistic transvestite.

The Kinsey studies added little to the literature on transvestism, although they probably reached a wider audience than previous writers. Some brief comments on transvestism were included in the volume on *Sexual Behaviour in the Human Female* (1953), but the subject did not receive the detailed scrutiny that other areas of sex and gender had been subjected to. Kinsey apparently justified his neglect of transvestism (along with sadism, masochism, voyeurism and exhibitionism) on the grounds of its statistical insignificance. According to Robinson (1976, p. 116), however, 'one senses a certain reserve, the more extravagant and picturesque expression of human sexuality simply did not capture his imagination', but in her autobiography Christine Jorgensen describes an interview with Kinsey at the latter's instigation (1967, p. 201).

Except as the person who first coined the term transsexual, David Cauldwell is never referred to in the academic literature. Yet in the late 1940s and early 1950s he wrote a great many booklets on most aspects of sexual behaviour (or at least deviant sexual behaviour) including transvestism. His booklets were clearly directed at the lay market and were based on his writings for the magazine, 'Sexology'. In the main they consist of accounts of 'famous transvestites in history', what Cauldwell calls 'confessions' sent to him by transvestites, and brief accounts of the nature of chromosomes, hormones, etc., interwoven with his own comments. The title of one of his booklets deserves quoting in full: 'Questions and answers on the sex life and sexual problems of transvestites – an exhaustive, revealing, surprising, informative, educational, entertaining and even shocking, encyclopaedic compilation of seldom-suspected facts' (1950a). Although probably the most amusing of his titles, it is typical of the others and conveys an impression of the style of the contents. Cauldwell stated that 'my work is to fight ignorance and intolerance' (1949a), and indeed his approach is generally tolerant although he warns strongly against 'sex change surgery' on a mixture of ethical and practical (it cannot make you a real woman) grounds. Transvestism is often described as a 'personality quirk' (1949a) or a 'harmless pastime of a group of lovable eccentrics' (1949b). In 1949 he reported that several readers had asked him to form a society for transvestites, and indeed Cauldwell's writings (which in content and style resemble the later sub-cultural publications, *Transvestia* and *Beaumont Bulletin*) are probably better located in relation to the emergence of a transvestite sub-culture than in relation to the scientific community. By 1950 Cauldwell was using the term transsexual to refer to 'individuals who are physically of one sex and apparently psychologically of the opposite sex' and who desire surgery to alter their physical characteristics to resemble those of the opposite sex' (1950b), although in 1951 he used the term 'sex transmutationist' to refer to the same individuals (1951). These terms do not seem to have made much impact at that time and up until around 1960 'sex changes' were reported in terms of transvestism.

The most famous of these was Christine Jorgensen, who received world wide publicity after the New York *Daily News* reported her story on its front page on 1 December 1952 under the headline 'ex G.I. becomes blonde beauty'. Jorgensen's 'sex change' was completed in three operations. The first, castration, took place in September 1951, the second, penectomy, in November/December 1952; both were carried out in Copenhagen. The third, the construction of an artificial vagina, was carried out in New Jersey in early 1954. The first published account of her case together with a general discussion appeared in May 1953 under the heading 'Transvestism, hormonal, psychiatric and surgical treatment' (Hamburger, Sturup and Dahl-Iversen 1953). The term transsexualism is not used in the article, the patient being described as a genuine transvestite or eonist (Ellis's term), a person who identifies completely with members of the opposite sex to the extent of wishing to live as one and who seeks surgical help to change the body. The authors subscribe to a biological theory of causation and, noting the impossibility of changing the patient's wishes, recommend surgical and endocrinological alteration of the body to resemble that of a person of the opposite sex, together with appropriate legal recognition of the 'change of sex'.

Much criticism of the treatment of the Jorgensen case was voiced, criticism which has continued to the present day. Wiedman (1953) comments that there appears no evidence for any constitutional causes and suggests that closer psychiatric investigation might reveal underlying schizophrenic processes. Masochism is evidenced, he asserts, by the patient's persistent demand to be castrated. More forcefully Ostow (1953) argues that Hamburger *et al.* too readily accepted the patient's own perception of his problem. Ostow sees the demand for castration as a symptom of underlying neurosis. Meeting the demand will not cure the neurosis. Ostow questions Hamburger's view that the patient wishes to live as a woman: 'The patient has no desire for sexual relations with men. There is no evidence of maternal interest'.

In contrast were the views of those who like Hamburger *et al.* saw the transvestite as some kind of hermaphrodite or intersex.[9] For example, in a letter to the *British Medical Journal*, Cawadias (1954) stated, 'In my opinion transvestites are as much hermaphrodites as those designated with this term'. Critics of this position have sought to demonstrate the psychological 'disturbance' of transvestites and transsexuals and hence the desirability of psychotherapy rather than 'mutilating' surgery. 'Transvestism is a psychical disease ... the abnormal minds should be treated in order to conform them with the normal body and not vice versa' (Allen 1954).

By this time the term transsexual had been introduced into the literature by Benjamin, but although some writers acknowledged the existence of the term, most writers continued to describe those who desired a change of sex as transvestites. In fact most papers of this period dealing with transvestism were concerned with those who had 'changed sex' or wished to do so. Exceptionally transvestism is defined solely in terms of the desire to change sex: 'Transvestites wish to assume the sex characteristics of the opposite sex and to wear its clothes, they feel as if mentally and bodily they belong to the opposite sex and look upon their sex characteristics as a contradiction to their "real" sex' (Hertz *et al*. 1961). There does not at this point in time appear to be a conception of a separate type of person who may be designated by a term such as transsexual. The social type is the transvestite, some of whom may request sex change surgery. There were, however, two major approaches to transvestism. One stressed the change of role and what Ellis called 'inversion in the effective and emotional sphere' (Ellis 1928), what we might characterize as the gender approach; and the other saw transvestism as sexual behaviour, classifying it as a form of an already existing sexual category, usually homosexuality (Stekel 1934), masochism (see examples in Lukianowicz 1959) or fetishism (Randell 1959), or including these other forms of behaviour within a wider clinical picture of the transvestite (Lukianowicz 1959).

With the creation of the transsexual category, the predominant view of the transvestite which remained was a sexual one laying the stress on masochism and particularly fetishism. Such a conception of transvestism made it seem well suited to aversion therapy; in 1961 Lavin *et al*. following Raymond (1956) reported on the use of this 'therapy' in a case of transvestism, and the following decade saw the publication of a number of similar reports.

The transsexual

The modern history of transsexualism begins about 1950, but before then there were several recorded attempts to meet certain individuals' requests that their bodies be made to resemble more closely those of the opposite sex. Hirschfeld (1938) mentions a woman who succeeded in having her breasts amputated; Benjamin (1969b) records his first attempt to induce gynaecomastia in a male patient by means of hormones in the early 1920s, although a paper in 1940 by C. W. Dunn entitled 'Stilbestrol induced gynaecomastia in the male' suggests that at that time it was still novel enough to merit an article. Castration has a long history, and Balfour Marshall (1913) states that the first recorded attempt to create an artificial vagina was in 1761, so that by 1913 he was able to cite several methods of creating an artificial vagina with varying degrees of success. It would appear then that by 1920 the surgical means of 'changing sex' were available, although in their infancy certainly. The techniques of plastic surgery were further improved as a result of two world wars. Judging by Benjamin's account (1969b), endocrinology was able to play its part from some time in the 1920s onwards.

In 1933 the book *Man Into Woman* was published (Hoyer 1933). This is the story of Lili Elbe, a (male) Danish painter who in the late 1920s had several operations to 'change' his sex, apparently without hormone treatment. The details of the operations are rather vague, but apparently they involved castration, penectomy and the implantation of 'ovarian tissue' and were carried out in Dresden. According to Norman Haire, in his introduction to the book, the presence of rudimentary ovaries were found, but whether today Lili Elbe would be classified as a hermaphrodite of some kind or as a transsexual is impossible to say on the basis of the information given. In many more recent books the case of Lili Elbe is usually cited as an early example of a transsexual (see Benjamin 1966; Bullough 1976).

In 1965 Pauly published a review of one hundred cases of male transsexualism[10] discussed in the literature. Twenty-eight of these were published before the case of Christine Jorgensen in 1953. Three cases came from Cauldwell's publications and only two others were of American 'transsexuals'. Of these twenty-eight cases, sixteen had obtained some form of surgery. All had been castrated, seven had penectomies; in six cases artificial vaginas had been created (two in 1931, one in 1947, two in 1950 and one in 1952). Of these sixteen cases, fifteen were either German (five), Swiss (eight) or Austrian (two). Only one was an American involving a case of auto-castration.

Sex change surgery then was certainly not new in 1950 although, even if the cases cited above were only the tip of the iceberg, it seems to have been comparatively rare. In addition to the countries where the cases cited by Pauly were operated upon, Benjamin (1966) mentions Sweden, Holland and Denmark as countries where earlier operations were performed. According to Bremer (1959) these countries all had legal provision for the castration of sex offenders and also for 'others who might desire it', which might go some way towards explaining the concentration of early sex change operations in these areas of Western Europe, although such operations (according to Bremer and Kinsey 1953) were also legal in Finland, Iceland, Norway and in certain states in the USA. Despite the lack of detail given in accounts of early sex changes and the consequent uncertainty about whether they involved what we would today describe as hermaphrodites of some kind, the idea of 'sex change' seems to have been current before the case of Christine Jorgensen.

A similar case to that of Christine Jorgensen gained some notoriety in Britain around the same time, that of Roberta Cowell. The details of this case are rather more obscure. Cowell in her autobiography (1954) insisted that she was 'basically and fundamentally female'. According to her the various medical practitioners concerned with her case were of the same opinion. The actual ways in which she was 'basically and fundamentally female' were not specified, but it seems that she regarded these as not only psychological. De Savitsch (1958) accepted Cowell's account and referred to her as an hermaphrodite although most other writers (Benjamin 1966; Bullough 1976) referred to her as a transsexual. She was operated upon late in 1951 or early 1952; the exact nature of the operations is unspecified. In May 1951 her birth certificate had been amended. According to her the operation was 'the first of its kind to be carried out in England and as far as was known in the world' (1954). No medical or psychiatric accounts of her case appear to have been published.

Whether or not Cowell, Elbe and others were biological intersexes in some way, the emphasis on being 'basically and fundamentally' female illustrates an important point about attitudes towards surgical treatment of transsexuals and hermaphrodites. Either genetically the patient should be of the sex compatible with the direction in which the genitalia are to be changed, or at least there should be some biological explanation for the patient's identification with the opposite sex. In the case of Agnes discussed by Garfinkel, Stoller and others, the medical personnel were convinced that the patient's conditions were biologically caused: 'Not being considered a transsexual her genitalia were removed' (Stoller in Garfinkel 1967). In this case, although genetically male, the presumed presence of biological causes was considered sufficient justification for surgical alteration of the genitalia. Others have insisted that, in the case of hermaphrodites, surgery be used to produce conformity with the genetic sex even when this conflicts with the patient's gender identity (Money and Tucker 1977, p. 76; Stoller 1968). As Garfinkel (1967, p. 127) remarks, 'It is not that normals and Agnes insist upon the possession of a vagina by females, they insist upon the possession of *either* a vagina that nature made or a vagina that should have been there all along, i.e. the *legitimate* possession' (see Balfour Marshall 1913). The actual grounds for legitimate possession were the subject of considerable controversy during this period.

Although the term 'transsexual' was coined by David Cauldwell, it was Harry Benjamin who introduced the term into the professional literature and promoted its use. Benjamin, an endocrinologist, had been seeing transvestites and transsexuals since the 1920s and had sometimes 'treated' them with female hormones. 'In 1953 I had probably examined more cases of gender identity disturbance than any other clinician in the United States' (Benjamin 1969b). Benjamin's first paper on the subject (1953) was written in part as a response to the Christine Jorgensen case and appeared in the *International Journal of Sexology*. According to Benjamin (1969b) this was 'the very first medical article on transexualism'. In this article Benjamin introduces the term transsexual as the most appropriate term for

the most extreme group of transvestites who wish to change their sex. Transvestism is the desire of a certain group of men to dress as women or of women to dress as men. It can be powerful and overwhelming, even to the point of wanting to belong to the other sex and correct nature's 'anatomical error'. [1953, p. 12]

Although unable to specify the mechanisms involved, Benjamin believes in a biological cause of transvestism and transsexualism. Environmental influences are important, he admits, but the genetic and endocrine constitution must provide a 'fertile soil' in order for them to have any effect. 'If the soma is healthy and "normal", no severe case of transsexualism, transvestism or homosexuality is likely to develop in spite of all provocations' (1953).[11] He regards surgical conversion as a last resort, is not opposed to all such operations, seeing them as the right solution in 'suitable cases', and expresses considerable sympathy for the transsexual faced with a

widely ignorant and often hostile society. Instead of treating the patient [including transsexuals, transvestites and homosexuals as well as other 'sexual deviants – 'where such behaviour does not intrude on the rights of others'], it would frequently be wiser and more constructive to 'treat' society, educationally, so that logic, understanding and compassion might prevail. [1953, pp. 13–14]

Benjamin's later writings (1954, 1966, 1969a, 1971) seem essentially to be elaborations of his first published ideas on the subject. There is a belief in a hidden biological intersexuality, with 'normality' and transsexualism representing the ends of a continuum and transvestism somewhere in between. The cause of transsexualism is then seen as some constitutional 'disorder' or variation. Benjamin's writings over a period of twenty or so years contributed little of a substantive nature to research on or theorizing about the transvestite or transsexual, and his influence has been rather in terms of his campaign for the recognition of the separate existence and the sympathetic treatment of the transsexual. So much so that *The Transsexual Phenomenon* (1966) became the transsexual's Bible (Sagarin 1969). It was some twelve or fifteen years, however, before the term became accepted. The sensational publicity surrounding the Jorgensen case and the coining of a new term certainly did not produce an outburst of research and publications on the subject. A few more cases were reported, usually as transvestites, but by the early 1960s the situation seemed little different from a decade earlier, except that some discussion had taken place concerning the desirability of the use of 'sex change' surgery.

Benjamin described the period thus:

Few references to transsexualism could be found in the medical literature during the ensuing years. It seemed not only a terra incognita but also a noli me tangere. Undoubtedly [sic] in the minds of many in the medical profession, the subject was barely on the fringe of medical science and therefore taboo. [1969b, p. 5]

Up to the end of 1964 Benjamin reported on fifty-one trans-sexuals who had obtained operations mostly in Denmark, Holland, Sweden and Casablanca. Operations had also been carried out in Japan, Mexico, Italy and very occasionally and secretly in the United States. Benjamin's picture of the U S A in this period would seem to fit Britain too. After Roberta Cowell (whose operation was performed in London), a few more British sex change cases were reported in the press, one of whom certainly had the operation in London (Georgina Turtle), but the majority seem to have been performed in North Africa. This is the period in which Casablanca became the transsexual's mecca.

Gender deviance

Around the mid 1960s the picture began to change. The most significant change was a more widespread acceptance that sex reassignment surgery could be used as a form of therapy for transsexuals and its actual use in a small number of 'respectable' medical centres. This change was intertwined with a number of terminological ones, the almost universal adoption of the term transsexual, the relative demise of the transvestite, the employment of a number of terms relating to the concept of gender and a further burst of categorizing activity.

In February 1965 the first 'sex change' operation was performed at the Johns Hopkins Hospital. This seems to have been the beginning of the use of the operation as treatment by 'respectable' medical personnel and several other centres followed this lead, but for several years the operation seemed to be available on a very uncertain and irregular basis. According to one . report, however, more than forty American medical centres now handle such cases, and operations are available under the Medicaid scheme (*Observer* Magazine, 17 September 1978). In Britain a gender identity clinic was established at Charing Cross Hospital in 1965 by John Randell, where operations have since been carried out fairly regularly averaging eight to twelve a year. Operations have also been carried out elsewhere but only very irregularly.

One consequence of the (relatively) wider availability of sex reassignment surgery and its (still precarious) acceptance into mainstream medicine has been the development of various criteria used to select suitable patients. The criteria used fall into basically two groups. The first group perhaps permits the widest use of the operation, and the criteria here could be described as essentially practical or behavioural. Randell (1973), for example, requires that patients be of single civil status, be free from 'severe psychiatric disease' and from 'antisocial propensities' and are able to 'prove themselves' by living and supporting themselves in the preferred gender role over a period of at least a year. The criteria which were used by the Johns Hopkins Hospital team as described by Money and Schwartz (1969) were similar, and also included 'that the patient be at least twenty one years of age, that they live within accessible travelling distance of the hospital to ensure follow up and that a next of kin be designated as an additional informant willing to give written operative consent'. I call this group of criteria practical or behavioural because, apart from criteria which are presumably designed to protect the medical practitioners involved, the main emphasis seems to be on the practicability or otherwise of the patient assuming the opposite gender role.

By contrast the second group of criteria is more concerned with diagnosing the 'true' transsexual according to some theoretical framework irrespective of the patient's ability to function successfully as a member of the opposite sex, although the other criteria referring to marital status, lack of psychiatric disturbance, etc., may be included within the definition of the true transsexual. This group may then be called 'diagnostic' or 'theoretical' criteria. The opinions of Stoller are perhaps the most well known of those writers who advocate the employment of these kind of criteria. In 1966 (published in 1968 in *Sex and Gender*) he wrote that 'I think that only those males who are the most feminine, have been expressing this feminity since earliest childhood, have not had periods of living accepted as masculine males, have not enjoyed their penises and have not advertised themselves as males (for example, female impersonation) should be operated upon', a view which he still held in 1975. These criteria summarize Stoller's clinical picture of the 'true' transsexual who is the product of a specific combination of aetiological factors. In 1975 he wrote, 'There must be a better way to diagnose the condition than to say a person is a transsexual because he requests sex transformation. I would rather attempt to diagnose by assessing the degree of femininity and how long and how completely it has existed.'

Up to probably the late 1950s at least, the category of transvestism was apparently vague enough to cover those who sought to change their bodies to resemble the opposite sex, as well as those whose gender deviance stopped short of these aims. Surgical methods of sex reassignment were initially legitimately available only to those who were considered to be biologically between the sexes (Hamburger *et al.* 1953; Cawadias 1954; Cowell 1954; Allen 1954), but with the development of the category of the transsexual, surgery gradually became available as a legitimate form of 'therapy' although often not seen as 'real' therapy (see Pauly 1969, p. 58). Concern then shifted, at least with those psychiatrists utilizing theoretical criteria, from sifting out the real biological intersexes to sifting out the 'real' transsexuals from the homosexuals, transvestites, schizophrenics and so on who may also apparently request sex change surgery.

Recently the conception of the 'real transsexual' has been formalized by the postulation of a distinction between primary and secondary transsexualism.

Primary transsexuals are essentially asexual and progress towards a transsexual resolution without significant deviation either heterosexually or homosexually. Secondary transsexuals are effeminate homosexuals and transvestites who gravitate towards transsexualism only after sustained periods of active homosexuality or transvestism. [Person and Ovesey 1974b, p. 174]

Another example of the breakdown of the category of the transsexual is to be found in a paper by Meyer and Hooper (1974), who refer to patients requesting sex change surgery by the term 'gender dysphoria syndrome'. This is then broken down into (a) transvestite (b) homosexual (c) sadomachoist (d) psychopath (e) schizoid or borderline (f) psychotic (g) eonist and (h) 'other'. The two groups of criteria characterize approaches falling between two extremes: that sex change surgery should be given to anyone who wants it (and of course who can pay for it) and that sex change surgery should be given to nobody. When outlining the John Hopkins criteria, Money and Schwartz rejected the first view explicitly and the second implicitly.

The philosophical question of freedom of the will and free choice with reference to a patient's right to acquire a sex change was not brought up for specific examination. It was simply assumed that according to the traditions of medicine, the experts would make the decision concerning the diagnosis, suitability and acceptance of applicants for surgery. Therefore sex reassignment may not be obtained as a whim or caprice of individual choice in the manner in which a person decides to get his body tattooed [1969, p. 261]

It seems, however, that there are surgeons who are prepared to perform sex change surgery simply on request with the required payment, but these surgeons do not appear to write in the medical literature. The opposite extreme is represented by Stafford-Clark who wrote:

There can be no greater tragedy and no greater mistake than to embark upon a series of mutilations or interferences with the shape of a person's body or the balance of their glands in a misguided attempt to make them into a travesty of something which they can never be however much they desire it. You cannot make a man into a woman or a woman into a man; and there can never be any ultimate justification for massive mutilation in the service of a delusional question for sexual mutation. [1964, pp. 71–2][12]

From the mid 1960s onward the volume of research and publications increased enormously. Reports were no longer on single patients but routinely involved large series. Yet mostly this activity was concerned with the transsexual; compared with the previous period this was the age of mass production sex change surgery. As noted previously, the transvestite had been the social type till the late 1950s, the wish for sex change surgery characterizing some extreme individuals; the transsexual emerged as a subtype of the transvestite and then began to stand as a separate category. Although still discussed together with homosexuality in relation to transsexualism, transvestism faded out of the picture somewhat.[13] Transvestism has usually been classed as a sexual perversion or disorder, and associations with masochism, fetishism and other perversions have frequently been made.

The conception of transvestism as a complicated form of fetishism is still widely held (Randell 1973; Allen 1969), and the fetishistic transvestite is mentioned as a type by a number of other writers (Benjamin 1966; Stoller 1968). But there seems to emerge another kind of transvestite, the one who is motivated by 'gender discomfort' (Benjamin 1966), and Benjamin classifies as the 'true' transvestite one who is so motivated. As we shall see in the next section, the main sub-cultural groups of transvestites have also stressed the gender aspects of their behaviour, and researchers who have studied non-clinical groups of subjects usually drawn from these have tended to argue that transvestism is a gender rather than a sexual anomaly. Brierley (1974, 1975), for example, argues that 'transvestism is a syndrome concerned with gender roles, with preferences to adopt the social and personal role of the opposite gender'.

The transsexual, however, while usually likewise included in textbook chapters on sexual perversions or disorders (for example, Sim 1974), seems never really to have been seen as a form of sexual expression (unless as a masked form of homosexuality), and from the mid 1950s the terms gender, gender role and gender identity have become increasingly popular (see Money 1973). Although the phenomena designated by these terms had been recognized before,[14] they were brought into greater prominence by the work of Money and the Hampsons on hermaphrodites and by the question asked by the women's and gay movements. Transsexualism is most likely to be represented as a '*gender identity* disorder'. For Stoller the transsexual represents the 'far side of the continuum of *gender aberration*' (1975). Treatment centres on *gender identity* clinics. The study of gender is a growth area in many social science disciplines, especially psychology and sociology, and transsexualism is often seen as being of theoretical importance now rather than a somewhat esoteric interest. By contrast, the transvestite, although on the fringes of this, remains in the sphere of sexual perversions.

Sub-cultural contributions

This section is concerned to look briefly at the rise of a sub-culture based on the categories of transvestism and transsexualism, and in particular at the influence of psychiatric and psychological conceptions of these categories on transvestites and transsexuals themselves, as well as the alternative conceptions which have arisen within the sub-culture. Transvestites and transsexuals have themselves of course contributed indirectly to the definitions of the categories by providing accounts of their experiences to those psychiatrists and others who have carried out research and written in this area. A number have published their memoirs or autobiographies from the Abbé de Choisy (1966) onwards. Most notable among recent examples of these have been those by 'Lili Elbe' (Hoyer 1933), Allen (1954), Cowell (1954), Jorgensen (1967) and Morris (1974). These and others have been published by general publishers presumably for general consumption; several others exist apparently published mainly for the semi-pornography market. From Elbe onwards these have all been by transsexuals. Autobiographies by transvestites (or at least by known transvestites) do not seem to exist, although there are many transvestite novels and short stories, which seem to serve a pornographic function.

Most transsexual autobiographies include accounts of 'scientific' views of the phenomenon, in particular those most sympathetic to the use of surgery, while stressing the uniqueness of their case. As noted earlier, those published up to about the late 1960s stress their physical characteristics appropriate to the sex role they are seeking to adopt. Infrequently transvestites or transsexuals have contributed to the medical and psychiatric literature. In 1957 Charles 'Virginia' Prince contributed an article to the *American Journal of Psychotherapy*, in which she separated transvestism from transsexualism and homosexuality. She argued that identification with different aspects of womanhood produced different 'deviations'. If a man identified with the sexual side of women, he became a homosexual; identification with the 'feminine attitudes of mind' resulted in transsexualism, and identification with the 'social woman', woman's role in society, resulted in transvestism.

At about this time, as we have noted, the concept of the transsexual emerged as more distinct from that of the transvestite, and the former term came to be more widely used amongst psychiatrists. Distinguishing transvestism from transsexualism was (and is) of almost as much concern to Prince and the organizations which were influenced by her as was distinguishing it from homosexuality. Again and again in her writings, Prince emphasized that transvestites are heterosexual and do not wish to change sex. The Beaumont Society, which is discussed below, excludes (at least formally) transsexuals from its ranks. But if transvestites were concerned to distinguish themselves from transsexuals, as was the psychiatric profession, they were unwilling to accept the view of transvestism which saw it as a complex fetish, putting gender and social role change into the category of the transsexual (see the quote from the Beaumont Society Constitution below).

In 1960 Prince founded the magazine *Transvestia* and shortly afterwards the Foundation for Full Personality Expression, a social organization which had branches in many parts of the world by the late 1960s.[15] FPE has now apparently become the Sorority for the Second Self. The British branch of FPE became the Beaumont Society around 1967, and has been very much influenced by Prince's views until comparatively recently (as have most other transvestite organizations). While several transsexuals have become celebrities through media exposure, Prince remains probably the only transvestite public figure.[16] She has consistently argued that transvestism is concerned with gender and not with sex, rejecting associations with fetishism and homosexuality. The transvestite is depicted as the most perfect example of human kind, combining both male and female characteristics. Prince has also coined the terms ' "femiphilia" for the condition and "femiphile" for the individual'. These mean 'love of the feminine and are applied to persons whose interest is solely in the feminine gender role and not in her sexual activity'. Some of Prince's views – that the transvestite symbolically identifies with his love object, a woman – recall Ellis's concept of aesthetic inversion.

Prince is also gently critical of 'society' for its rigid gender roles; thus the transvestite is one who seeks expression for those aspects of his personality which are culturally supposed only to exist in women (it is always 'he' because Prince thinks that the cultural constraints are less rigid for women). She criticizes, in addition, its over-emphasis on competitiveness and aggressiveness. 'If the finer, gentler, more considerate qualities of humankind were not set aside and labelled feminine so that the man cannot express them we would not have so much pugnacity in the world' (1957).[17] Prince's criticism of the gender role system, however, seems to be confined to its lack of allowance for mobility and to the competitive/aggressive aspects of the male role. The content of the traditional female role seems to be acceptable to Prince, who in a number of her books and *Transvestia* writings urges her fellow transvestites to cultivate correct lady-like patterns of behaviour and styles of dress.

The Beaumont Society is 'an association of heterosexual

transvestites whose motivation for crossdressing is primarily of a gender rather than a sexual nature' (Beaumont Society constitution 1975). It is principally a social organization, but other goals in the constitution include disseminating information and increasing public understanding and tolerance. Particularly in recent years, the views of those who depart from Prince's ideal have become visible in the Society's publications (those who could be roughly described as transsexuals, fetishists or homosexuals).

Around 1974–5 a number of transvestite/transsexual groups were formed in Britain independently of the Beaumont Society and were usually critical of its philosophy. Most seemed to be influenced by the kinds of discussions which were taking place in the gay and women's movements. It seems to have been only during this period that transsexuals became organized (the main group being a branch of the American Transsexual Action Organization, although a number of others were planned or existed for brief periods). Transsexuals never seem collectively to have felt the need to stress their separateness from transvestites, although this remains an individual need, particularly perhaps when trying to obtain surgery.

A predominant concern was to provide information about facilities for surgery and to campaign for reform of certain legal or administrative obstacles to sex changes, but the publications of these groups[18] are unmistakably influenced by the gay and feminist writings of the early 1970s. Such influences probably helped to shift the Beaumont Society away from its rather rigid pre-1974 stance, but it remains basically a social society with few members concerned to analyse the nature of transvestism and transsexualism beyond offering speculations as to aetiology. A handful of items in the *Beaumont Bulletin* in recent years shows, however, that there are some transvestites and transsexuals who are attempting to grapple with the questions raised by the women's and the gay movements. The response from these groups to transvestites and transsexuals has, however, tended to be far from welcoming. The women's movement has criticized transvestites and transsexuals for identifying with cultural stereotypes of women which form part of their oppression. The radical gay movement has made similar criticisms and has sometimes seen the transvestite, and particularly the transsexual, as a special kind of 'closet queen', switching gender roles to avoid the label of homosexual. In many ways the response of some gays and feminists (but by no means all) to transvestites and transsexuals parallels that of the more reactionary psychiatrists and psychologists. Transvestites or transsexuals have been treated by these groups with contempt or, at best, have been denied any authenticity by having their feelings and behaviours 'explained away' as a response to various aspects of the sex role system or as a psychological method of repressing or legitimizing homosexuality. Not that any woman of even mildly feminist tendencies wouldn't be horrified by reading the *Beaumont Bulletin*, but the kind of response which has been prevalent may have lessened the impact on transvestites and transsexuals of ideas which deserved a better hearing. Overall, however, they seem to remain wedded to a 'condition' view of themselves, seeking only more acceptance and help within the existing order of things.

Conclusions

Although this section concludes the present paper, there is nothing 'conclusive' about the following remarks. Indeed this whole paper is only the beginning of an attempt to outline the development of contemporary conceptions of transvestism and transsexualism. First, there was the emergence of a separate category of people who wished to dress, behave or physically resemble persons of the 'opposite sex'. At first such people seemed not to be regarded as suffering from a medical or psychiatric condition. It may be that Ellis was exceptional, but the general impression gained from his writings is of the eonist as, certainly, a different kind of person but not of one struck by some pathological condition. At first the category covered persons with a wide range of feelings and behaviours, but with the development of methods of sex change surgery and increasing numbers of requests for its use, the separate category of the transsexual emerged along with attempts to define it more closely and to devise criteria by which to select candidates for surgery. By the mid 1960s the 'condition' perspective seemed well established. One recent writer expressed this approach particularly well: 'There is no doubt that gender dysphoria is a painful condition, which previously has been underestimated and often ridiculed and that patients with this condition need medical help' (Hertoft 1976, p. 231).

At the same time, as I have outlined in the section on gender deviance, the late 1960s and early 1970s saw a new period of classification and refinement. Foucault sees such activities not simply as attempts to condemn and stamp out a certain kind of phenomena but as mechanisms for controlling it.

The machinery of power that focussed on this whole alien strain did not aim to suppress it, but rather to give it an analytical, visible, and permanent reality . . . a natural order of disorder [is being created. But whilst] discourse transmits and produces power [it] also undermines and exposes it, renders it fragile and makes it possible to thwart it . . . . [Thus] there is no question that the appearance in nineteenth century psychiatry, jurisprudence and literature of a whole series of discourses on the species and sub-species of homosexuality . . . made possible a strong advance of social controls into this area of 'perversity'; but it also made possible the formation of a 'reverse' discourse: homosexuality began to speak on its own behalf, to demand that its legitimacy or 'naturality' be acknowledged, often in the same vocabulary, using the same categories by which it was medically disqualified. [1979, pp. 44, 101]

Although the term transvestism was coined in 1910, it was not until the 1950s with the advent of suitable methods of sex change surgery that medical and psychiatric interest in the field became aroused. And it was not until the mid 1960s that the British or American transsexual ceased to sneak off to Casablanca for his operation, out of the control of established medicine, and was able to obtain his operation (subject to various controls) as 'treatment' in his own country. But if this 'proliferation of discourse' on transsexualism and, by extension, transvestism, along with attendant 'surgical treatment', has enabled control over gender mobility to be retained rather than relinquished to foreign surgeons, a 'reverse discourse' has also begun to emerge, as was seen in the last section. Transvestites and transsexuals have been created, and like homosexuals are now beginning to 'speak on their own behalf', albeit at least as yet not so challengingly. The contributions of transvestites and transsexuals must be seen as part of a 'multiple and mobile field of force relations, wherein far-reaching, but never completely stable, effects of domination are produced' (ibid., p. 102).

Clearly this article has avoided one major problem as discussed in the introduction: the situating of the events described in the context of wider social processes, the linkage of psychiatric and sub-cultural conceptions of transvestism/transsexualism with cultural conceptions of sexuality and gender, and their relation to aspects of social structure. A problem on a less macro scale concerns the actual use of public categories, for interactionism warns us that there is no simple fit between public and private meanings. Everyday life is not to be explained as a simple application of a blueprint provided by the culture of a society at any given time.

While the meaning of things is formed in the context of social interaction and is derived by the person from that interaction, it is a mistake to think that the use of meaning by a person is but an application of the meaning so derived. [Blumer 1969, p. 5]

The general tone of the psychiatric and other writings on which I have drawn in this article is a liberal sympathetic one, but there is no doubt that the experiences of many transvestites and transsexuals in their encounters with the medical profession have been far from happy ones (see any of the autobiographies cited in the bibliography). How then are these public psychiatric categories actually employed in psychiatric practice? Likewise we need to ask, what is the relationship between the 'public' conceptions of transvestism and transsexualism in the sub-cultures in this area and the ways in which their members actually interpret their experiences?

While the impact of the early writers was probably small even within their 'professional' communities, the publicity given to cases of sex change, the rise of transvestite and transsexual organizations and particularly media interest in 'gender identity problems' in the 1970s probably brought about at least the beginning of the emergence of the transvestite and particularly the transsexual as 'social types'. The nature of these social types requires further examination, and again the actual nature of their use remains problematic. These problems are not the only ones, but they are crucial ones in terms of the perspective taken in this article and indeed in this book as a whole. They point towards a wider theoretical and empirical endeavour, of which this article is a fumbling beginning, on the social construction of transvestism and transsexualism.

8 Male dominance and the gay world

Gregg Blachford

Homosexual sub-cultures – like other sub-cultures[1] – have typically been seen as massive collective problem-solving devices. Plummer (1975), among others,[2] has suggested that gay sub-cultures may resolve all those problems which flow from the homosexual taboo: secrecy, guilt, identity and access. This is fine as far as it goes, but it generally does not go far enough because it fails to connect the sub-culture back to the dominant culture. The task of this article then will be to begin the empirical and theoretical task of examination of the links between some parts of the male gay sub-culture and the wider social order,[3] a task already begun in the area of delinquent sub-cultures by the Birmingham Centre for Contemporary Cultural Studies (Hall and Jefferson 1975; Hall *et al.* 1978). Their framework suggests that all sub-cultures are located at the intersection of the dominant order (which generates problems) and other located cultural forms (which mediate the problems).

Willis (1978), for instance, studied the sub-cultures of hippies and bikeboys and illustrated how they operated at this intersection, claiming that they understand something of their own conditions of existence through the logic of their actions: their 'cultural profanity' and creativity. They, like other oppressed and minority groups,[4] can construct their own 'vibrant culture', rather than simply act as the rejects or 'fall guys' of a social system that is overwhelmingly stacked against them. His optimism and enthusiasm for their actions against 'the system' is reflected throughout his work.

In the very transformations of their cultural fields – no matter what was actually expressed – [the bikeboys] were striking back at the heart of the whole commodity form and its detailed domination of everyday life. Instead of yielding control and allowing commodities . . . to determine the pattern of commonplace life and modes of living and behind this detail to enforce much larger ideological patterns, they seized a kind of control. [Willis 1978, p. 171]

But he also stressed that in these attempts to win space inside a dominant culture, sub-cultures are ultimately restricted in what they can actually *do* about the fundamental problems that their members face.

The problematic of a subordinate class experience can be 'lived through', negotiated or resisted; but it cannot be *resolved* at that level or by those means. There is no 'sub-cultural career' for the working class lad, no 'solution' in the sub-cultural milieu for problems posed by the key structuring experiences of the class . . . . Sub-cultural strategies cannot match, meet or answer the structuring dimensions emerging in this period for the class as a whole . . . . [Clarke *et al*. 1975b, p. 47]

So sub-cultures solve, but in an 'imaginary way'[5], problems of (in this case) working class boys, which at a more fundamental level remain unresolved.

Following this model, my discussion of the male gay sub-culture[6] will begin by briefly sketching some themes of the dominant culture in which the gay world must be located. It will then proceed to examine two processes at work in the gay world: those of *reproduction* and *resistance*. The first section examines some characteristics of the male gay sub-culture and how they can be seen to reproduce directly parts of the dominant culture, thereby reinforcing the dominant order through its arch conformity. The second section examines the resistances, alterations and modifications that the homosexual sub-culture makes to the dominant culture that it confronts. It does this as an expression of a partly negotiated opposition to those values. In this case, as with the bikeboys, there is a challenging of the dominant order.

A final section will then consider the limitations of these resistances, for despite opposition and challenge the gay world remains firmly tied to the dominant order. As Peter York says, with reference to the 'gay scene' in the USA:

The fact that American capitalism can co-opt almost anything no matter how ostensibly subversive is a truism so bizarre, so fascinating in its implications as to give many sensitive souls perpetual culture shock. [1977, p. 58]

The dominant culture

Justice cannot be done to the complexity of the social order of industrialized societies in this short section.[7] I will only attempt to identify certain core values of the social order that can be said to make up its dominant culture, that is, the behaviour that counts as normal, natural, 'common sense', against which all other behaviour is measured. It is necessary to identify these values to note how the gay sub-culture is linked to them.

In capitalist societies there is an emphasis on values such as individual achievement, a never ending desire for more consumer goods and a market mentality that extends beyond the commodity market-place to include areas of sexual behaviour and emotional relationships. The majority religion, Christianity, stresses monogamy, sexual fidelity and potentially procreative sexual behaviour within marriage. The homosexual taboo, itself a core value, has its roots in religious doctrine.[8] Finally, age stratification is also prevalent with its stigma against being old in this society and a worship of the idea of youth itself.

Each of these core values (class relationships, consumerism, Christian morality and devaluation of the old) could be examined to see how the gay sub-culture, at the same time, both reproduces and resists them. But in this article I will mainly be dealing with another core value, male dominance, and how it is dealt with by the gay world. In subsequent research, links to the other core values could be examined.

Male dominance as part of the dominant culture

As with other core values, sex role stereotyping and the resulting domination of men over women is a complex area that cannot adequately be summarized in a few lines.[9]

Men dominate the crucial decision making centres of power in industrialized societies. The economic contributions that women make to society, both at the work-place and at home, are undervalued, if recognized at all. Any status that a woman has is that which comes to her from her husband or father. Despite attempts in the 1970s in Britain, through the Equal Pay Act and the Sex Discrimination Act, to try to give equal opportunities to women, women are still subject to the ideology that sets out their main role as housewife and mother. But the economic sector is not the only one that men dominate. Their power is all-encompassing.

According to usage and conventions which are at last being questioned but have by no means been overcome, the social presence of a woman is different in kind from that of a man. A man's presence is dependent upon the promise of power which he embodies [which] may be moral, physical, temperamental, economic, social, sexual – but its object is always exterior to the man . . . . To be born a woman has been to be born, within an allotted and confined space, into the keeping of men. The social presence of women has developed as a result of their ingenuity in living under such tutelage within such a limited space . . . . One might simplify this by saying: men act and women appear. [Berger 1972, pp. 45–7]

Because of the submissive position that women are given in all aspects of society, their associated gender characteristics of femininity (which are culturally and historically specific) are seen as inferior ways of behaving – for example women's gestures, interests, concerns, dress, mannerisms, language – regardless of whether they are actually taken on by women or men.

The masculinization of the gay sub-culture

Before beginning the examination of the homosexual sub-culture, it is necessary to comment briefly on how far masculine characteristics have permeated the gay sub-culture in the late 1970s compared with the sub-culture in the earlier decades of this century. Elsewhere in this book, John Marshall argues that masculinity only became separated from homosexual orientation in the second half of this century. This was the precondition for the masculinization of the gay world that began in the 1970s in America and Britain. Ironically this has occurred at the same time as patriarchal privilege is being progressively undermined (Tolson 1977, p. 16). This is not to say that masculinity and male images were not seen as desirable fantasy images by many gay men before this time (note the muscle 'porn' magazines of the 1950s and 1960s), but rather for the first time homosexuals themselves moved away from the previous stereotype of 'swish and sweaters' towards a new masculine style which has become the dominant mode of expression in the sub-culture (see Humphreys 1971). The

'Homosexual role', discussed by McIntosh earlier, has to be seen then as in no way permanent, for the expectations of that role now prohibit or certainly limit effeminancy. This change is a key point that aids understanding of the gay sub-culture in the late 1970s (see Nichols 1979).

Reproduction of male dominance in the gay sub-culture

The task now is to see how this particular aspect of the dominant culture, male dominance, is reproduced and resisted in the homosexual sub-culture. I will begin, as I stated earlier, by pointing out how the gay sub-culture *reproduces* male dominance. To do this, I will examine three aspects of the style of the homosexual sub-culture: the practices of language, 'pick-ups, cruising and objectification' and, third, the 'expressive artefacts and concrete objects' (Willis 1977, p. 172) found in the gay sub-culture.[10]

The style of language

A group's specialized language or slang reflects much about its culture. The homosexual sub-culture, like all others, has its own slang which reflects that manner in which homosexuals perceive and structure the world in which they live. Much of the slang of the male homosexual directly reproduces traditional male attitudes to women. For example, women are often referred to by their sexual organs; 'fish' is a common term for a woman and 'cunty' is used as an adjective referring to something that possesses the qualities of a woman. The derogatory term 'fag hag' is used to describe a woman who enjoys the company of gay men. Besides these peculiarly gay male expressions, most references to women are similar to the way in which heterosexual men can be seen to respond to women: 'cow', 'old woman', 'slag', 'tart', 'cheap', 'scrubber'.

Sonenschein (1969) in his study of homosexual language characterized it by four main processes: utilization, effeminization, redirection, invention. The one that is at work here is 'utilization', whereby terms used by other groups, in this case heterosexual men, are borrowed and used in a similar way. It reflects a negative attitude to women, who are seen as insignificant, passive objects, not fit for anything except sexual intercourse and/or looking after children. Since gay men neither want sex with women nor have any procreative use for them, they serve no purpose at all; in fact, they may be accused of taking men away from possible homosexual encounters.

There is also slang that refers pejoratively to effeminate homosexuals because they are 'like women' and therefore are not worthy of considerate treatment. The slang used is the same as that used by heterosexuals against *all* homosexuals, that is, 'queer', 'bent', 'poof' and 'fairy'. Bruce Rodgers in *The Queen's Vernacular: A Gay Lexicon* gives examples: 'I'm gay, but you're queer'; 'We're not the queer ones; they are!' (1972, p. 166). This is said by 'normal' homosexuals to those whom they believe are 'truly perverted'. These would include not only these effeminate homosexuals, but also transvestites, transsexuals and paedophiles.

Perhaps the 'normal' homosexual feels threatened by the overtness of the effeminate homosexual. Because of the expectations involved in 'being a man', with its attendant homosexual taboo, gay men may want to distance themselves as far as possible from the stereotyped role of the homosexual which they have internalized as negative and undesirable. So effeminate homosexuals are going to be stigmatized by the more 'normal' homosexuals, and in rejecting effeminancy they imitate so closely the world of the dominant male culture. Mike Brake relates how one member of a respectable homophile organization (notoriously anti-drag) puffed furiously at his pipe while complaining of being barred from a pub which had banned gays: 'They said I was effeminately dressed. I was furious. I may be queer but at least I'm a man' (1976, p. 186).

Aspects of homosexual slang then show the internalization and reproduction of male culture with its particular attitudes towards women and its rejection of deviants who do not fit the prescribed masculine pattern of behaviour.

By laughing at homosexuals one ceases to be one, or at least establishes ... 'role distance' between oneself and other homosexuals. By reserving ridicule for some homosexuals such as the ... exhibitionistically effeminate 'screaming queen', a distance is placed between oneself who is presumably adjusted and manly, and certain other homosexuals deserving of contempt. [Sagarin 1970, p. 41]

So the everyday language of homosexual males is in many ways continuous with the everyday language of the heterosexual male culture. Their slang ties them to the dominant order and offers no challenge to a society which labels *all* homosexuals as deviants and oppresses them as such, although effeminate homosexuals are more likely to be singled out for the brunt of any attack because of their visibility.

The style of pick-ups, cruising and objectification

Male dominance affects the nature of sexual relationships between men and women. One form of sexual relationship, that of the casual sexual encounter, departs from the strongly sanctioned norms that declare deviant 'anything other than monogamous, legally sanctioned, obligated relations' (Hooker 1967, p. 177). But a man is less likely to suffer sanctions if he engages in promiscuous behaviour, as his powerful position allows him to be the pursuer and the chooser. This stronger position enables him to see his potential female partner as a sexual object with its emphasis on physical appearance to the almost total neglect of other aspects of her character. I want to look for evidence of this form of 'sexual objectification' in the gay sub-culture.[11]

The prevalence of homosexual promiscuity has not gone unnoticed. Recent research has found that the average, white, male heterosexual has five to nine sexual partners over his lifetime. The average, white, male homosexual, on the other hand, encounters 1000 partners over his life, most of them strangers (Bell and Weinberg 1978, p. 12).[12] So sexual activity is important. The sub-culture and common understandings among homosexuals facilitate these encounters.

Two men passing on the street may momentarily glance at each other, drop cues that each is homosexual and interested in each other, hesitate for confirmatory signals and, within a half hour, consummate their 'spontaneous' love in the many available niches that are legion in congested N.Y.C. [Delph 1978, p. 9)]

Delph's work – an ethnography of public homosexual encounters – describes in detail the social and sexual interactions which occur in a wide variety of settings including streets, public toilets, public parks, subways, cinemas, beaches, empty lorries, public buildings, as well as the more expected gay bars and baths. One characteristic common to almost all of these settings is that verbal utterances are virtually absent. The study illuminates

how individuals learn to use the special self-presentations, bodily posturing, gestural cues, the manners and informal (but sanctionable) rules unique to the settings; how the distinctive meanings of space, time, and manner (or 'self') separate these erotic worlds from the conventional ones; how public sexuality produces a metamorphosis of the individuals who partake in it, thus transforming normal selves into erotic selves. [J. M. Johnson in Delph 1978, p. 16][13]

Does sexual objectification occur in these casual encounters? People in these situations will not be attracted to someone unless they are attracted by some external feature that fulfils some sexual fantasy. It follows that there must be an emphasis on surface or cosmetic characteristics. And because the criteria of selection can be highly specific, one is, in turn, concerned to present an image of oneself that will attract others. Therefore appearance, dress, manner and body build are very important. The partner is only a means to an impersonal, purely sexual end. 'In this meeting of strangers, the disengaged character of activities from any ascriptive characteristics is promoted' (Hooker 1967, p. 177).

The ultimate sexual objectification in gay male casual sexual encounters is the glory hole in public toilets.[14] As a wall separates the two participants, they have no contact except for a mouth, a penis and perhaps a hand. Almost total anonymity is maintained as no other attributes are taken into consideration.

Some gay men note the emphasis on outward appearances and resent it.

The gay scene is a market and both sellers and buyers have become used to the coinage of appeal and neither can change it without losing out. The way the compulsive cruisers present themselves is geared to the way the buyers choose: looking no further than skindeep, ignoring what might or what might not be underneath .... The majority of gays are placing their cosmetic selves, not their real selves, on the line. [Houston 1978, p. 14]

In this reproduction of the sexual objectification that even goes beyond that characteristic of heterosexual casual encounters, one is not challenging the ideology of male dominance in our society and its resulting homosexual oppression.

Engaging in public sex [the public eroticist], does so with no intention of contesting discrimination against homosexuality. There is no drive to change existing moral conditions. The homosexual adapts to the contingencies of the existing order of things. He maintains socially prescribed and expected demeanor in the round of settings through which he travels. [Delph 1978, p. 28]

Gay men have an invested interest in the system as it exists. And so the arch-conformity of the gay sub-culture is further reinforced.

The style of 'expressive artefacts and concrete objects'

The overall style that is most recognizable and far reaching in the public gay sub-culture in the 1970s is the copying of traditional masculine clothing and its associated artefacts. There are a variety of forms, from 'hard' to 'soft' masculinity, but the studied virility is to be found almost everywhere. Its extreme is represented by the 'leather men' of the gay sub-culture who adopt images of sexual violence and dominance including neo-Nazi adornments, metal-toed boots, studded belts, handcuffs and chains. Then there are those who wear clothes associated with masculine working class labouring occupations such as construction workers (overalls, hard boots, construction helmet, tools hanging from belts), mechanics (coveralls) or cowboys (denim jeans, vest and jacket, plaid shirt, cowboy boots, short neck scarves and, in some cases, a cowboy hat and breeches). Different kinds of athletes are represented, and one sees people dressed as joggers (shorts, sleeveless top, white running shoes) or boxers complete with authentic boxing shorts, a vest or nothing over the chest, long socks and boxing shoes.

Other styles would be a military look including complete uniforms of one of the services. *Him Exclusive*, a British gay magazine, outlines the details of this style for its readers:

If uniforms are your thing the best place you could go seems to be Hampstead Heath .... Talking about uniforms I must admit I do have a liking for sailors; there's something about nice short hair and bell bottoms .... Somehow a sailor's uniform seems to fit right round the arse and crotch. [September 1975, p. 27][15]

A popular American disco group in the late 1970s, 'Village People', wore clothing and carried artefacts that were clearly intended to represent these gay male styles. The members of this group include a cowboy, Indian chief, policeman, biker/leather freak, GI soldier and construction worker.

But these extremes are not common except in the large 'trendy' discos of metropolitan cities. More usual is for an individual to wear only a certain item rather than the complete outfit. Denim from the 'Western style' is an example. Peter York describes the general look.

The costume was Basic Street Gay (or 'lumberjack'): straight jeans, cheap plaid shirt, construction worker's yellow lace-up boots, short cropped hair – and the moustache, always the moustache .... One of the tightest dress-codes in the world was evolving, and with the costume ... the mythology of the hard man, *macho*. [1979, p. 59]

These objects and styles have clear meanings in the wider culture: toughness, virility, aggression, strength, potency – essentially, masculinity and its associated machismo. It seems as if there is an attempt, as with language, to achieve through these objects a differentiation between oneself, who becomes a 'real man' in these outfits, and the absurd, condemned and ridiculed role of other homosexuals. There is a celebration of masculinity that allows them to distance themselves from the stigmatized label of homosexual. Again the dominant culture with respect to male dominance becomes reproduced in the gay sub-culture.

Reactionary macho had made a cultural reappearance .... Mass macho ... [was] set solid by the late Seventies into the most archaic possible stereotype: the gay as Ultraman. [Although] there was nothing new, in principle, about gays taking up worker chic, they had been doing it for years ... a funny reference to an icon, the straight working man, gays [were now] internalising him, his clothes, his hardman values, his contempt for sissies. [York 1979, pp. 59–60]

Challenges through camp

The previous section dealt with some of the ways in which the male gay sub-culture, through its styles, reproduces characteristics of the dominant culture which are associated closely with male assertiveness and (tacitly at least) female subordination. In this way the gay world reinforces the dominant order through its conformity. But the processes at work in the sub-culture are more complicated than might appear at first glance, for there is some evidence that the gay sub-culture negotiates an oppositional challenge to some aspects of the dominant order. The best way to understand this innovatory style is to examine one phenomenon of the gay sub-culture – camp – and to show how it transforms conformity into a challenge.

What is camp?

Very little has been written specifically about camp. It conjures up images of limp wrists and swivelling hips, but camp, Christopher Isherwood says, is much more than

a swishy little boy with peroxided hair, dressed in a picture hat and a feather boa, pretending to be Marlene Dietrich. [1954, p. 125]

Susan Sontag in 'Notes on camp' made the first major attempt to discuss it in 1964, but admitted that it is very hard to talk about because it is a sensibility (as distinct from an idea).

To talk about Camp is therefore to betray it ... [or, at best], one runs the risk of having, oneself, produced a very inferior piece of Camp. [1967, pp. 275, 277]

Jack Babuscio claims that camp does two things for homosexuals; it gives them a general understanding about what the world is like and their place in it, and it helps them to deal with that world.

What the world is like   By being polarized by society into the negative category of homosexuality, which is opposite to the category of heterosexuality and its associated characteristics of normality, natural and healthy behaviour, gay people become aware that to be homosexual is to bear a stigma.

Homosexuals come to see how the world is socially constructed, and become aware of some of the rules by which it is so constructed, being placed as they are in positions of constantly having to consciously perform roles. Being stigmatised results in the uncommonsense knowledge of commonsense social structures. [Plummer 1975, p. 160]

But one also comes to learn very quickly that the stigma can be avoided by 'passing for straight', playing a role, pretending to be something that one is not.[16] This two-sided nature of many homosexuals' lives can be productive of the gay sensibility which

Babuscio defines as

a creative energy reflecting a consciousness that is different from the mainstream; a heightened awareness of certain human complications of feeling that spring from the fact of social oppression: in short, a perception of the world which is coloured, shaped, directed and defined by the fact of one's gayness. [1978, p. 18]

With this particular awareness, one may be better able to look for the double meaning or polarization or two sides in any activity, individual, object or situation. If it can be found, then it is 'camp'. Of course not all gay men will understand camp nor will all see it in the same object. It, like beauty, is often in the eye of the beholder. But there is an underlying unity of perspective, especially among sub-culturalized homosexuals, that sees in someone (like a filmstar) or something (like Art Deco furniture) a characteristic camp or double flavour.

Dealing with that world   Camp can also help homosexuals deal with a hostile environment that forces one to live a 'closeted' or two-sided life. It does this by criticizing through mockery the hypocrisy, pretension, self-deceit and prudery that gay people have come to know exist in the wider world. It is a gesture of self-legitimization which has not just a touch of propaganda value. The 'normal' world, which makes homosexuality illegitimate and forces homosexuals to pass for straight, is made into the common enemy. 'Camp is a solvent of morality. It neutralizes moral indignation, sponsors playfulness' (Sontag 1967, p. 290), at least when one is in the sub-culture.

Camp also deals with the world because it is an assertion of identity. It will always be done in the company of others 'in the know' where one can 'drop the mask' and feel superior to those outside. It is 'something of a private code, a badge of identity even, among small urban cliques'. (Sontag 1967, p. 275).

The sissies in the Blue Parrot had little choice [about coming out], except perhaps to stay home. They could not conform though they could pretend to. Such a survival led fatally to rage and self-contempt. The theatricality of camping helped keep some sanity and humanity; it was an awareness of one's helplessness. [Kleinberg 1978, p. 18]

The problem with Babuscio's account is that it is not made clear whether homosexuals are conscious of this process as it operates in their own lives or whether it can operate at a subconscious level. Also how pervasive is camp in the sub-culture? And, third, has the camp style faded out as a result of the masculinization of the gay sub-culture? I would claim that camp as a process is still strong, although what constitutes camp has changed, as we will see. Nevertheless an important aspect of camp is the awareness of another side of what, to 'normal' people, has only one meaning.

It should now be possible to look again at the styles of the sub-culture to see if there is an additional way of interpreting the behaviour that we have already examined – especially to see if there is any evidence of these styles challenging, through mockery or otherwise, the dominant male culture, rather than simply copying it.

The style of language

While it seems likely that the male gay slang reproduces the dominant male order, it may be at least as plausible to view it simultaneously as containing elements which could be seen as critical: mocking and ridiculing the idea of masculinity, femininity and heterosexual institutions.

There is a massive amount of feminization of nouns, adjectives, pronouns and names among gay men. For example, gay men will constantly 'camp it up' by referring to themselves and others as 'she', 'girl', 'woman', 'Miss', etc., as well as by changing men's names to women's. Henry becomes Henrice; Stephen becomes Stephanie. 'Miss' will be used as a title preceding the first or last name of a gay man. It is also used with nouns or adjectives to describe the characteristics or pecularities of another homosexual. Bruce Rodgers lists fifty 'Miss . . .' in his index (1972, pp. 241–2), although it is certain that few homosexuals would know all of them. 'Miss Politics' is a homosexual involved in the homophile movement. 'Miss Priss' is a prim or prudish homosexual.

Closely connected in usage and meaning is the term 'queen', which is a designation among male homosexuals for one another and does not necessarily imply that the individual is effeminate. A 'muscle queen' is a gay body builder. It is most frequently, but not always, used affectionately amongst sub-culturalized homosexuals. It can also be put before someone's name. 'Queen

Cecil didn't give up cigarettes – he gave up quitting' (Rodgers 1972, p. 164). Or it can be a suffix naming one's locality. 'That Hampstead queen is visiting us tonight.' It can also indicate one's sexual preference and/or idiosyncracy. A 'size queen' is someone who prefers sex with men who have large penises. A 'drama queen' is a fussy person who makes a 'scene' at the slightest provocation.

This effeminization can be read as critical of heterosexual norms because it is a recognition that masculinity is a learned behaviour pattern and not necessarily the 'normal' or only possible way for men to behave. There are two points to emerge from this. First, it reflects a sharp awareness of conventional expectations that could only come about if one felt divorced from them as a result of being a homosexual. This is illustrated by noting that these same terms (with different meanings) are used to describe heterosexual men. In this case, the slang is used to satirize and point out the ridiculousness of straight men who play at 'being a man'. It can also be used in this sense to satirize homosexuals who are attempting to hide their homosexuality by engaging in virile activities and responsibilities 'Who does that butch queen think she is – playing football of all things. She'll ruin her manicure.' Secondly, this slang indicates that the individual does not think it is an insult to be referred to or thought of as a woman. Masculinity and femininity are just roles to be donned or shunned at different times. Many sub-culturalized homosexuals can 'camp it up' or 'butch it up', be 'butch' or a 'screamer' at will.

So the effeminization of language which occurs within the homosexual sub-culture can be seen both to reflect and transform the attitudes about gender and gender expectations of the wider cultures, both to accept and question the position in which homosexuals find themselves.

The style of pick-ups, cruising and objectification

Earlier I argued that the promiscuous behaviour of the male homosexual is similar to the heterosexual casual sexual behaviour with its emphasis on seeing others only as physical objects and seeing oneself as a marketable commodity. But the meaning of these rituals is again more complex. There is a sense in which this behaviour is in opposition to the dominant culture's view of sexual behaviour.

First of all, the assumption that a casual sexual encounter involves the 'use' of people which is seen as a 'bad thing' is giving it a meaning which is not necessarily there. That view reflects the dominant culture's definition of legitimate sex as only that which occurs in the context of love and possible reproduction inside a long-term monogamous relationship, with the resulting stigmatization of sexual behaviour outside of these bounds. Gay casual sex can be seen as a rejection of this narrow definition of legitimate sex, as it expands its range of possible meanings. It includes seeing sex as a form of recreation, simply a game or hobby, as fun. It is divested of all its moral and guilt overtones and is enjoyed as an end in itself. Perhaps the possibility has arisen for this wider and creative range of public meanings because the reproductive aspect of sex is impossible for gay men. This recreational view of sexual behaviour is reflected in an editorial in *Him Exclusive* where Alan Purnell argues that we should 'put the SEX back into homosexual'.

There are those who insist on retaining their sexuality, who lustily enjoy gay sex and by doing so, step outside the comfy mould of social acceptance. *Him* is . . . a full-blooded magazine about sex and the enjoyment thereof. [no. 9, p. 43]

Generally then promiscuous sex can be seen as the actual devaluation of the centrality of sex in a society that gives us meaning as primarily sexual beings. Foucault (1979) argues that public sex, anonymous sauna orgies, etc., decentre sex, desubjective us as sexed beings, and therefore they are radical or challenging of the society.

Lee's *Getting Sex – A New Approach: More Fun, Less Guilt* offers a legitimation for the sex delivery system of the gay sub-culture in the terms outlined above.

. . . it is time to argue that in at least one way, the gay world *is* better. Gay people are generally less inhibited about the enjoyment of playful and uncommitted sex. Sex with more joy and less guilt is something gay people can teach the rest of the world. [1978, p. viii]

Instead of being defensive about accusations of promiscuity by insisting that many gay people have long-term relationships (which is true but beside the point, he argues), he feels that it is time to ask what is so wrong with promiscuity. He claims that one cannot talk about objectification and 'using and discarding' people when there is a voluntary and reciprocal enjoyment of each other's bodies. Although there are disadvantages and shortcomings, the gay 'ecosystem' provides the social arrangements to facilitate mutual sexual pleasure without fear of rape, high costs or unfulfilled expectations. Lee emphasizes the point that

... treating sex as a commodity does not mean it is only a commodity. Nothing said of sex in this book prevents anyone from enjoying sex as part of a long-term relationship or faithful marriage. [ibid., p. 12]

Lee claims that there is a great deal of affection in casual sexual relationships that goes unnoticed by outside observers who may only see a continuous flow of bodies. Tripp has also noted that there can be an intensity and a closeness unmatched in even some longer-term relationships.

Sometimes promiscuity includes surprising elements of affection. Even in fleeting contacts ... affection often develops as a by-product of sexual activity. [1977, p. 146]

But promiscuity is criticized because this affection will only last the length of the encounter and the person may soon be forgotten. Lee asks why sex is centred out for such attention. If we forget the plot of a good book we have read or meet acquaintances through work and forget them a week later, no one is surprised or shocked.

A second challenge to the dominant order through casual gay encounters is that there is no necessary connection between sexual activities and social roles. Male/male sex is more able to ignore the so-called 'natural' connection between sexual position (inserter, insertee, for example) and gender role. In other words, if one partner gets fucked, he is not necessarily expected to make the breakfast the next morning or act effeminately. (Haist and Hewitt 1974). In male/female sex there is more likely to be an automatic link between sexual position and gender role. And since there is a power differential between heterosexual women and men, the 'use' of the woman by the man is more likely to occur than in male/male sex where, if 'use' does occur, it is more likely to be mutual. Sex is invested with different meanings for heterosexual men and women, and although this is changing, women are still meant to see sex as part of an intense emotional relationship, which can lead to unfulfilled expectations in a casual sexual relationship.

There is then the possibility of re-reading the practice of casual sex as an example of a creative transformation of and an opposition to the dominant culture's view of what constitutes legitimate sexual behaviour.

The style of 'expressive artefacts and concrete objects'

The account of the reactionary nature of the 'macho-mania' of the male gay sub-culture assumes that the objects used in the style of the sub-culture have the same meaning there as they do in the wider cultures. An alternative account is that the objects used by gay men have meanings quite different from their original meanings. This process of 'stylization' has been described with reference to working-class youth cultures and their 'generated' styles.

The generation of subcultural styles involves differential selection from within the matrix of the existent. What happens is not the creation of objects and meanings from nothing, but rather the *transformation and rearrangement* of what is given (and 'borrowed') into a pattern which carries a new meaning, its *translation* to a new context, and its *adaptation*. [Clarke *et al.* 1975, p. 178]

What adaptations then take place? First of all, the clothes are worn differently in the gay sub-culture from the way they are worn by 'real men'. They are much tighter fitting, especially tailored to be as erotic and sensual as possible. Parts of the body will be purposely left exposed in an attempt to attract others. Some type of jewellery is likely to be worn, including chains on the neck, ear-rings and finger-rings or combinations of these, all of which are unlikely to be found on heterosexual workers or athletes.[17]

These subtle changes and transformations of objects infuse the style with a new meaning of eroticism and overt sexuality – that is, they are used explicitly to make one appear sexy and attractive to other men. This can be seen as distinct from any celebration of masculinity as such. Instead it may be an attempt to show that masculine or 'ordinary' men can be homosexual too – a breaking down of the stereotyped image of the homosexual. It forces the wider culture to question its stereotypes and question the legitimacy of linking femininity and homosexuality.

The disco group, Village People, mentioned earlier, fit this description. They are 'new' or 'transformed' macho men *and* homosexual.

At one level the Village People are camp; they take straight icons and up-end them; these men aren't cops and construction workers, they're disco folk. It's very funny and they do it very well. [York 1979, p. 58]

Their difference from 'straight' men is neatly portrayed in a recent edition of *Playgirl* where they are shown, through a purple filter, disco-dancing with each other as they progressively take off their macho drag – pulling at each other's jockstraps, belts and chains. Actual full frontals are never shown. Compare this to the portrayal of the other 'normal' men in the rest of the magazine: serious expressions, virile stances, in outdoor and sporty shots in natural surroundings. The accompanying articles shows an understanding of the double meaning.

The roles the six gentlemen recreate on stage are presented with tongues in cheek, winks in eye and lots of ham sans cheese, on wry .... The Village People are harmless, though lyrical barbs and stereotypical stances inherent in the roles they portray while on stage are sharp and keen. Have you ever seen a policeman's billy club stroked to the beat of a bass drum? Or an Indian chief excited in a war-dance frenzy not unlike a spiritual orgasm? Or how about a construction worker, all taut and sinewy underneath his hard hat, seemingly ready to kick some ass with a smile on his face? [*Playgirl* vol. 6, no. 9, p. 52]

So the behaviour of these men can be glaringly unlike the behaviour of the equivalent heterosexual male.

It is true that many gay men find the big, butch, straight image of the macho man very attractive and appealing. But it is possible to separate this fantasy image from the reality of that fantasy, which many of these same gay men would reject. In other words, many of those who don these 'costumes' may have no real desire actually to take on the associated characteristics of virile masculinity. It is accepted and seen only as a fantasy and remains at that level.

Many of the articles in *Him* and *Q International* are aware of the fantasy and both the role it plays in love-making and the dangers that may emerge if it becomes too prevalent.

The fantasy factor is obviously an important part of all sex. The ability to create mental sex images is vital to well-adjusted sexuality . . . . The only drawback in 'mind-fucking' and fantasy is that it can be habit-forming. There is a point where tools that should serve the cause of sexual fulfilment become the master . . . . Keep an impartial eye on yourself or your partner for signs of the reality slipping. [*Him* no. 11, pp. 42–3]

In conclusion, objects taken from the male culture can be transformed and given a new oppositional force by their users in an attempt to overcome feelings of stigma and, at the same time, find an alternative life style.

The limitations of oppositional style

In the introduction I pointed out that although sub-cultural styles can strike back at the dominant order, there are limitations to these resistances in that the basic problem facing subordinate groups cannot be resolved by these means. This section will illustrate the limitations of the styles of the gay sub-culture. This necessitates a further look at camp.

Andrew Britton, in a critique of Sontag's and Babuscio's statements on camp, argues that they

ignore the crucial distinction between the kind of scrutiny which dissolves boundaries in order to demonstrate their insubstantiality, or the value-systems which enforce them and the kind of scrutiny which merely seeks to confirm that they are there. [1979, p. 13]

Camp belongs to the second category, he says, and therefore 'gay camp seems little more than a kind of anaesthetic, allowing one to remain inside oppressive relations while enjoying the illusory confidence that one is flouting them' (ibid., p. 12).

He rejects Babuscio's idea that a 'gay sensibility' emerges automatically because of the fact of one's oppression.

Although oppression creates the potential for a critical distance from (and action against) the oppressing society . . . 'consciousness' . . . is not determined by sexual orientation. The ideological place of any individual at any given time is the site of intersection of any number of determining forces, and one's sense of oneself as 'gay' is a determinate product of that intersection – not a determinant of it. [ibid.]

He argues that camp's positive features (an insistence on one's otherness and a refusal to pass as straight) are 'irredeemably compromised by complicity in the traditional, oppressive formulations of that otherness' (ibid., p. 14). So although camp style may be a covert defiance of a society that humiliates homosexuals – a technique for survival – it is not an effective means of ending oppression.

For example, the style of language works effectively in mocking the wider cultures and in providing a sense of identity and solidarity. But although gay men may 'suss out' the learned aspect of gender roles through their particular slang, they continue to reinforce those same roles and, by extension, the inferior position of women in this society. Gay men may not mind being thought of as women, but they have the choice of switching back to being men and do so readily.

Camp simply replaces the signs of 'masculinity' with a parody of the signs of 'femininity' and reinforces existing social definitions of both categories. The standard of 'the male' remains the fixed point, in relation to which male gays and women emerge as 'that which is not male'. [ibid., p. 11]

On re-examining the clothing styles of the gay sub-culture, it again seems that the oppositional force of showing that homosexuals can be as manly as any heterosexual is limited in that it hardly threatens the overall social order. The role-distancing from the image of the homosexual is not to a new role, but to the role of the very source of oppression that homosexuals suffer: masculine gender roles. R. Houston suggests that it is to the uniforms of the oppressor that the oppressed run to in the hope of safety

like the boy who laughs and jokes with the school bully in the hope that by siding with him he'll go unmolested. But the boot-licking doesn't save him when the school bully takes it into his head to beat him up. [1978, p. 15]

Another gay writer, disenchanted by this increase in the relentless pursuit of masculinity, feels that this adoption of masculine images conveys an eroticization of the very values of straight society that have tyrannized their own lives.

The suppression or denial of the moral issue in their choice is as damaging as the perversity of imitating their oppressors [and it] guarantees that such blindness will work itself out as self-contempt. [Kleinberg 1978, p. 17]

He rejects what he sees to be the rationalization that 'being butch' is just another idea of play, another version of 'the gay uniform'. The choice of this particular new 'drag' is significant. Regardless of its meaning within the sub-culture, it uses the *idea* of gender roles that exist in society already. He also notes that the enemy will not exempt macho gays from its wrath.

The lessons of Negroes who disliked blackness or Jews who insisted they were assimilated, really German are ignored. To some whites, everything not white is black; to Nazis, Jews are Jews, sidelocks or not. Welcoming the enemy does not appease him; often it makes him more vicious, furious that his victim approves his scorn. [ibid., p. 18]

The values that created the situation gay people find themselves in are mocked but not challenged. One makes the best of a bad lot instead of transforming the whole lot. Babuscio notes that this is the message that many a Tennessee Williams female makes in his plays. For example, in the film version of *The Night of the Iguana*, the character of Maxine Faulk is played by Ava Gardner who

tells Burton that sooner or later we all reach a point where it is necessary to 'settle for something that works for us in our lives – even if it isn't on the highest kind of level'. [Babuscio 1978, p. 22]

Changes in the homosexual sub-culture

Employing the same analysis that I have for styles in the gay sub-culture, I now want to turn to a discussion of the homosexual sub-culture in general and its relation to the wider cultures. The changes that have occurred will be put into the context of the changing societal reaction to homosexuality and broader issues of sexuality and gender.

The homosexual sub-culture remains overwhelmingly male and urban. It is still centred around providing sexual contacts and continues to be a part-time sub-culture for most people in that it is entered into only during one's leisure time. Despite these continuing similarities with the gay sub-culture of the 1950s and 1960s, it has undergone massive changes in the last decade. First of all, there has been a large increase in the sheer number of commercial facilities of all kinds available to gay people, at least in urban areas. These range from more pubs, clubs and discos to more accessible cruising areas. The *Spartacus Guide*, which has been publishing annually since 1970, lists homosexual meeting places around the world, and it has vastly increased in size over the years. My impression is that the atmosphere in gay bars and clubs is much more open and relaxed. Facilities seem to be of a higher quality with very few places still up narrow staircases and behind two sets of locked doors with peep-holes. It is not uncommon to see queues of gay men outside known gay discos on busy streets in London.

As well as these commercial enterprises, there are many more community based gay services available, mainly centred around counselling and providing information and support (in the UK gay switchboards around the country, Friend and Ice-breakers, to mention just a few). There are also interest groups organized for gay Christians, Jews, trade unionists, professionals, Labour and Conservative Party members, etc., which have both supportive and propagandistic functions. Gay community centres have sprung up in the larger urban areas providing an alternative to the commercial 'scene'. A gay centre in South London lasted for more than four years with support from mainly gay people. Another still exists in Birmingham. Located in an old house, it provides a disco, meeting rooms, offices and a small cafe.

Information about homosexuality and homosexual meeting places is more readily available from gay newspapers. The fortnightly *Gay News* in the UK helps to strengthen this trend, as it confirms the view that one is not an isolated individual, and one learns that it is possible to 'come out' to some extent without always suffering serious repercussions. It is also possible to get information about homosexuality from certain sections of the mass media. The topic is far from taboo. *Time*, the American weekly news magazine, printed its third cover story in the 1970s on homosexuality in April 1979.

Press coverage of homosexuality is wider now than ever – thirty years ago, the word could hardly be mentioned, now 'gay' is even used in headlines . . . . Homosexuality is slowly being treated more positively in films and T.V., although most of the time we are portrayed as limp-wristed caricatures by a whole breed of camp comics. The assumption behind such images is that feminine traits in men are inherently laughable. [Collective editorial, *Gay Left*, no. 6, p. 3]

The importance of homosexuality being discussed cannot be

over-estimated even if what is presented is not the most 'progressive'. Readers 'reinterpret' what they read anyway, either more positively or more negatively. Knowledge, although it does not necessarily mean acceptance, has grown enormously.

Continuing repression

This discussion of the increasing openness of the gay sub-culture and greater tolerance in some areas should not blind us to the increasing societal reaction against these changes.

Homosexuality, American right-wingers had found, was an effective 'red button' issue – like abortion and the bussing of black children into white neighbourhood schools – on which to raise the irrational vote .... Gays were presented as a threat to the sanctity of the family and to the stability of country – like liberated women, only worse. [York 1979, p. 60]

The best known of these 'fightbacks' was Anita Bryant's campaign, 'Save Our Children', which successfully sought to have legislation repealed in Dade County, Florida which had protected homosexuals from discrimination in housing and employment. Gay groups were more successful in having Proposition 6 in California defeated. It would have barred homosexuals from any kind of public sector teaching job and also would have barred any heterosexuals who might have supported them.[18]

In the United Kingdom the state has partially withdrawn from the regulation of sexual behaviour by granting in 1967 a free space for gay men, over twenty-one, in England and Wales, in private, to engage in consenting sexual acts. Despite this, active discrimination is still practised. Many state jobs are closed to known homosexuals, for example, the diplomatic service, branches of the Civil Service, the Armed Forces. Many gay meeting places are heavily patrolled by the police – a constant reminder that toleration is strictly limited. Reports of the latest raids, arrests and prosecutions can always be found in *Gay News*. In 1979 the Discrimination Commission of the Campaign for Homosexual Equality in Britain published its report, 'Queers need not apply', which dealt with discrimination against homosexuals in employment, public services, commercial and other services, the press and the police (CHE 1979).

Public attitudes are equally ambiguous, as a *Gay News* survey of public opinion has suggested. Stereotypes of homosexuality (still seen as a largely male activity, associated with effeminancy and mental derangement) are deeply embedded in the public mind. The heavily publicized trial in 1979 of the former leader of the Liberal Party in the UK, Jeremy Thorpe, on a conspiracy to murder charge had both the prosecution and the defence portraying homosexuality in a negative and stereotypical manner.

A controlled space

The male gay sub-culture today then still performs the same functions as before, but now simply does a much better job at providing solutions to the problems that its members face. At the same time, though, there is a growing and vocal opposition to these changes. An explanation of these apparently, although not necessarily contradictory processes lies in the point that, as with the practices discussed earlier, *the sub-culture itself, through its own actions, cannot alleviate the conditions that led to these problems*. Because the sub-culture does not exist independently of the wider society, it is heavily fashioned by it. The dominant culture remains influential in channelling these changes into avenues that are moulded and defined explicitly by its own values. Gays are offered an improved situation only if they surrender to it completely. One surrenders to it completely by accepting (but not in a straightforward manner) the reproduction of larger gender, class, age divisions in the sub-culture.

'Homosexuals' were once controlled and defined by 'experts' – now they need no longer do it, for *the* homosexual has assumed that role for him or herself. Ghettoized and reified, the 'homosexual' remains firmly under control in 'liberated' capitalism. [Plummer, this volume]

In this chapter I have shown how the male gay world – in part – reproduces masculinity and patriarchy, but as I mentioned in the introduction, the gay world also sustains systems of consumer capitalism, hierarchies of social class and divisions of age. Each one of these could be an area for further research. For example, with regard to consumer capitalism, Peter York has emphasized how the gay movement in the USA has been co-opted just like black pride, the women's movement, ecology groups, etc. The slow acceptance of and resulting changes in these minorities have been allowed because they are a market, a growth industry.

The process began early in the Sixties, with the recognition that to sustain the American Way in the age of leisure industries, the U.S. positively *needed*, not Puritan Ethic consumers but hedonists .... The commercial assimilation of minorities tends to come from a more basic American process. America's minorities want to be the majority, billion-dollar babies like everyone else .... And it works. These people sure as hell buy! [York 1979, p. 58]

One issue of an American gay magazine, *Blueboy*, had advertisements for 'Contourex, a new exercise system designed to give you tighter, shapelier buns'; a book called *The Joy of Gay Sex*; 'The Guard Hose for rectal douches'; 'Jac-Up pills to make you a sex fiend'; and a leather cover for one's jar of 'Crisco' (a favourite American lubricant).

Gay men are 'better' consumers because of their higher disposable income and fewer commitments. York claims that

between 1974 and 1976 the market analysts, the publishers, the property developers, the record companies got homosexuals in their sights. Gays, they realised, were good Americans: they consumed and there were an awful lot of them .... And what the gays bought today, the 'wise' straights would watch and copy and in a couple of years there would be a mass market among the lumpen .... Gays have been the harbingers of all the growth stocks in the culture industry. [York 1979, p. 59]

Clarke refers to this latter process as the 'defusion' of style where it loses its original symbolic importance as it is torn from the group from which it emerged. He deals with youth cultures where

a particular style is dislocated from the context and group which generated it, and taken up with a stress on those elements which make it 'a commercial proposition', especially their novelty. ... The symbolic elements, especially dress and music are separated out from the context of social relations, as elements most amenable to 'promotion' for the broader base of the youth market. [1975, p. 188]

Fashion trends which originated in the gay sub-culture, where they were intimately connected to other elements of the style such as language and sexual practices, would not be amenable to promotion or commercialization on a wider base. So they are torn from the context of these other practices. Commoditization of objects of gay style, to the small extent that it has occurred, such as jewellery, hair and clothing styles and toiletries, can render their specific meaning useless, and the limit of style as an oppositional force (if indeed it was a force in the first place) becomes evident.

The transformation of gay from outcast to cultural commodity happened very quickly, and can best be seen as the result of the triumph of the demands of a consumer-oriented capitalism over one based on production. This encouragement of sexual hedonism is also linked with the development of adequate and widely available birth control methods. These have broken the 'natural' link between sexuality and procreation for women, and by extension there is a similar destruction of that part of the dominant ideology which branded homosexuality as 'unnatural' by virtue of its non-reproductive nature. Sex has become technologically 'freed' to become a commodity at the same time as capitalism no longer demands that sexuality be totally bent to the needs of the reproduction of labour power. It is no longer necessary to force everyone into the role of producing and raising children.

Conclusion

I have attempted to show how the practices of the male homosexual sub-culture both reproduce and resist the masculinity of the dominant culture. I trust that future research can spell out the ways in which other aspects of the dominant culture are 'dealt with' by the gay sub-culture. But although the language, casual sexual patterns, the styles of clothing and camp itself can be seen as a real struggle to try to work out solutions to the oppressive situations in which homosexual men find themselves, the solutions cannot represent a very significant threat to the dominant culture. To change that situation requires a much more revolutionary attack on the ideological and political institutions of society. In fact Willis claims that sub-cultures are essential in the reproduction of the dominant order.

Cultural forms cannot be reduced or regarded as the mere epiphenomenal expression of basic structural factors. They are not the accidental or open-ended determined variables in the couplet structure/culture. They are part of a necessary circle in which neither term is thinkable alone. It is in the passage through the cultural level that aspects of the real structural relationships of society are transformed into conceptual relationships and back again. The cultural is part of the necessary dialectic of reproduction. [1977, p. 174]

At present the practices mildly mock and ridicule the dominant culture. But, through them, homosexuals find a way of coping with their world, a world that, despite recent changes, still makes life very difficult.

Appendix 1 Researching into homosexualities

One major purpose of this volume has been to suggest further avenues of investigation into homosexuality – both theoretical and empirical. Collectively we have advocated a position that suggests a turn away from matters of individual aetiology – a point espoused by the Hooker Report (1969a) albeit there are others who would still view aetiology as an important area (Bell 1976a) – towards matters of the diverse social organization of diffuse homosexual experiences. In particular we have stressed the need to look at the ways in which historically changing homosexual categorizations are tied to wider changes in economy, family and gender, and have influences upon the contemporary expression of diverse sexualities. The essays in this book speak in different ways to such issues, but they all represent speculative beginnings rather than definitive conclusions. It is our hope that this volume will spawn fuller and more substantial investigations which may even resolve some of the problems we have raised.

To this end, this appendix is written in a different vein: it is not concerned with matters of substance, but with matters of method. Since every contributor to this volume has been (or is) actively engaged in research, we have tried here to discuss *some* of the methodological problems with which we have been confronted.

At the start of any investigation, four broad sets of problems will confront the researcher (see Faraday and Plummer 1979), and they will remain as issues throughout. They are:

1 *Social science problems* which are concerned with the intellectual (and epistemological) justifications of the research. What status does the kind of knowledge we are producing have?
2 *Technical problems* which are concerned with *how* we actually conduct the research. What claims to reliability and validity does the research have?

3   The *ethical and political problems* which are concerned with 'extra-scientific' reasons for doing the research and 'extra-scientific' dilemmas confronted while doing it.
4   The *personal problems* which are concerned with the way the research can impinge upon the personal life of the researcher.

We will raise a few issues entailed with each of these problems.

Social science dilemmas

So much has been written on the philosophy of the social sciences – and so much of it remains inconclusive – that it would be a fruitless (and impossible) endeavour to summarize it here. However, most research into homosexuality seems to us to display a curious naivety about even the existence of such debates and produces its 'findings' as if all were unproblematic – knowledge is knowledge, and that's that. This view must be firmly corrected.

The bulk of homosexual research works from a tacit philosophy that is best (if crudely) regarded as positivist; excellent examples of it can be found in England through the work of Michael Schofield (1965) and in America in the recent Kinsey surveys (Bell and Weinberg 1978; Weinberg and Williams 1974). The hallmark of such work lies in its objectivity and methodological rigour; there is a scrupulous concern with gaining a reliable sample, designing a valid questionnaire and presenting statistically significant results. Sometimes such findings are linked to a tightly woven deductive theory, where hypotheses may be falsified (Harry and DeVall 1978); more often a control sample of heterosexuals is used and comparisons drawn (Saghir and Robbins 1973). This research is usually concerned with the characteristics of the homosexual, but sometimes it may be concerned with the characteristics of the societal reaction (Steffensmeier 1974).

Such studies are the most 'scientific' looking and usually contain much interesting information. But anyone opting for such methods must be cautious, for they have been the object of much criticism within sociology (for example, Cicourel 1964). Thus even within its own frame of reference, it can be argued that such research can never gather a reliable sample and hence all findings are only relevant to the group under study. From the perspective of other philosophies of science, however, its view of the world is heavily suspect: it lacks a concern with meaning and intention, is overtly behaviouristic, usually provides 'absolute truths' rather than relative (perspective-based) ones, conceals values behind a mask of objectivity, views 'facts' as unproblematic and favours methodological exactitude over theoretical understanding. None of the studies in this book represent this viewpoint.

Another approach – which is found through much of this book – is that of conventionalism. It is a highly sceptical viewpoint which believes that any absolute truth is in principle inaccessible to human beings – even through reason alone – and that hence all 'truths' are necessarily from some perspective, some experience, and some point of view (Charan 1979). With homosexuality either it thus tries to capture 'objectively' the perspective of certain (historically and culturally located) homosexual experiences like Warren's middle class gay community and Humphrey's 'cottaging homosexuals', or it tries to capture the perspective of certain groups responding to 'homosexuals' like Spector's account of psychiatrists viewing homosexuals. It may attempt to 'reconstruct' history or indeed to 'construct a general theory', but if it does so, it will always acknowledge that this too is from *a* perspective: other 'accounts' are always possible (see Rock 1976).

Such a posture – identified especially with pragmatism, symbolic interactionism and phenomenology – is anathema to another view: the 'realists'. For them the positivists deal only with surface manifestations, while the conventionalists totter towards an uncritical and defenceless relativism. While they may use the 'findings' of both schools, they will be tied to an underlying social dynamo that makes things happen the way they do. The unconscious (even if 'structured like a language'), 'the mode of production' and 'patriarchy' are some favourite candidates for this 'dynamo'. Like the positivists, the perspective claims 'the truth', but unlike the positivists, it does not rely upon empirical work but on denser and denser layers of theoretical abstraction. So far it has rarely been found in studies of homosexuality – although Hocquenghem's *Homosexual Desire* is a good example of it.

These three postures – positivism, conventionalism, realism (see Keat and Urry 1975) – hold antagonistic views of each other; and while these positions have been oversimplified, it is important, however, for any research to be loosely located this way, since each makes different claims on our credulity.

Some technical problems: the sources of data

Doing research into homosexuality will inevitably raise all of the standard technical problems of data collection and data analysis which are discussed in many social science methodological cook books. Here we will restrict our focus to the main sources of data.

Homosexual people: the standard source

Most students head in one of two directions when they embark upon gay research. Historically the most favoured route led to the psychiatrist's couch or the prison cell, and it resulted in generalizations being made about homosexuality that were wildly awry. The now classic observation ponders what we would know about heterosexuality if we restricted our research to psychiatric cases and imprisoned heterosexuals! It is not, however, surprising that this was the main source for a long time, since most 'homosexuals' were 'hidden from history' and most researchers were clinically inclined.

The other major research route, which now dominates inquiries, turns toward the rapidly expanding gay community (Levine 1979b; Lee 1979; Wolf 1979). Entry to this diverse community provides an array of sources: questionnaires can be distributed or interview volunteers sought through gay and feminist organizations (for example, Weinberg and Williams 1974), through bars and baths (Bell and Weinberg 1978), through gay magazines (Spada 1979; Jay and Young 1979) and through 'snow-balling' friendship networks (Westwood 1960).

While prison and psychiatric samples are highly suspect, samples drawn from the gay community also probably only capture a particular segment of gay experience. Indeed it must be recognized that none of them can provide random samples and therefore none of them can produce generalizable statements *per se*. More important, however, from the perspective of this book, they often work from an initial assumption that people can be identified as 'homosexuals';

whereas a major burden of our arguments in this book is that research should be directed towards homosexual *experiences* rather than homosexual *people*, and indeed that much research should not even be concerned with this, but rather focus upon the groups involved in defining, identifying and responding to homosexuality. This leads therefore to two new sets of sources: (a) homosexual *experiences* and (b) homosexual *categorizers*.

Homosexual experiences

Here, three distinctive sources are available:

Settings and sites Humphreys's study of impersonal sex between men in public conveniences (Humphreys 1975), is perhaps the most celebrated example of researching the homosexual experience rather than the homosexual person. He sampled public conveniences in a limited area (by time and place) and observed the sexual encounters occurring. One of the most important findings of the research pointed to the large number of 'heterosexual' men who regularly participate in homosexual experiences – men who would almost certainly never have come to the researchers' attention through the samples discussed earlier. Prior to Humphreys's work the main setting to be investigated was the prison (for example, Giallombardo 1966), which also showed the frequency of homosexual experiences independent of homosexual identities; but since Humphreys's work a number of settings have been investigated involving gay baths (Weinberg and Williams 1975), highway 'rest stops' (Corzine and Kirby 1977), parking lots (Ponte 1974), 'discos' (Lee 1978) and prostitution (Lloyd 1977) – as well as homosexual bars (Achilles 1967). The trouble with many of these studies, however, is that they focus upon sources which are primarily 'homosexual' – constructed by and for those with homosexual identities. They can easily therefore become samples of homosexual 'people' once again.

Large scale sampling Perhaps the best and probably the only way to resolve this problem of behaviour *v.* identity is to gain access to as wide a sample of sexual behaviours as possible and to question incidentally on homosexuality. This was of course the main strategy of Kinsey's studies, and it is his study which has thrown up the largest recorded estimate of both male and female homosexual behaviours (37 per cent and 13 per cent respectively). Later large scale studies, however, have come up with such small figures that, given the high cost of such research, it becomes an impractical strategy for gay research.

Biographies   At the other extreme from large samples is the need to conduct research on individual lives (see Plummer forthcoming) and to study them in such detail as to tease out of them the dense matrix of homosexual/heterosexual responses (behaviours, cognitions, identities, emotions) across the life cycle. If the arguments made frequently throughout this book are valid, then almost any life will have some inter-connections with homosexual experiences (with self or other). No claim can be made here of course for any kind of generalizability.

Homosexual categorizers

Here, five key sources seem available:

Population samples   A number of attempts have been made to gather large scale random samples of public attitudes to homosexuality – the most important being the one produced by the Kinsey Institute in the early 1970s (see Levitt and Klassen 1974). Much more common is the study of a small select sample – usually of captured students – that is available to the researcher: a hundred or so students are asked for their views on homosexuality (see Kituse 1962; Steffensmeier 1974) or given a 'homophobe' scale to complete (McDonald and Games 1974). As, however, Plummer has suggested elsewhere (1975), such studies may have only a very limited value.

Agency studies   Much more imaginative than the above are studies directed at agencies involved in the (formal or informal) defining and processing of homosexuals: social services, counselling agencies – voluntary and statutory – the police, psychiatrists, hospitals, or schools. Models of such analysis have been set up in other substantive areas – police responses to delinquents, social work responses to the blind, etc. – but to date little of such analysis has been directed towards homosexuality.

Family and informal groupings The above directs the researcher to formal agencies, but it is equally important to conduct research with the informal definers of homosexuality – the community, the peer group, the family. In other areas – for instance, alcoholism, handicaps and physical illnesses – studies have been conducted of small groups of families (sometimes – as in Davis's *Passage Thru Crisis* – with a sample of only fourteen) to see how they manage a 'crisis'. Every 'homosexual' belongs to some kind of family, yet to date we have no studies of how families respond. How do families 'cope' with a 'homosexual' son or daughter?

Mass media All media – press, literature, film, radio and TV, 'gay media' – need scrutiny for the images they represent of 'homosexuality'. This is now a heavily worked area of study in the 'sociology of deviance' but still, surprisingly, little of significance has been researched for homosexuality (see Pearce 1973). Of special value here are the media collections at the Albany Trust (16–20 Strutton Ground, London SW1), the contemporary 'gay magazines' housed at the offices of *Gay News* (la Normand Gardens, Greyhound Road, London W14 9SB) and of course the British Library (Colindale 'depot').

Moral crusaders Homosexuality, both in recent history and now, has been the subject of many 'moral campaigns' similar to those conducted over prohibition and pornography (see Spector and Kitsuse 1977, appendix). 'Mary Whitehouse' has already been the topic of research in England (Morrison and Tracey 1979), but there are many other campaigns which could be analysed (like Anita Bryant in America; see Bryant 1977).

Historical sources

Only very recently has the significance of researching historical aspects of homosexuality come to be taken seriously. Such histories can be constructed from a variety of sources. On the one hand, we need to trace the various forms of social regulation of sexual behaviours – legal, moral, medical and popular. On the other, given the constantly changing forms and meanings of homosexuality as a subjective experience, we need to find traces of individuals involved. Both involve complex problems of interpreting the evidence (some of which are discussed in Weeks' paper in this volume). But often as difficult is the task of finding the evidence with which to start. To take an obvious example: to grasp the significance of the passing of the restrictive Labouchere Amendment to the Criminal Law Amendment Act of 1885, we need (at least) to be able to trace the political purposes of the leading figures (Henry Labouchere, government ministers), the significance of the voting patterns, the complex political situation, the significance of the moral panic around public vice that was raging at the time and the reaction to the passing of the Amendment! This has to be built up from myriad pieces of evidence: private papers, official records, parliamentary reports and newspaper and journal accounts. This means in turn that one can rarely turn to a simple source and find an article or book implicit within – an angel in the marble. On the contrary, historical work demands a constant dialogue between the articulation of the historical problem and the investigation of the remains of the past, and this leaves aside the epistemological problems concerning the status of those remains, whether in fact a history is possible (see Rock 1976).

Having said this there are a number of aides to researchers which can ease one's path to relevant archives. In England and Wales the Royal Commission on Historical Manuscripts (Quality House, Quality Court, Chancery Lane, London WC2) receives regular reports on accessories to repositories from various libraries, and publishes annual lists of these. It also runs a frequently updated National Register of Archives, which allows one to find the whereabouts of known collections of records, both of institutions and of individuals. The problem with this system is that it is passive and relies on libraries and local record offices providing information to the Commission. The information itself is often sketchy and is only organized on a subject basis. (The subject index has no entry for 'sexuality', needless to say.) The usefulness of the Commission is twofold. It is the most comprehensive centre of information about archives in England and Wales. (The NRA (Scotland) at Edinburgh fulfils a similar function in Scotland). And it publishes useful lists about specific archives and addressees as well as information about public and national libraries and record offices. So once the researcher has decided on the type of archive he or she needs to trace, the Commission can be useful.

In recent years the information side of the Commission has been supplemented by the publication of various guides to archives, of which the most comprehensive for the twentieth century have been the volumes produced by the British Library of Political and Economic Science under the general editorship of Chris Cook (Cook *et al*. 1975–7, vols. 1–4; Cook and Weeks 1979, vol. 5). Volume 1 provides information on the whereabouts and contents of the archives of pressure groups – social, political, moral, religious – which are highly relevant for research on social regulation of sex. Volume 5 provides information on the papers of various theorists, publicists and moral entrepreneurs who played a major part in defining attitudes to sexual morality. Other volumes (on public servants and MPs) also contain relevant information.

The major source for national policy decisions, from the Middle Ages onwards, is the Public Record Office (Ruskin Avenue, Kew, Richmond). The staff at the PRO, and the lists it publishes, allow the researcher to trace relevant material. Of particular relevance to modern research are the files of the Home Office, the Director of Public Prosecutions and the Admiralty and the War Office (especially for court martials). The files of the Metropolitan Police are generally closed, and most records dealing with individuals are closed for one hundred years. But useful information can be obtained from general files.

Every county and major town has a local record office, with statutory duties to preserve local records. Here can be found invaluable legal, administrative and often precious papers which throw light on prosecutions for sexual offences and on local variations of attitudes. The other major public and private libraries also contain much relevant material, whether it be the records of the medical profession, psychiatry, religious organizations or reform organizations (for example, the collection of Carpenter's papers at Sheffield University and the women's documents at the Fawcett Library, City of London Polytechnic). There are, of course, also large collections of papers still in private hands. But by using the Historical Manuscripts Commission and its adjuncts, and through judicious employment of published guides, together with individual initiative, a vast store of largely untapped records are available, which should throw new light on the regulation of sexuality.

One final historical source is to be found through 'oral history' (see Thompson 1978). Here the task is to track down elderly 'homosexuals', crusaders and the like in order to document their experiences from the end of the nineteenth century onwards. In many ways this is the most pressing task: to capture the personal experiences of homosexuality in earlier times before they are irredeemably lost.

Personal experience

A most important source of much sociological data is the sociologist's own personal experience, and with the writers in this volume this has been no exception. Yet usually – for diverse reasons – this important source of sociological knowledge is minimized or evaded. As Jack Douglas says:

> I know of any number of studies in which the author's fundamental way of knowing the things he [sic] reports was through direct personal involvement, a fact that has been carefully hidden from the readers because revealing it would stigmatize him as a creep, weirdo or maybe even a criminal. In all instances I know of, these sociologists have been unhappy that they felt it necessary to do this and in each case with which I am familiar they have not lied. They have merely evaded the issues. [1976, p. xiii]

One of the most valuable and honest accounts of homosexual experiences is Joseph Style's discussion of his 'insider' role in researching gay baths. He contrasts the earlier phases of his study where he used an *outsider* strategy – 'observation without sexual participation, and a correspondingly heavier reliance upon informants as original sources of ideas as well as a means of testing these notions' – with an *insider* strategy – 'observation and sexual participation in the baths, the heavy use of these as a source of original typologies and images, and the employment of informants as a way of testing, revising and evaluating these typologies and images' (Styles 1979, p. 151) – and he argues that *both* strategies are needed.

There are both advantages and problems associated with such 'opportunistic research' (Riemer 1977). The advantages include easier access to the sub-culture. Membership gives an in-built, face-value trust that may not be extended to those outside of a deviant sub-culture. Likewise the language and symbolic meanings of the sub-culture are more familiar, and so meaningless and irrelevant questions can be avoided. Difficult areas can be probed with greater sensitivity. Understanding the double-edged wit of 'camp', for example, helped Blachford in his examination of it as a practice of the homosexual sub-culture.

But at what costs have these advantages been gained? Many positivist methodological 'cookbooks' list the dangers of this type of work in their focus on the differences that should exist between the social scientist and those observed. The sociologist must be detached from the world studied because of the dangers of 'over-rapport' whereby one can be contaminated. One must remain external, value free and objective. These moral and political issues (also discussed in this appendix) must be dealt with. Riemer, an advocate of opportunistic research, admits that the most critical disadvantage of this method 'is the potential for the researcher to become emotionally involved with the members being studied, to the point that one's objectivity may be affected. The researcher may simply become too involved' (1977, p. 474). Validity is also a problem because it is often difficult if not impossible to replicate the research as the observations are partially unique to the investigator. And how does one keep records? Blachford found that he would not always be concerned after experiences within the homosexual sub-culture to withdraw sufficiently from it and set down his observations and reflect upon his conclusions.

There is the need for a careful self-analysis and intensive self-scrutiny for sufficient objectivity to be maintained within the framework of one's own perspective. Since the research in this book is largely based on conventionalism, there is a rejection of the idea that it is impossible to become *completely* objective. One must know one's basic assumptions or they can become serious biases, remembering of course that we have rejected the idea that a total lack of involvement is going to lead to the most objective research.

Other disadvantages include the likelihood that one's research will be discredited by other sociologists. Are these researchers, though, willing to extend their argument to say that only homosexuals can study heterosexual sexual behaviour because the heterosexuals themselves may be blinded 'by personal interests'? And would it mean that only women could study men, only blacks could study whites objectively? Not surprisingly, it seems as if only more powerful majority groups can study the less powerful minitory groups 'objectively'.

The key dilemma is clear. To say that you have used your

personal experiences and that you are homosexual can invalidate your research in the eyes of other sociologists. But not to give credit to personal experience is to perpetrate the hypocrisy in much sociological research whereby personal experiences remain unacknowledged.

Moral and political issues

There are a great many political problems attendant on any research, and these have been widely discussed (for example, Barnes 1979). The table below briefly raises some of these dilemmas which the researcher ought to confront *generally*. More specifically however, our focus here will be upon the moral and political dimensions raised by our topic: homosexuality. For clearly the phenomenon of homosexuality in this culture is surrounded by extreme dimensions of moral and political debate. Many theologians condemn it as sin, although increasing numbers do not; many psychiatrists view it as a sickness, but an 'official consensus' disagrees; many moral crusaders still perceive it as a pernicious corrupting force, while the gay movement itself positively elevates it.

The existence of such diverse and often hostile reactions inevitably place the researcher on delicate moral ground. But more than this, they raise, in a particularly vivid form, the whole question of the relationship between fact and value in sociological inquiry. In the face of competing moral

A table of general ethical and political issues

1 For whom is the research being conducted?	(a) Self: to gain a degree, to advance a career
	(b) Scientific community: to advance 'scientific' knowledge for its own sake
	(c) Ruling groups: to provide knowledge for decision makers' policies (for control or care?)
	(d) Studied group: to provide knowledge to assist group in attaining desired goals

Note: There may be multiple groups involved and goals may therefore contradict.

2 How far should you disclose to others what you are doing?

   (a) Total disclosure: a complete honesty to all involved – the researched, other researchers and the wider community

   (b) Selective disclosure: a general honesty about the research to all involved – but selectively concealing some aspects of it

   (c) Partial disclosure: honesty to some groups (e.g. those who fund the research) but dishonesty to others (e.g. covert observation on a group)

   (d) Covert research: concealing the actual nature of the research from all parties

3 To what extent will the research change the subjects' lives?

   (a) Nil change: the unlikely (and possibly undesirable) situation where the research has absolutely no consequences for anybody!

   (b) Non-reactive: the use of archives, unobtrusive measures by which no change is effected in the subjects' lives during the research, though the research findings subsequently influence their lives

   (c) Accidental change: through the research, the subjects' lives become explicitly changed

   (d) Praxis: there is an explicit and direct commitment to research and change simultaneously

4 What kind of relationship will you have with the subject?

   (a) The 'professional' relationship: no involvement, instrumental, often one-sided

   (b) The 'exchange' relationship: a contract of mutual expectations evolves into the 'research bargain'

   (c) The 'friendship' relationship: highly involved, expressive, high levels of reciprocity perspectives, how can the researcher be sure of objectivity? What role do the researcher's own values have in determining the conclusions reached? And to what extent, if at all, can morals be drawn from sociological work? These are certainly difficult questions and we do not propose to enter them in depth. However, since the issue is important, we would like to offer a few comments.

Throughout the debates on homosexuality during the 1950s and 1960s, observers often called for a dispassionate study of the facts, without unfounded presuppositions and without value biases. The demand reflected the feeling in both philosophy and science that ethics are a separate domain, that matters of fact are logically separable from matters of value and that scientific findings are necessarily distorted when values intervene.

This faith in scientific neutrality has since been the subject of increasing unease and even the most primitive empiricist is now likely to admit that the distinction between fact and value is considerably more problematic. However, the precise point at which values become relevant and the way in which they become relevant are still matters of considerable disagreement. At the most elementary level, few would dispute that values dictate our selection of topics for research and will often guide the specific form of the questions we ask. Likewise, we can acknowledge that research findings often have practical ethical implications, in the sense that researchers are often drawn into political and moral debates as 'experts' or 'authorities' in their various fields of study. To this extent at least, researchers are morally implicated in the decision making process. Concessions of this sort, however, do not challenge the belief in the logical separation between fact and value. Indeed in conceding these points and no more, one stays firmly within the traditional positivist mode. The relation between factual study and normative belief is still viewed in the orthodox way: values are held to be 'relevant' but 'facts' remain neutral between them.

A more serious threat to the doctrine of value freedom comes when researchers acknowledge that values play a more crucial role in determining the outcome of study. It may be thought, for example, that the academic appraisal of homosexuality is deeply influenced by value perspectives and that different conclusions follow, not from competing 'scientific' interpretations, but from different moral baselines. Thus, it is argued, a baseline which views homosexuality as unfortunate or pathological will lead to a portrait which differs greatly from that offered by a baseline emphasizing harmless variation. Most of the contributors to this volume would agree that values have this degree of centrality. However, there is a lack of consensus over the precise epistemological status given to values in this type of assessment.

Some would follow the conventionalist position outlined on page 213 by arguing that there are no absolute truths and that different value baselines simply offer different but equally plausible 'accounts'. This is not to deny that once a value perspective has been selected, the researcher should do everything possible to eliminate bias and maintain objectivity. But according to this interpretation, there are no objective ways in which to determine the truth or falsity of an elected value baseline. Indeed, if this position is upheld, it makes no sense to speak of values being 'true' or 'false'; each account is merely viewed as a 'different way of seeing'.

Other contributors feel reluctant to accept such conclusions. They argue that the conventionalist position, while certainly challenging the doctrine of value freedom, does little to clarify the relation between fact and value. Indeed by distinguishing so boldly between the 'value baseline' and the 'objective' portrait drawn from that baseline, it is held that the conventionalist position simply restates, in a slightly different form, the orthodox belief in the logical separation between fact and value. For although the conventionalist sees an inevitable relation between factual interpretation and normative belief, the position still views them as separate, and logically different, enterprises. Value baselines are regarded as somewhat arbitrary (or at least 'unscientific'), whereas factual propositions (although based ultimately upon value perspectives) are thought to be amenable to the usual rules of scientific method. A clear division is therefore maintained between normative statements and scientific propositions, even though the latter are seen in a non-positivist manner.

An alternative way of viewing the fact-value relation, the argument runs, is to deny any practical distinction. Rather than regarding factual and normative elements as 'separate but related', this position sees them as intrinsically connected, and, more important, it sees them grounded not in arbitrary moral baselines but in alternative theoretical frameworks. To put the matter as briefly as possible, the argument is put that different theoretical frameworks define the salient features of a phenomenon, select the key variables for explanation, specify the type of causal relations which hold, *and also provide the grounds for intelligible statements of value*. In the study of homosexuality, for example, a biologist theoretical framework which pinpoints the urge to survive and reproduce as the major underlying dynamic of social life might well conclude that a pattern of exclusive homosexuality is intrinsically disordered and pathological. A conclusion of this sort, however, would certainly not follow from a competing theoretical framework which emphasized the diversity and flux of socially constructed meanings. In other words, this position denies that values are merely arbitrary baselines and asserts instead that theoretical frameworks both guide our perception of the world and simultaneously dictate our value assessments.

Such an approach to the fact-value relation, while superficially similar to the conventionalist position, actually differs greatly from the approach offered by both conventionalists and positivists. For while the latter positions concede that values can influence findings (a matter which the positivist views with alarm but which the conventionalist regards as inevitable), the third position moves in the other direction. It maintains that values can, and are, derived from factual interpretation and that disputes over interpretation can only be settled in the theoretical sphere.

Some personal problems

Conducting any social science investigation can never be viewed as a mechanical, impersonal task; inevitably it has some impact upon the researcher's life (even if only to bore and disillusion or to bring fame and fortune). Increasingly social scientists have been paying attention to such 'personal' concerns (see Vidich, Bensman and Stein 1964; Newby and Bell 1977). Here we would like merely to point to a few that are specifically connected with the subject matter of 'homosexuality'.

Stigmatized research

Since homosexuality in this culture remains largely 'taboo' and subject to hostility and attack, it is not surprising that those who elect to conduct research into this area will also be subject to such condemnation (see Farberow 1963). We know, for instance, of undergraduate projects into homosexuality that have been brought to a halt when 'discovered' by moral entrepreneurs, and we have our suspicion that many university and government administrations are reluctant to endorse such research (see Warren 1977, p. 98). Although 'support systems' for such research have developed during the 1970s (in America, for instance, around *The Journal of Homosexuality* and in various academic unions as *The Gay Sociologists Caucus*, and in England around *The Gay Research Group*), it is still possible for research into homosexuality to invite condemnation from colleagues, community and family. Anybody embarking upon such research – gay or not – should thus give serious consideration to being 'discreditable' or 'discredited'.

'Know thyself' is perhaps a first injunction to those embarking upon sociological research into homosexuality. Broadly the question of the researchers' (a) actual, (b) potential, and (c) non-homosexuality needs to be raised and carefully considered. Thus if the researchers know that they enjoy homosexual experiences (and indeed may even accept the label 'homosexual'), then the problems centre around the issue of 'coming out' – to whom, when and where? If the researchers are unsure of their own sexuality, then they should be wary because the research is likely to transform or clarify it for them. It is not unknown for 'curious heterosexuals' to explore homosexual worlds for research purposes only to become confirmed 'gays' by the end of their inquiries. The research provided a legitimation for entry into the gay world until sufficient support had been gained for the researchers to enter the homosexual role. Nor is it unheard of for self-declared homosexuals to 'convert' to heterosexuality while studying the area! If, on the other hand, the researchers are absolutely sure that they have nil personal interest in homosexual experiences, then they will still have to deal with the fact that many people – research subjects, family, colleagues and 'public' – will think they are. Anybody entering this field may become 'guilty through contamination'.

To 'come out' or not to 'come out?

Until the advent of gay liberation, few researchers – if any – were willing to let their homosexuality be known; since that time, a few – but only a few – have 'come out'. Many studies still begin with a preliminary disclaimer which dedicates the study to 'spouse and child'. Of course many researchers do not have homosexual authorship, but many do and it is often concealed. It is these which we are concerned with here.

The issue was brought out into the open when Sagarin in a lengthy review article remarked, 'Some of the works that defend and even glorify homosexuality are written by men who make a complete heterosexual identification, *and among the others, there are the secret and the overt*' (Sagarin 1973, p. 11; our italics). There is in fact a little known irony to Sagarin's remark (as he does not disclose his former masked identity as Donald Webster Cory, a leading homophile spokesperson in the early 1950s, and his subsequent 'conversion' to heterosexuality), and so the issue of concealment is very well taken! (See Bullough 1976, p. 667.)

Gay researchers can 'come out' to different degrees and to different audiences. At one end of the spectrum is the 'gay' who says that this is his or her identity in the research report/book and is happy to make it known to all (Styles 1979); at the other is the 'homosexual' who refuses to mention this to anybody and who has to 'pass as straight', maybe employing standard strategies to maintain 'closed awareness' (Glaser and Strauss 1965), such as references to spouse or children. In between there are researchers who are 'out' to selective audiences (maybe family, maybe academic peers alone, maybe research subjects) but who maintain a 'front' to others. Each of these postures raises serious problems.

For the gay who is completely 'out' the major issue is the potential for the discrediting of his or her public identity and hence for losing any claims to play the role of 'expert'. There is an embedded – and largely false – assumption here that to be gay renders one incapable of 'adequate objectivity'; one is left open to the accusation of bias and prejudice. Such *ad hominem* charges can obviously be sufficient to discredit the research in the eyes of both 'straight' public and 'scientific community', and this is so because of the conceptions of 'objectivity' (usually false) that are widely held. Any position therefore that is 'out' challenges this orthodox view of knowledge *and* renders one's own work suspect in that view. That is the paradox of 'coming out' in gay research and it parallels the classic liberal/radical debates: to work within the orthodoxy or to work beyond it.

Of course those who choose to work within will develop enemies from outside. The most obvious problem here is the refusal of some gay groups to assist in any way those 'closet' cases who want to do research *on* them rather than *with* them. Increasingly, since the rise of the gay movement, there has been the growing feeling amongst gays that they themselves are in the best position to do their own research; non-gays are suspect and 'closet' cases are treacherous (see Jay and Young 1979). Whichever way one turns, therefore, some personal tensions will be generated.

Further reading on researching homosexuality

Most sociological studies of homosexuality include a (usually brief) section which discusses the methods and problems of the research. Of greatest value are the sections on field work contained in Warren (1974) and Delph (1978), and the sections on sampling contained in Bell and Weinberg (1978) and Harry and DuVall (1978). In addition, the second edition of Humphreys's (1975) volume *Tea-Room Trade* contains detailed discussion of unorthodox methods of research, along with critiques and responses.

Articles to deal with specific aspects of homosexual research are:

Bell, A. (1974), 'Homosexualities: their range and character', in I. Cole and R. Dienstbier (eds.), *Nebraska Symposium on Motivation*, Nebraska Press

Lee, J. A. (1979), 'The gay connection', *Urban Life*, 8:2, pp. 175–98

Leznoff, W. (1956), 'Interviewing Homosexuals', *American Journal of Sociology*, vol. IXII, pp. 202–5

Masters, W., Johnson, V., and Kolodny, W. (1977), *Ethical Issues in Sex Research*, Boston: Little, Brown

Sagarin, E. (1968), 'Ideology as a factor in the consideration of deviance', *Journal of Sex Research*, 4, pp. 84–9

Styles, J. (1979), 'Outsider/insider: researching gay baths', *Urban Life*, 8:2, pp. 135–52

Warren, C. (1972), 'Observing the gay community', in J. Douglas (ed.), *Research on Deviance*, New York: Random House

Warren, C. (1977), 'Fieldwork in the gay world: issues in

phenomenological research', *Journal of Social Issues*, vol. 33, no. 4, pp. 93–107

Weinberg, M. S. (1970), 'Homosexual samples: differences and similarities', *Journal of Sex Research*, vol. 6, no. 4, pp. 312–25

Weinberg, M. S. (1972), 'Fieldwork among deviants', in J. Douglas, *Research on Deviance*, New York: Random House

Appendix 2 Select guide to research sources

Below is provided a highly selective guide to further sources in researching sociological aspects of homosexuality. It should point the reader towards most of the major writings.

General bibliographies

There are a number of bibliographical sources on homosexuality. Most central are:

Bullough, V. L., Dorr Legg, W., Elcano, B. W., and Keeper, J. (1976), *An Annotated Bibliography of Homosexuality*, New York: Garland Press

Parker, W. (1977), *Homosexuality Bibliography: Supplement 1970–1975*, New Jersey: Scarecrow Press (an earlier 'Selective bibliography of over 3,000 items' was produced by the same publishers in 1971)

Weinberg, M. S., and Bell, A. P. (1972), *Homosexuality: An Annotated Bibliography*, London: Harper & Row

Journals

The core academic journal is the *Journal of Homosexuality*, Haworth Press. Volume 1 covers 1974–6, and since then each volume has been produced annually with four editions.

Related academic journals which occasionally include debates about sexuality and homosexuality include:

Alternative Life Styles, Sage Publications, Beverly Hills, California. Quarterly.

Archives of Sexual Behaviour, Plenum Publishing Corp., 227 West 17th Street, New York, NY 10011. Bi-monthly.

Homosexual Counselling Journal, HCCC, Inc., 30 East 60th Street, New York, NY 10022. Quarterly.

Journal of Sex and Marital Therapy, Human Sciences Press, 72 Fifth Avenue, New York, NY 1011. Quarterly.

Journal of Sex Research, Charles Ihlenfeld, MD, Treasurer, Society for the Scientific Study of Sex, Inc., 12 West 72nd Street, New York, NY 10023. Quarterly.

Journal of Sexual Medicine, Medical News Tribune, Strand, London
WC2, Bi-monthly – started 1972.

Medical Aspects of Human Sexuality, Hospital Publications, Inc., 609
Fifth Avenue, New York, NY 10017. Monthly.

Sex Roles: A Journal of Research, Plenum Publishing Corp., 227 West
17th Street, New York, NY 10011

Signs, University of Chicago Press. Quarterly – started 1975.

Some journals that have started fairly recently and which have a
feminist stance include:

Feminist Review, 65 Manor Road, London N16. Three issues per year –
started 1979.

Feminist Studies, Women's Studies Program, University of Maryland,
College Park, MD 20742. Three issues per year.

Ideology and Consciousness, 1 Woburn Mansions, Torrington Place,
London, WC1. Three issues per year – started 1977.

International Journal of Women's Studies, Eden Press, Women's
Publications, Box 51, St Albans, Vermont 05478. Bi-monthly –
started January 1978.

MF, 69 Randolph Avenue, London w9. Two issues per year – started
1978.

Women's Studies: International Quarterly, Pergamon Press, Headington
Hill Hall, Oxford OX3 0BW. Quarterly – started 1978.

Working Papers in Sex, Science and Culture, Box 83, Wentworth
Building, 174 City Road, Darlington 2008, Australia. Quarterly –
started January 1976.

Gay magazines, papers and journals

There have been a great many short-lived homosexual magazines –
some of which are listed in Edward Sagarin's *Odd Man In* (1969) – but
during the 1970s the most prominent and durable included:

The Advocate, One Peninsula Place, Bldg 1730, Suite 225, San Mateo,
Ca 94402. Fortnightly – started 1967.

Body Politic, Box 7289, Station A, Toronto, Ontario, Canada M5W 1X9.
Ten issues per year.

Gay Left, 38 Chalcot Road, London, NW1. Periodic: started Autumn
1975; no. 8 – Autumn 1979.

Gay News, 1a, Normand Gardens, Greyhound Road, London, W14 9SB.
Fortnightly – started 1972. (An index to *Gay News*, nos. 1–160, was
published in consecutive issues of *Gay News*, nos. 151–61.)

Gay Sunshine, Box 40397, San Francisco, Ca 94140. Quarterly.

Lesbian Tide, 8855 Cattaraugus, Los Angeles, Ca 90034. Bi-monthly.

Sappho, 39 Wardour Street, London W1V 3HA. Quarterly – started
1972.

Classic studies

Most of the 'founding fathers' of research into human sexuality have had a great deal to say about homosexuality. An excellent introduction to the growth of contemporary sex research is Paul Robinson's (1976) *The Modernization of Sex*, and a quicker tour is E. M. Brecher's (1970) *The Sex Researchers*. The main original sources are:

Ellis, H. (1936), *Studies in the Psychology of Sex*, vol. 2, and *Sexual Inversion*, New York: Random House

Ford, C. S., and Beach, F. A. (1952), *Patterns of Sexual Behaviour* (especially chapter 7), London: Methuen

Freud, S. (1977), 'Three essays on the theory of sexuality', in vol. 7 (*On Sexuality*) of The Pelican Freud Library, London: Penguin Books

Hirschfeld, M. (undated), *Sexual Anomalies: The Origins, Nature and Treatment of Sexual Disorder*, London: Torch Publishing Company

Kinsey, A. C., Pomeroy, W. P., and Martin, C. E. (1948), *Sexual Behaviour in the Human Male* (especially chapter 21), London: W. B. Saunders

Kinsey, A. C., Pomeroy, W. P., Martin, C. E., and Gebhard, P. H. (1953), *Sexual Behaviour in the Human Female* (especially chapter 11), London: W. B. Saunders

Masters, W., and Johnson, V. (1979), *Homosexuality in Perspective*, Boston: Little, Brown

The psychoanalytic 'sickness' views are most significantly presented in:

Bieber, I., *et al.* (1962), *Homosexuality: A Psychoanalytic Study of Male Homosexuality*, New York: Basic

Caprio, F. (1954), *Female Homosexuality: A Modern Study of Lesbianism*, New York: Grove Press

Socarides, C. (1978), *Homosexuality*, London: Jason Aronson

Reviews and textbooks

Although there is a distinctly male bias to them (as is true of so much work in this area), the following are very useful general overviews of the field:

Churchill, W. (1967), *Homosexuality in the Male Species: A Cross-Cultural Approach*, New York: Hawthorn

Karlen, A. (1971), *Sexuality and Homosexuality: The Complete Account of Male and Female Sexual Behaviour and Deviation*, London: MacDonald

Tripp, C. (1976), *The Homosexual Matrix*, New York: Signet Books

West, D. J. (1977), *Homosexuality Re-Assessed*, London: Duckworth

Surveys of social characteristics

Most of the large scale surveys on homosexuality have been conducted in the United States. Central here are the large sample of men and women in studies produced at the Kinsey Institute during the late 1960s and early 1970s. These include:

Bell, A., and Weinberg, M. (1978), *Homosexualities: A Study of Diversity Among Men and Women*, London: Mitchell Beazley

Gagnon, J., and Simon, W. (1973), *Sexual Conduct: The Social Sources of Human Sexuality*, Chicago: Aldine

Weinberg, M. S., and Williams C. J. (1974), *Male Homosexuals: Their Problems and Adaptations*, Oxford: University Press

Aside from this, interesting data can be found in:

Jay, K., and Young, A. (1979), *The Gay Report*, New York: Summit Books

Rosen, D. (1974), *Lesbianism*, Illinois: Charles C. Thomas

Saghir, M. T., and Robins, E. (1973), *Male and Female Homosexuality*, Baltimore: Williams and Wilkins

Schofield, M. (1965), *Sociological Aspects of Homosexuality*, London: Longman

Spada, J. (1979), *The Spada Report*, New York: Signet Books

Wolff, C. (1971), *Love Between Women*, London: Duckworth

Studies of the male homosexual sub-culture

While again mainly American, most aspects of the contemporary male gay world have been the subject of some preliminary inquiries. General accounts may be found in:

Harry, J., and DeVall, B. (1978), *The Social Organisation of Gay Men*, New York: Praeger

Hooker, E. (1967), 'The homosexual community', in J. Gagnon and W. Simon, *Sexual Deviance*, New York: Harper & Row

Lee, J. A. (1978), *Getting Sex*, Ontario: Musson Book Company

Levine, M. P. (1979), *Gay Men: The Sociology of Male Homosexuality*, London: Harper & Row

Plummer, K. (1975), *Sexual Stigma: An Interactionist Account*, London: Routledge & Kegan Paul

Warren, C. (1974), *Identity and Community in the Gay World*, London: Wiley

Accounts that focus on more specific aspects of the gay world include:

Achilles, N. (1967), 'The development of the homosexual bar as an institution', in J. Gagnon and W. Simon, *Sexual Deviance*, New York: Harper & Row

Delph, E. W. (1978), *The Silent Community: Public Homosexual Encounters*, London: Sage

Humphreys, L. (1975), *Tea-Room Trade*, 2nd ed., Chicago: Aldine

Plummer, K. (1978), 'Men in love: observations on the male homosexual couple', in M. Corbin (ed.), *The Couple*, London: Penguin

Sonnenschein, D. (1976), 'The ethnography of male homosexual relationships', in M. S. Weinberg, *Studies from the Kinsey Institute*, Oxford University Press.

Weinberg, M. S., and Williams, J. (1976), 'The social organization of impersonal sex: gay baths and other contexts', in M. S. Weinberg, *Studies from the Kinsey Institute*, Oxford University Press

Studies of the female homosexual sub-culture

The lesbian community has only recently – and then rarely – been the topic of study, and again the research is almost wholly American. The main studies are:

Ettorré, E. M. (1980), *Lesbians, Women and Society*, London: Routledge & Kegan Paul

Gagnon, J., and Simon, W. (1973), *Sexual Conduct*, Chicago: Aldine

Ponse, B. (1979), *Identities in the Lesbian World*, Westport, Conn.: Greenwood Press

Wolf, D. G. (1979), *The Lesbian Community*, University of California Press

The homosexual role and the homosexual identity

The original paper (reprinted in this volume) by Mary McIntosh, 'The homosexual role', is to be found in *Social Problems* (1968), vol. 16, pp. 182–92. It is criticized by F. L. Whitham (1977) in 'The homosexual role: a reconsideration', *Journal of Sex Research*, vol. 13, no. 1, pp. 1–11. Discussion of role identity, 'coming out' and homosexual socialization include:

Cass, V. C. (1979), 'Homosexual identity formation: a theoretical model', *Journal of Homosexuality*, vol. 4, no. 3, pp. 219–36.

Dank, B. M. (1971), 'Coming out in the gay world', *Psychiatry*, vol. 34, pp. 180–97

Plummer, K. (1975), *Sexual Stigma*, London: Routledge & Kegan Paul

Shively, M. G., and DeCecco, J. P. (1977), 'Components of sexual identity', *Journal of Homosexuality*, vol. 3, no. 1, pp. 41–8

Warren, C. (1974), *Identity and Community in the Gay World*, London: Wiley

Weinberg, T. S. (1978), 'On "doing" and "being" gay: sexual

behaviour and homosexual male self identity', *Journal of Homosexuality*, vol. 4, no. 2, pp. 143–56

Discussions of female identity, 'coming out' and socialization include:

Cronin, D. M. (1974), 'Coming out among lesbians', in E. Goode and R. Troiden, *Sexual Deviance and Sexual Deviants*, New York: Morrow, pp. 268–78

Kelly, D. H. (1978), 'The structuring and maintenance of a deviant identity: an analysis of lesbian activity', in D. H. Kelly, *Deviant Behaviour*, New York: St Martins Press

Moses, A. E. (1978), *Identity Management in Lesbian Women*, New York: Praeger

The homosexual life-cycle

The key preoccupation of research has been with the earlier phases of the gay experience – notably 'coming out'. There has been one preliminary study of other aspects of the gay life-cycle:

Kimmel, D. C. (1978), 'Adult development and ageing: a gay perspective', *Journal of Social Issues*, vol. 34, pp. 113–31

The representation of homosexuals in cultural products

There are now a number of studies which discuss the way in which homosexuality has been presented in literature, drama and film. Useful sources here are:

Austen, R. (1977), *Playing the Game: The Homosexual Novel in America*, Indiana: Bobbs-Merrill

Damon, G., Watson, J., and Jordan, R. (1975), *The Lesbian in Literature: A Bibliography*, 2nd edn, Nevada: The Ladder

Dyer, R., (ed.) (1977), *Gays and Film*, London: British Film Institute

Foster, J. H. (1958), *Sex Deviant Women in Literature*, London: Frederick Muller

Rule, J. (1975), *Lesbian Images: Critical Studies of Lesbian Literature and Lives*, New York: Doubleday

Sarotte, G. M. (1978), *Like a Brother, Like a Lover: Male Homosexuality in the American Novel from Melville to Baldwin*, New York: Doubleday

Stambolian, G., and Marks, E. (1979), *Homosexualities and French Literature*, New York: Cornell University Press.

Tyler, P. (1972), *Screening The Sexes: Homosexuality in the Movies*, New York: Holt, Rinehart and Winston

Young, I. (1975), *The Male Homosexual in Literature: A Bibliography*, New Jersey: Scarecrow

The gay movement

There are now a number of useful 'catalogues' and 'compendiums' on the gay movement. Most useful are:

Abbott, S., and Love, B. (1972), *Sappho Was a Right-On·Woman*, New York: Stein & Day

Covina, G., and Galana, L. (1975), *The Lesbian Reader*, California: Amazon Press

Jay, K., and Young, A. (1972), *Out of the Closets: Voices of Gay Liberation*, New York: Douglas Links

Johnston, J. (1973), *Lesbian Nation*, New York: Touchstone

Richmond, L., and Noquera, G. (1973), *The Gay Liberation Book*, San Francisco: Ramparts Press

Sanders, D. (ed.) (1977), *Gay Source: A Catalogue for Men*, New York: Berkeley Publishing Group

Vida, G. (ed.) (1978), *Our Right to Love: A Lesbian Resource Book*, New Jersey: Prentice-Hall

Most of the lesbian literature here connects strongly to feminism. See especially:

Birkby, P. and Harris, B., *et al.* (1973), *Amazon Expedition: A lesbian feminist anthology*, New York: Times Change Press

Myron, N., and Bunch, C. (1975), *Lesbianism and the Women's Movement*, Maryland: Diana Press

On history and sociology of the gay movement, the most useful volume is:

Weeks, J. (1977), *Coming Out: Homosexual Politics in Britain from the Nineteenth Century to the Present*, London: Quarter

Useful additional sources include:

Humphreys, L. (1972), *Out of the Closets: The Sociology of Homosexual Liberation*, New Jersey: Spectrum Books

Lauritsen, J., and Thorstad, D. (1974), *The Early Homosexual Rights Movement*, New York: Times Change Press

Societal reactions to homosexuality

Recent work on homosexuality has turned attention away from studying 'the homosexual' to a concern with the nature of people's responses (including their attitudes) towards homosexuality, and to explanations of their hostility. Good examples of the 'attitudes' studies are:

Gerassi, J. (1968), *The Boys of Boise*, New York: Collier Books

Kitsuse, J. I. (1964), 'Societal reaction to deviant behaviour: problems of theory and method', in H. S. Becker (ed.), *The Other Side*, New York: Free Press

Levitt, E. E., and Klassen, A. D. (1974), 'Public attitudes towards homosexuality', *Journal of Homosexuality*, vol. 1, pp. 9–27

Steffensmeier, D. and R. (1974), 'Sex differences in reaction to homosexuals: research continuities and further developments', *Journal of Sex Research*, vol. 10, no. 1, pp. 52–67

And on the origins of this hostility, see:

Greenberg, D., and Bystryn, M. (1978), 'Social sources of the prohibition against male homosexuality', as of 1979 an unpublished paper, obtainable from New York University, NY 10003

Plummer, K. (1976), 'The homosexual taboo', *Gay News*, no. 106

Weinberg, G. (1973), *Society and the Healthy Homosexual*, New York: Doubleday

Historical research

The three major studies are:

Bullough, V. (1976), *Sexual Variance in Society and History*, New York: Wiley

Katz, J. (1976), *Gay American History*, New York: Avon Books

Weeks, J. (1977), *Coming Out*, London: Quartet.

Each of these contains very detailed reading lists. A useful collection of reprints of rare and privately circulated books from the late nineteenth and early twentieth centuries has been undertaken by Arno Press, 330 Madison Avenue, New York, NY 10017. A catalogue is free on request. On more classical history, see the bibliography in *Journal of Homosexuality*, vol. 3, no. 1, pp. 78–89, and the recent study by K. J. Dover (1978), *Greek Homosexuality*, Duckworth.

General research into sexuality

This book cannot provide anything more than a few global source points on research into sexuality in general. The widest ranging general source books have been produced at the Institute for Sex Research (Bloomington, Indiana) and published by G. K. Hall, Boston. They include:

Catalogue of the Social and Behavioural Sciences Monograph Section of the Library of the Institute for Sex Research (1974, 1976), Boston: G. K. Hall

Beasley, R. (ed.) (1976), *International Directory of Sex Research and Related Fields*, Boston: G. K. Hall

Brooks, J. A., and Hofer, H. C. (eds) (1976), *Sexual Nomenclature: A Thesaurus*, Boston: G. K. Hall
For a small fee, the Institute will usually provide select reading lists on any topic.

More accessible source books are:
Green, R. (ed.) (1975), *Human Sexuality A Health Practitioner's Text*, Baltimore: Williams & Wilkins
Katchadourian, H. A., and Lunde, D. T. (1975), *Fundamentals of Human Sexuality*, 2nd edn, New York: Holt, Rinehart and Winston
Money, J., and Musaph, H. (1978), *Handbook of Sexology*, 5 vols., New York: Elsevier

Of greatest value to sociologists are:
Foucault, M. (1979), *The History of Sexuality*, London: Allen Lane
Gagnon, J., and Simon, W. (1973), *Sexual Conduct*, Chicago: Aldine

Notes

Chapter 1: Building a sociology of homosexuality

1 On the contribution of Hooker – which never culminated in a book, but which did lead to the 'Hooker Report' (1969a) – see the personal interviews with her (Hooker 1975, 1978).

2 This work is reviewed by Mark Freedman in his (1970) study. Freedman was, in fact, a gay psychologist, and his work became more outspokenly gay during the early 1970s. Before his untimely death in 1976, he produced the first pictorial guide to gay love-making (Freedman and Mayers 1976). A feminist version of homosexuality being psychologically positive can be found in Love (1975).

3 Indeed very little has appeared since. In English sociology, for instance, we still do not have a single instance of published research on the homosexual community, its bars, etc., except perhaps for my own studies of homosexual couples (Plummer 1978), the research of Betsi Ettore (1980) and some of the work in this volume.

4 He returns to the problem in his paper for Hooker (1969a) and, more conceptually, in Schur and Bedau (1976).

5 I discuss this distinction more fully in Plummer (1979b), and the central issue is to be found in Kitsuse and Schur's critiques of Gove et al. in Gove (1976).

6 These quotes are from the debates in Gove (1976) above.

7 Ibid.

8 Although the earlier work of Michael Schofield (1965) in England provides empirical data which corroborates the theory.

9 See the section on the gay movement in Appendix 2 (page 237) for examples of such writing. Of particular value too are the discussions to be found in the pages of *Gay Left*, *Body Politics* and *Gay Sunshine*.

10 For details on the American Gay Sociologists Caucus, write to GSC, 440 East 87th Street, New York NY 10028. An attempt was made to start such a group in England through the Gay

Research Group, but it remained very small and ineffective. At present it can be contacted via Peter Davies, Sociology Department, University College, Cardiff.

11   For an example of a feminist defence of sado-masochism, see Barbara Ruth (1977, pp. 10–11).

12   This is attributed to Samuel Butler in Hughes and Brecht (1976).

13   For an interesting example of this contradiction, see the discussion by Sagarin on 'transsexual' categories (1978).

Chapter 2:   The homosexual role

1   This is a grossly simplified account. Edwin Lemert provides a far more subtle and detailed analysis in *Social Pathology* (1951), Chapter 4, 'Sociopathic individuation'.

2   For discussion of situations in which deviants can lay claim to legitimacy, see Talcott Parsons, *The Social System* (1951, pp. 292–3).

3   The position taken here is similar to that of Erving Goffman in his discussion of becoming a mental patient (1961, pp. 128–46).

4   For evidence that many self-confessed homosexuals in England are not effeminate and many are not interested in boys, see Michael Schofield (1965).

5   The lack of cultural distinction is reflected in behaviour; Gordon Westwood found that only a small proportion of his sample of British homosexuals engaged in anal intercourse, and many of these had been active and passive and did not have a clear preference. See Westwood (1960, pp. 127–34).

6   See especially Ellis (1936), Bloch (E. Duhren, pseud.) (1938), Taylor (1965b), Garde (1964).

7   Evelyn Hooker has suggested that in a period when homosexual grouping and a homosexual sub-culture have not yet become institutionalized, homosexuals are likely to behave in a more distinctive and conspicuous manner because other means of making contact are not available. This is confirmed by the fact that lesbians are more conspicuous than male homosexuals in our society, but does not seem to fit the seventeenth century, where the groups are already described as 'clubs'.

8   However, 'fairy' and 'pansy', the commonest slang terms used by non-homosexuals, have the same meaning of effeminate as the earlier terms.

9   Bloch (1938, p. 328) gives several examples, but attributes their emergence to the fact that 'the number of homosexuals increased'.

10   The more general drawbacks of Kinsey's data, particularly the

problem of the representativeness of his sample, have been thoroughly canvassed in a number of places: see especially Cochran *et al*. (1954).

11 This cannot be taken in a rigorously statistical sense, since the categories are arbitrary and do not refer to numbers, or even proportions, of actual sexual acts.

12 But an interesting beginning has been made by Evelyn Hooker (1967, 1965); there is much valuable descriptive material in Cory (1953) and in Westwood (1960), as well as elsewhere.

13 There is an illuminating ethnomethodological discussion of this problem in Kessler and McKenna (1978, pp. 21–41).

14 Whitham's view is presented in Whitham (1977) and he has recently commented on the need to recognize homosexual beings existing now in all cultures (Whitham 1980).

Chapter 3: Homosexual categories

1 This shift from derogatory terms to positive self-constructed ones is discussed in Berzon and Leighton (1979) and in Morin and Schultz (1978).

2 The denial of civil liberties is being slowly documented in England by the Campaign for Homosexual Equality (1979), and in American by the Center for Homosexual Education, Evaluation and Research through the pages of the *Journal of Homosexuality* (see Petersen and Licata 1979). The 'atrocities' delivered on 'homosexuals' in other times are only slowly coming to light but see, for example, Katz (1976) and the Martin Sherman play, *Bent*.

3 I use this phrase only in the most general sensitizing way; I do not wish to imply the discovery of a rigid definition which would negate the central thesis of this chapter.

4 While both authors – Levine and Humphreys – see aspects of this segregation as arising from social hostility, Humphreys at least sees the formation of a gay 'satellite culture' as a very positive development for gay men, and does not contemplate its control role.

5 John Alan Lee (1979, pp. 179–80) vividly described this 'institutional completeness' of the Toronto gay scene. He writes:

A gay citizen of Toronto can buy a home through a gay real estate agent familiar with the types of housing and neighbourhoods most suitable to gay clients. He can close the deal through a gay lawyer, and insure with a gay insurance agent. If he is new to the community and cannot ask acquaintances for the names of these agents, he can consult the Gay Yellow Pages, a listing of businesses and services which is available in many larger cities. Or he can approach a typical source of connection with the gay community, such as a gay bookstore, or he can consult a local gay newspaper or periodical. From any of these sources of information he will also learn where he can buy lumber and renovating supplies from a company catering to a gay clientele. He will find gay suppliers of furniture, houseplants, and interior decorating. He will find gay sources of skilled labour or gay cleaning services.

Having moved in, our gay citizen can clothe himself at gay-oriented clothing stores, have his hair cut by a gay stylist, his spectacles made by a gay optician. He can buy food at a gay bakery, records at a gay phonograph shop, and arrange his travel plans through gay travel agents. He can buy newspapers and books at a gay bookstore, worship in a gay church or synagogue, and eat at gay restaurants. Naturally he can drink at gay bars and dance at gay discotheques. He can obtain medical care from a gay physician or if he prefers, a gay chiropractor. If he wishes to remain entirely within the gay culture, he can seek work at many of these agencies and businesses, but he will have to bank his earnings at a nongay bank, though he may be able to deal with a gay credit union. He can contribute money to tax-deductible gay foundations, participate in gay political groups, and enjoy gay-produced programs on cable television. To keep him up to date on everything happening in his gay community he can telephone the Gay Line, which is updated weekly. If he feels the need for counselling to adjust his lifestyle to the nongay environment, he can get help anonymously, or in person, as he prefers.

6 An illuminating interactionist account of this lobby is to be found in Spector and Kitsuse (1977).

7 The term seems to hail from Wainwright Churchill's 'homoerotophobia' (1967).

8 Sections of the following are reproduced from Plummer (1976).

9 Szasz has discussed homosexuality in a number of places, but see especially Szasz (1979).

10 The literature which supports these statements is now quite vast. See Bell and Weinberg (1978), Dank (1974), Ovesey (1969), Reiss (1962), Humphreys (1972), Blumstein and Schwartz (1976), T. Weinberg (1978).

11 I will discuss this non-congruency much more fully in a forthcoming book.

12 The orientation model implies people become 'types of being'. This is akin to Sagarin's 'tyranny of isness' (1975), a view which has been criticized by Humphreys (1979a).

13 This model is primarily allied to symbolic interactionist theory, but variants of it connect to the sociology of knowledge (Blumstein and Schwartz 1976), interpersonal congruency theory (Cass 1979) and existential sociology (Warren and Ponse 1977).

14 The standard source of this argument is C. W. Mills (1940).

Chapter 4: Discourse, desire and sexual deviance

1 See, for example, Public Record Office HO 79/1/66: Lord Hawkesbury to Lord Sydney, 8 November 1808.

2 Public Record Office: transcript of *Regina* v. *Boulton and Others*, 1871, DPP4/6, Day 1, p. 82; Day 3, p. 299.

3 On youth, see Gillis (1974) and Gorham (1978), and on housework and motherhood, see Oakley (1976) and Davin (1978).

4 For comments on this theme, see Kuhn (1978, pp. 61–2), Coward (1978), Adams and Minson (1978).

5 For Wilhelm Reich's comments on homosexuality see Reich (1969, p. 211). 'It can be reduced only by establishing all necessary prerequisites for a natural love life among the masses'. For a useful comment on the historical context of Reich's views, see Mitchell (1974, p. 141). A similar leftist view that homosexuality was 'a symptom of arrested or distorted development' can be seen in Craig (1934, p. 129). Herbert Marcuse's views are to be found in Marcuse (1969). Reiche (1970) expresses a viewpoint that homosexuality is a product of capitalist distortion of the libido. For comments on the biologism of Reich and Eric Fromm, see Laclau (1977, pp. 85–6). For an attempted Marxist appropriation of Freud to explain the oppression of homosexuality under capitalism, see Fernbach (1972).

6 Compare Plummer's slightly different account in the SSRC Report (Plummer 1979a).

7 Campioni and Gross (1978, p. 100) in their paper on 'Little Hans: The Production of Oedipus' propose a useful critique of Mitchell. See also Hall's point (1978, pp. 118–19):

> Surely, we must say that, without further work, further historical specification, the mechanisms of the Oedipus in the discourse both of Freud and Lacan *are* universalist, trans-historical and therefore 'essentialist'. . . the concepts elaborated by Freud (and reworked by Lacan) cannot, in their *in-general and universalist form*, enter the theoretical space of historical materialism, without further specification and elaboration – specification at the level at which the concepts of historical materialism operate.

8 For a discussion of the structuralist approach to history, see Johnson (1979). For an inspired polemic, see Thompson (1979, pp. 193ff). On Foucault's rather tenuous relationship to structuralism, see Gordon (1979).

9 'Desire' is an ambiguous concept carrying with it notions of the pre-individual. A careful dissection of its elements is provided in Foss and Gross (1978, p. 157):

> Deleuze-Guattari contrast their concept of desire with those founded in the

literature of Freud, surrealism, Bataille and the counter-culture. They argue for a non-adequated, a non-Utopian diagram with which desire would not be treated finally as univocal in language or as homogeneous with the social infra-structure. For example, they believe that desire should no longer be thought as existing in a necessary relationship with lack and law, and therefore as inevitably linked to interdiction (Bataille, Lacan), nor should it be celebrated as natural and spontaneous insofar as it may seem to be 'released' through increased leisure and sexuality. . . nor, again they argue, can any politics of desire be forged so long as one reduces desire to the ready-made (and ultimately Aristotelian) category of *pleasure as sensation*, under which the arena of revolution is relocated to the intensive arena of festival alone . . . . Rather, for the desire is the 'effective operator', it is always *desire for something* and never exists in a pure state or as an absolute quality. Desire is 'assembled, machined upon a plan of immanence or composition, which must itself be constructed at the same time as desire assembles and machines . . . one only desires as a function of an assemblage where one is enclosed (there it is a association of brigandage or of revolt).

Chapter 5: Liberating lesbian research

1 This paper is not intended to be 'objective'; my aim is to counter the often implicit bias of recent sociological literature. I want, however, to make my bias explicit; it comes from a radical feminist perspective similar to that underlying the work of Robin Morgan (1978) and Mary Daly (1979). My perspective has emerged not only from academic or published work, but, more importantly, from discussions and involvement in the women's liberation movement.

2 I use this term cautiously; 'rejection' of heterosexuality is not always primarily conscious and may be experienced as rejection by the opposite sex, or more positively as attraction to the same sex. However, my concern here is not with how lesbian identities become consolidated, but with how those identities are popularly conceived.

3 Nancy Chodorow (1978) provides an interesting feminist psychoanalytic discussion of gender formation and the universally asymmetrical and tension ridden nature of heterosexuality, arising from the fact that only women perform primary parental functions via the social role of mothering.

4 My concern here is with behaviourist/sociological studies; for a feminist critique of psychological research on lesbians, see Barbara Sang, 'Lesbian research – a critical evaluation', in *Vida* (1978).

5 Charlotte Wolff (1971) has of course provided an alternative definition based on emotional attachment, but one which arises from a traditional psychoanalytic approach, assuming the

'naturalness' of 'femininity' – a position which this paper would in no way support.

6   The following statement demonstrates this particular form of teleology: 'There is every gradation between a simple goodnight kiss or a friendly embrace and a kiss or an embrace which is definitely sexual in its intent and consequences. But whenever physical contact had led to orgasm, there was rarely any doubt of the sexual nature of the situation' (Kinsey *et al*. 1953, p. 510).

7   Their complete statement deserves quoting as an example of determinism writ large. 'Since we have shown that there are considerable differences in effectiveness of such psychologic stimuli between females and males, we may believe that this, the most striking disparity which exists between the sexuality of the human female and male must depend on cerebral differences between the sexes' (ibid., p. 712).

8   Research on women's sexual fantasies, most notably that of Nancy Friday (1974, 1975), suggests that while such fantasies often take a submissive form, it is crucial that we not only examine their situational function within certain kinds of oppressive relationships, but that we also view them within the context of women's sexual training, and not as 'inevitable' or 'natural'. Moreover, research into men's and women's use of pornography (Kutschinsky 1970, p. 50), demonstrates the differing functions for men and women; men use it primarily for masturbation purposes, whereas women tend to use it as an adjunct to heterosexual coitus where a man is necessarily present. The differences in the role which porn has for men and women become more apparent when contextualized.

9   This argument has also been asserted by sexologists studying men's and women's written descriptions of orgasm; see Vance and Wagner (1976).

10   For a more explicit example of this position, see Victor (1978), who extends and develops Gagnon and Simon's approach and suggests that men's sexual 'needs' are determined in the final analysis by the nature of their genitals. 'The larger size and external anatomy of the penis means that male children are more easily and consistently exposed to bodily excitation from genital stimulation', and hence that 'as young men and women become involved in genital petting and initial sexual intercourse, their different body consciousness predisposes them to attribute different kinds of meanings to that experience' (p. 153).

11   For a more general feminist critique of the deviance perspective as a whole, see Millman (1975).

12   Research on lesbians which does purport to look at meaning, for example, Rosen (1974), still tends to use the terms 'masculine' and 'feminine' as totally unproblematic constructs.

13   This view is made explicit by Donna Tanner: 'Lesbians are women who must face all the problems that single women face. They also must spend a great deal of their time in the straight world. . . . Thus, lesbians can be called double-deviants: both as single women and as lesbians in a society that regards each status as deviant' (1978, p. 43).

14   It is revealing that Hedblom presented the following paragraph, from the main body of his study, entirely *in brackets*:

(This study also explored attitudes of female homosexuals toward male homosexuals. The findings supported the contention that lesbians have more in common with female heterosexuals than they do with male homosexuals. In fact lesbians appear to view the male homosexual as being more promiscuous, more flighty, having more extremes in behaviour that would tend to identify him as deviant. He was interpreted as having more 'one night stands', as tending less toward the generation of a stable relationship. The data support the contention that female homosexuals tend to view male homosexuals perjoratively.) [1973, p. 334]

He then continues to talk about 'homosexuality' as if it were a discrete phenomenon.

15   This image building, as well as being the result of research into highly specific groups, is also a reflection of researchers' initial interests and myth conceptions; Kelly's work is concerned with those whom she describes as 'butch' women, thus imputing 'masculine' traits; Ponse chose to study secrecy and then focused on lesbians; Tanner states that her sample was from a gay women's organization and that 'politically active or radical lesbians were systematically excluded' (1978, p. 48); Wolf tells us that 'some women disapproved of the fact that I was studying their community' (1979, p. 9), and yet continues to draw conclusions about 'lesbian-feminists'.

16   Wolf states, for example, that 'men biologically are more genitally oriented than women, whose needs are more diffuse' (1979, p. 88).

17   For a concise outline of the development of lesbian-feminist theory since the Radicalesbians' statement, see Charlotte Bunch, 'Lesbian-feminist theory' in *Vida* (ed.) (1978).

Chapter 6: Pansies, perverts and macho men

1   These components are a modified version of those discussed by Shively and DeCecco (1977). The models based upon these components (see Tables 1–3) are ideal types. They are not intended to be exhaustive or historically specific.

2   Contemporary strategies of neutralization are discussed by Plummer (1975, pp. 137–41).

3   The traditional stress on gender ambiguity is indicated by various historical writings on the early homosexual sub-culture (see McIntosh, this volume).

4   This distinction was to play an important role in religious debate. See, for example, Bailey (1955).

5   Such ideas are still prevalent in certain societies especially those, like the countries of Latin America, with a strong 'macho' tradition. For an introduction to this area, see G. Hannon, 'Oppression in Mexico', *Body Politic* (Toronto), May–June 1974, and the Latin American issue of *Gay Sunshine* (San Francisco) Winter 1975–6. In contemporary Britain and the United States, the evidence suggests that few male homosexuals now think exclusively in terms of the active–passive dichotomy. See, for example Jay and Young 1979.

6   It is not suggested that these components are 'real' entities, which awaited scientific 'discovery'. However, once the distinctions were made, new realities effectively came into being.

7   In practice, however, this departure from the 'third sex' tradition was often more apparent than real. Although the psychodynamic theories stood in sharp contrast to the earlier congenital theories, many psychoanalysts nevertheless accounted for male homosexuality in terms of female gender identification (see Harry and DeVall 1978, pp. 1–7).

8   See, for example, the discussions in *The Medical Press* (3 September 1947) and *The Practitioner* (April 1947).

9   A good summary of typical medical beliefs during this period is found in the joint submission of the Institute for the Study and Treatment of Delinquency and the Portman Clinic (see Glover 1957).

10 Useful discussions on changing attitudes towards sexuality can be found in Robinson (1976) and in North (1972). The changing position of women in the post-war period is documented by Wilson (1977) and by the Birmingham Feminist History Group (1979). On the youth culture and especially the scenario of 'swinging London', see Aitken (1967).

Chapter 7: Gender confusions

1   See Pearce (1973). A number of transsexuals interviewed by me have also indicated that their families and friends seem to tolerate their cross-dressing and adoption of the social role of the opposite sex, but draw the line at sexual relationships with members of the same (chromosomal) sex.

2 Green (1969), Ford and Beach (1952), Devereaux (1937), Hill (1935), Forgey (1975).

3 As Green (1969), and Bullough (1974, 1975) have done.

4 In this and the following sections, the emphasis is very much on *male* transvestites and transsexuals. Although early writers like Ellis and Hirschfeld included case histories of women in their works, women have received scant attention in the literature on this area. Only two contemporary writers consider women transsexuals in any detail (Pauly 1969; Stoller 1968, 1975), and there is disagreement over whether the female *transvestite* actually exists or whether she is simply not noteworthy, being allowed to cross-dress with impunity (see Stoller 1968; Randell 1973; Bullough 1974).

5 So far as I am aware, this has not been translated so I am dependent on secondary accounts and Hirschfeld's later *Sexual Anomolies and Perversions* (1938) for his views on transvestism.

6 Carpenter, quoted by Ellis (1928, p. 12).

7 Quoted by Ellis (1928, p. 13).

8 For example, Horton and Clark (1931), Yawger (1940), Olkon and Sherman (1944).

9 The term hermaphrodite was in use (as referring to those who possess some mixture of the physical characteristics which usually distinguish the sexes) by at least 1876, when Klebs proposed a typology of the major forms (see Snyder and Browne 1977).

10 This is how Pauly describes them, although in terms of the perspective taken in this book, there are problems involved in scanning history for cases of 'transsexuals'.

11 Compare this with Ellis (1928, pp. 309–10): 'The same seed of suggestion is sown in various soils; in the many it dies out, in the few it flourishes. The cause can only be a difference in the soil.'

12 For objections from a psychoanalytic point of view more traditional than Stoller's, see Socarides (1969, 1970).

13 In the section of Bullough's *et al.* (1967) bibliography on transvestism and transsexualism (about 450 references), there are only eight references to articles on transvestism in the professional literature since 1965 and two books (which may be popular titles). There are also six references which include transvestism *and* transsexualism since that time. This is miniscule compared with the number of articles on transsexualism.

14 See Freud, cited by Stoller (1968, p. viii).

15 For more on FPE and one chapter in particular, see Feinbloom (1976).

16 'Transvestism is her creed and its acceptance by the world, her mission' (Beigel 1969, pp. 118–19). Riddell (1971) calls her the arch-transvestite of the ghetto.

17 Actually this article is credited to Virginia Bruce, but the ideas and often the words are identical to Prince's other publications so that I am sure they are the same person.

18 See especially 'Gemini', published by the Leeds Transvestite/ Transsexual Group in 1975.

Chapter 8: Male dominance and the gay world

1 Most sub-cultural studies have been American and in the field of delinquency, for example, the work of A. K. Cohen (1955), Cloward and Ohlin (1961) and Downes (1966).

2 Some important homosexual sub-cultural studies have been done by Achilles (1967), Hooker (1967), Leznoff and Westley (1967), Hoffman (1968), Warren (1974), Dank (1971), Plummer (1975). See also Chapters 1 and 2 in this book where there is a discussion of homosexual sub-cultural theories. The problem of when a distinctive homosexual sub-culture emerged is discussed in the McIntosh–Weeks–Marshall debate, also summarized in Chapter 1.

3 For early work along this line in the area of delinquency, see Matza (1961).

4 See Barry Adam (1978) for a similar discussion, in a macro-historical way, of the ways in which Jews, blacks and gays have been dominated and the resistance that they have made.

5 Stan Cohen has criticized these 'imaginary ways'. See Cohen (1980).

6 I will be concerning myself with the male homosexual sub-culture only, as the female gay sub-culture has different characteristics and origins, and also there is no possibility of me gaining access to this sub-culture. Gagnon and Simon (1967b) point to the wider cultural influences of 'femininity' (and all that that entails in America) on lesbian behaviour which puts lesbians nearer to heterosexual women rather than to homosexual men. I will use the term gay sub-culture rather loosely, but here I stress that it cannot be said to exist in any limited number of settings or times. 'The gay world' is multi-faceted, multi-tiered and pluralistic mainly because of its location at the intersection of a large number of other cultural forms. I draw examples most frequently from the public and visible gay world to be found in gay bars, discos and public sex areas. Most homosexuals though (and indeed most people) spend their leisure time with lovers, cliques and friends in a private and less visible world where their behaviour may differ from the more public world.

7 A more detailed discussion can be found in Rock (1974).

8 See Pearce and Roberts (1973).

9   Some of the literature in the sexual divisions field is discussed in Barker and Allen (1976) and Kuhn and Wolpe (1978).

10 The research technique used for this study would have ideally been a full-scale ethnography. What I have relied on as a substitute in this situation is my own retrospectively interpreted personal experiences and observations as a participant homosexual in different aspects of the homosexual sub-culture. This methodological approach and its advantages and disadvantages are outlined and discussed by Riemer (1977) and in the section on methodology in this book.

11 See Schofield (1976) on heterosexual promiscuity.

12 This is an average figure. Many homosexuals, of course, would match the heterosexual average. And many of the '1000 partners' could easily be totted up over a twenty-year period by a fleeting contact with, say, five men on a monthly visit to a gay sauna. Each of the 1000 would not therefore represent an entire night's encounter.

13 Humphreys (1975) discusses casual sexual encounters in public toilets.

14 A 'glory hole' is a hole bored through a dividing wall or door of a toilet cubicle that is large enough and placed at the right height to permit passage of the penis through it.

15 Other British gay magazines are *Zipper*, *Sam*, *Men in Uniform* and *Mister*. In USA some magazines are *Blueboy*, *Macho* and *Numbers*.

16 Erving Goffmann discusses 'passing' in relation to stigmatized groups in *Stigma: The Management of Spoiled Identity* (1963b).

17 Interestingly enough, heterosexual workers are taking on some of these 'adaptations' themselves. This is not new. In the 1960s aftershave lotion was only for 'fairies', but now its use by heterosexual men is close to universal.

18 A discussion of societal reaction in the USA is not directly applicable to the UK situation. However, differences exist not only between societies but within them as well. New York City and San Francisco are different from Plains, Georgia.

Bibliography

Unless otherwise stated, the place of publication is London.

ABBOTT, S., and LOVE, B. (1971). 'Is women's liberation a lesbian plot', in V. Gornick and R. Moran, *Woman in Sexist Society*, Mentor, pp. 601–21.

ACHILLES, N. (1967), 'The development of the homosexual bar as an institution', in J. H. Gagnon and W. S. Simon (eds), *Sexual Deviance*, (1967a), pp. 228–44

ADAM, B. (1978), *The Survival of Domination: Inferiorization and Everyday Life*, New York: Elsevier

ADAMS, R., and MINSON, J. (1978), 'The "subject" of feminism', *M/F*, vol. 2, pp. 43–61

ADORNO, T. W. *et al.* (1950), *The Authoritarian Personality*, London: Harper and Row

AITKEN, J. (1967), *The Young Meteors*, Secker & Warburg

ALBURY, R. (1976), 'Two readings of Freud', *Working Papers in Sex, Science and Culture*, vol. 1, no. 1, pp. 4–9

ALLEN, C. (1949), *Sexual Perversions and Abnormalities*, Oxford University Press

ALLEN, C. (1954), Correspondence, MMJ 1 May, p. 1040

ALLEN, C. (1958), *Homosexuality: Its Nature, Causation and Treatment*, Staples Press

ALLEN, C. (1969), *A Textbook of Psycho-sexual Disorders* 2nd edn, Oxford University Press

ALLEN, R (1954), *But For the Grace*, W. H. Allen

ALTMAN, D. (1971), *Homosexuals: Oppression and Liberation*, Outerbridge & Dienstfrey

ALTMAN, D. (1978), 'The state, repression and sexuality', *Gay Left*, vol. 6, pp. 4–8

ANON. (c. 1880), *My Secret Life*, 11 vols. privately printed, Amsterdam

BABUSCIO, J. (1978), 'The cinema of camp' *Gay Sunshine*, Summer, pp. 18–22

BAILEY, P. D. SHERWIN (1955), *Homosexuality and the Western Christian Tradition*, Longmans

BARKER, D. L., and ALLEN, S. (1976), *Sexual Divisions and Society: Process and Change*, Tavistock

BALFOUR MARSHALL, G. (1913), 'Artifical vagina: a review of the various operative procedures for correcting atresia vagina', *Journal of Obstetrics and Gynaecology*, vol. 23, pp. 193–212

BARNES, J. A. (1979), *Who Should Know What? Social Science, Privacy and Ethics*, Penguin

BARNHART, E. (1975), 'Friend and lovers in a lesbian counter culture community', in N. G. Malbin, *Old Family/New Family*, New York: D. Van Nostrand Co., pp. 90–115

BARRETT, M. (1979), *Ideology and Cultural Production*, Croom Helm

BECKER, E. (1973), *The Denial of Death*, New York: Free Press

BEIGEL, H. (1969), 'A weekend in Alice's wonderland', *Journal of Sex Research*, vol. 5, pp. 108–22

BELL, A. P. (1973), 'Homosexualities: their range and character', Nebraska Symposium on Motivation, 1973

BELL, A. P. (1976a), 'Research into homosexuality: back to the drawing board', *Archives of Sexual Behaviour*, vol. 4, pp. 421–31

BELL, A. P. (1976b), 'The appraisal of homosexuality', paper given at Kinsey Summer Conference, 1976

BELL, A. P., and WEINBERG, M. S. (1978), *Homosexualities: A Study of Diversity Among Men and Women*, Mitchell Beazley

BELL, C., and NEWBY, H. (1977), *Doing Sociological Research*, Allen & Unwin

BENJAMIN, H. (1953), 'Tranvestism and transsexualism', *International Journal of Sexology*, vol. 7, pp. 12–14

BENJAMIN, H. (1954), 'Transsexualism and transvestism as psychosomatic and somato-psychic syndromes', *American Journal of Psychotherapy*, vol. 8, pp. 219–30

BENJAMIN, H. (1966), *The Transsexual Phenomenon*, Julian Press

BENJAMIN, H. (1969a), 'New aspects of the transsexual phenomenon', *Journal of Sex Research*, vol. 5, pp. 135–41

BENJAMIN, H. (1969b), 'Introduction' to R. Green and J. Money, *Transsexualism and Sex Reassignment*, Maryland: John Hopkins University Press

BENJAMIN, H. (1971), 'Should surgery be performed on transsexuals', *American Journal of Psychotherapy*, vol. 25, pp. 74–82

BERGER, J. (1972), *Ways of Seeing*, Penguin

BERGER, P. (1965), 'Towards a sociological understanding of psycho-analysis', *Social Research*, vol. 32, pp. 26–41

BERGER, P. L., BERGER, B., and KELLNER, H. (1973), *The Homeless Mind*, Penguin

BERZON, B., and LEIGHTON, R. (1979), *Positively Gay: New Approaches in Gay Life*, California: Celestial Arts

BIEBER, I. (1965), 'Clinical aspects of male homosexuality', in J. Marmor (1965), pp. 248–67

BIEBER, I., *et al.* (1962), *Homosexuality: A Psychoanalytic Study of Male Homosexuals*, New York: Basic Books

BIRKBY, P., *et al.* (1973), *Amazon Expedition: A Lesbian Feminist Anthology*, New York: Times Change Press

BIRMINGHAM FEMINIST HISTORY GROUP (1979), 'Feminism as femininity in the 1950s', *Feminist Review*, vol. 3, pp. 48–65

BLOCH, I. (1938), *Sexual Life in England, Past and Present*, Francis Alder

BLOOMFIELD, J. (1977) (ed.), *Class, Hegemony and Party*, Lawrence & Wishart

BLUMER, H. (1969), *Symbolic Interactionism*, New Jersey: Prentice-Hall

BLUMSTEIN, P., and SCHWARTZ, P. (1976), 'The acquisition of sexual identity: the bisexual case', unpublished paper for ASA Conference

BRAKE, M. (1976), 'I may be queer but at least I'm a man: male hegemony and ascribed "v" achieved gender', in D. L. Barker and S. Allen. *Sexual Divisions and Society: Process and Changes*, Tavistock, pp. 174–98

BRECHER, E. M. (1970), *The Sex Researchers*, Andre Deutsch

BREMER, J. (1959), *Asexualisation*, Macmillan

BRIERLEY, H. (1974), 'The heterosexual transvestite: a gender anomaly', unpublished

BRIERLEY, H. (1975), 'Gender as a component of sexual disorders', unpublished

BRISTOW, E. J. (1977), *Vice and Vigilance: Purity Movements in Britain since 1700*, Dublin: Gill & Macmillan

BRITTAN, A. (1977), *The Privatised World*, Routledge & Kegan Paul

BRITTON A. (1979), 'For interpretation – notes against camp', *Gay Left*, vol. 7, pp. 11–14

BROWN, N. (1959), *Life Against Death*, Connecticut: Wesleyan University Press

BROWNMILLER, S. (1976), *Against Our Will: Men, Women and Rape*, Penguin

BRUCE, V. (1967), 'The expression of femininity in the male', *Journal of Sex Research*, vol. 3, pp. 129–39

BRYANT, A. (1977), *The Anita Bryant Story*, New Jersey: Fleming H. Revell Co.

BULLOUGH, V. L. (1974), 'Transvestites in the Middle Ages', *American Journal of Sociology*, vol. 79, pp. 1381–94

BULLOUGH, V. L. (1975), 'Transsexualism in history', *Archives of Sexual Behaviour*, vol. 4, no. 5, pp. 561–71

BULLOUGH, V. L. (1976), *Sexual Variance in Society and History*, Wiley

BULLOUGH, V. L. *et al.* (1976), *An Annotated Bibliography of Homosexuality*, Garland Press

BULLOUGH, V. L., and VOGHT, M. (1973), 'Homosexuality and its confusion with the "secret sin" in pre-Freudian America', *Journal of the History of Medicine*, vol. 27, no. 2

BUNCH, C. (1978), 'Lesbian feminist theory' in G. Vida (ed.), *Our Right to Love: A Lesbian Resource Book*, New Jersey: Prentice-Hall

BURTON, R. (1888), *A Plain and Literal Translation of the Arabian Nights Entertainment with Terminal Essay*, Benaves, Kamashastra Society, 1885–8

BSSP (1915), *The Social Problem of Sexual Inversion*, British Society for the Study of Sex Psychology

CAMPAIGN FOR HOMOSEXUAL EQUALITY (1979), *Queers Need Not Apply*, Manchester CHE publication

CAMPIONI, M., and GROSS, L. (1978), 'Little Hans: The production of Oedipus', in P. Foss and M. Morris (eds.), *Language, Sexuality and Subversion*, Darlington, Australia: Ferral Publications, pp. 99–122

CARPENTER, E. (1908), *The Intermediate Sex*, Allen & Unwin

CARPENTER, E. (1914), *Intermediate Types Among Primitive Folk*, Allen & Unwin

CARPENTER, E. (1924), *Some Friends of Walt Whitman: A Study in Sex Psychology*, British Society for the Study of Sex Psychology, pamphlet no. 13

CARPENTER, E. (1952), 'The intermediate sex', in E. Carpenter, *Love's Coming of Age*, Allen & Unwin

CASS, V. C. (1979), 'Homosexual identity formation: a theoretical model', *Journal of Homosexuality*, vol. 4, pp. 219–36

CAULDWELL, D. O. (1949a), *What's Wrong with Transvestism*, Haldeman-Julius

CAULDWELL, D. O. (1949b), *Unconventional Modes of Sexual Expression*, Haldeman-Julius

CAULDWELL, D. O. (1950a), *Questions and Answers on the Sex Life and Sexual Problems of Tranvestites*, Haldeman-Julius

CAULDWELL, D. O. (1950b), *Questions and Answers on the Sex Life and Sexual Problems of Transsexuals*, Haldeman-Julius

CAULDWELL, D. O. (1951), *Sex Transmutation – Can One's Sex Be Changed?*, Haldeman-Julius

CAWADIAS, A. P. (1954), 'Correspondence', *British Medical Journal*, 10 April, p. 876

CHARAN, J. M. (1979), *Symbolic Interactionism: An Introduction, An Interpretation, An Integration*, New Jersey: Prentice-Hall

CHODOROW, N. (1978), *The Reproduction of Mothering: Psychoanalysis and the Sociology of Gender*, University of California Press

CHOISY, A. DE (1966), *Memoires de l'Abbé de Choisy habille en Femme* (1735), republished and edited by Georges Mongredien, Paris: Mercure de France

CHURCHILL, W. (1967), *Homosexuals in the Male Species: A Cross Cultural Approach*, New York: Hawthorn

CICOUREL, A. (1964), *Method and Measurement in Sociology*, New York: Free Press

CLARKE, J. *et al.* (1975a), 'Style' in S. Hall and T. Jefferson, *Resistance Through Rituals* (1975), pp. 175–91

CLARKE, J. *et al.* (1975b), 'Subcultures, cultures and class: a theoretical overview', in S. Hall and T. Jefferson, *Resistance Through Rituals* (1975), pp. 9–74

CLOWARD, R., and OHLIN, L. E. (1961), *Delinquency and Opportunity*, Routledge & Kegan Paul

COCHRAN, W. G., MOSTELLER, F., and TUKEY, J. W. (1954), 'Statistical problems of the Kinsey report', Washington D.C.: American Statistical Society

COHEN, A. K. (1955), *Delinquent Boys: The Culture of the Gang*, Collier-Macmillan

COHEN, S. (1980), *Folk Devils and Moral Panics*, 2nd edn, Martin Robertson

COLLECTIVE EDITORIAL (1978), 'In the balance', *Gay Left*, no. 6, pp. 2–4

COOK, C., JONES, P., SINCLAIR, J., and WEEKS, J. (1975, 1977), *Sources in British Political History*, vols. 1–4, Macmillan

COOK, C., and WEEKS, J. (1979), *Sources in British Political History*, vol. 5, Macmillan

CORY, D. W. (1953), *The Homosexual Outlook: A Subjective Approach*, Nevill

CORY, D. W. (1964), *The Lesbian in America*, New York: Citadel Press

CORY, D. W., and LEROY, J. P. (1963), *The Homosexual and His Society: A View from Within*, New York: Citadel Press

CORZINE, J., and KIRBY, R. (1977), 'Cruising the truckers: sexual encounters in a highway rest area', *Urban Life*, vol. 6, pp. 171–92

COWARD, R. (1978), 'Sexual liberation and the family', *M/F*, vol. 1, pp. 7–24

COWELL, R. (1954), *Roberta Cowell's Story*, Heinemann

COX, C. (1966), *The Enigma of the Age: The Strange Case of the Chevalier d'Eon*, Longman

CRAIG, A. (1934), *Sex and Revolution*, Allen & Unwin

CRISP, Q. (1968), *The Naked Civil Servant*, Fontana

CROMPTON, L. (1969), 'Homosexuality and the sickness theory', *Albany Trust Talking Point*, Albany Trust Publication

CRONIN, D. (1974), 'Coming out among lesbians', in E. Goode and R. Troiden, *Sexual Deviance of Sexual Deviants* (1974), pp. 268–77

DALY, M. (1979), *Gyn/Ecology*, The Women's Press

D'AMICO, R. (1978), 'Review of Foucault', *Telos*, no. 36, pp. 169–83

DANIEL, M. (1965), 'Essai de methodologie pour l'etude des aspects homosexuals de l'histoire', *Arcadie*, vol. 133, January, pp. 31–7

DANK, B. (1971), 'Coming out in the gay world', *Psychiatry*, vol. 34, 2 May, pp. 180–97

DANK, B. (1974), 'The homosexual', in E. Goode and R. Troiden, *Sexual Deviance & Sexual Deviants* 1974)

DANK, B. (1976), 'The social construction of the homosexual', Unpublished paper, California State University, Long Beach

DAVID, D. S., and BRANNON, E. (1976), *The Forty-Nine Percent Majority – The Male Sex Role*, Addison-Wesley

DAVIN, A. (1978), 'Imperialism and motherhood', *History Workshop*, vol. 5, pp. 9–65

DELEUZE, G., and GUATTARI, F. (1977), *Anti-Oedipus: Capitalism and Schizophrenia*, New York: Viking Press

DELPH, E. W. (1978), *The Silent Community*, Sage

DE SAVITSCH, E. (1958), *Homosexuality, Transvestism and Change of Sex*, Heinemann

DEVEREUX, G. (1937), 'Institutionalised homosexuality of the Mohave Indians', *Human Biology*, vol. 9, pp. 498–627, and reprinted in Ruitenbeck (1963)

DOUGLAS, J. (1976), *Investigative Social Research*, Sage

DOVER, K. G. (1978), *Greek Homosexuality*, Duckworth

DOWNES, D. (1966), *The Delinquent Solution: A Study in Subcultural Theory*, Routledge & Kegan Paul

DUNN, C. W. (1940), 'Stilbestrol induced gynaecomastia in the male', *Journal of the American Medical Association*, vol. 115, pp. 2263–4

EAST, N., and HUBERT, W. (1939), *Psychological Treatment of Crime*, HMSO

ELLIS, H. (1920), *Studies in the Psychology of Sex*, vol. 2, *Sexual Inversion* 3rd edn. Pennsylvania: F. A. Davis

ELLIS, H. (1928), *Studies in the Psychology of Sex*, vol. 7, *Eonism and Other Supplementary Studies*, Pennsylvania: F. A. Davis

ELLIS, H. (1936), *Studies in the Psychology of Sex*, vol. 2, *Sexual Inversion*, New York: Random House

ETTORE, E. (1980), *Lesbians, Women and Society*, Routledge & Kegan Paul

FARADAY, A., and PLUMMER, K. (1979), 'Doing life histories', *Sociological Review*, vol. 27, pp. 773–98

FAREBEROW, N. L. (1963), *Taboo Topics*, New York: Atheling Books

FARRELL, R. A. (1971), 'Class linkages of legal treatment of homosexuals', *Criminology*, vol. 9, pp. 49–67

FARRELL, R., and HARDIN, C. (1974), 'Legal stigma and homosexual career deviance', in M. Riedel and T. Thornberry (eds.), *Crime and*

Delinquency: Dimensions of Deviance, New York: Praeger, pp. 128–40

FARRELL, R. A., and MORRIONE, T. J. (1974), 'Social interaction and stereotypic responses to homosexuals', *Archives of Sexual Behaviour*, vol. 3, p. 425

FARRELL, R. A., and NELSON, J. F. (1976), 'A causal model of secondary deviance: the case of homosexuality', *Sociological Quarterly*, vol. 17, pp. 109–20

FEINBLOOM, D. H. (1976), *Transvestites and Transsexuals: Mixed Views*, Delta Books

FENICHEL, O. (1934), *Outline of Clinical Psycho-Analysis*, Routledge & Kegan Paul

FENICHEL, O. (1954), *The Psychology of Tranvestism in Collected Papers*, vol. 1, Routledge & Kegan Paul (first published 1930)

FERNBACH, D. (1972), 'Towards a Marxist theory of gay liberation', *Gay Marxist*, vol. 2, and reprinted in *Capitalism and the Family* (1976), San Francisco: Agenda Publishing

FERENCZI, S. (1963), 'The nosology of male homosexuality', in Ruitenbeck (1963), pp. 3–15

FISHER, S. (1973), 'Understanding the female orgasm', New York: Basic Books

FORD, C. S., and BEACH, F. (1952), *Patterns of Sexual Behaviour*, Methuen

FORGEY, D. G. (1975), 'The institution of berdache among the North American Plains Indians', *Journal of Sex Research*, vol. 11, pp. 1–15

FOSS. P., and MORRIS, M. (1978), *Language, Sexuality and Subversion*, New South Wales: Feral Publications

FOUCAULT, M. (1977a), *Discipline and Punish: The Birth of the Prison*, Allen Lane

FOUCAULT, M. (1977b), 'Power and Sex: an interview with Michel Foucault', *Telos*, no. 32, Summer, pp. 152–61

FOUCAULT, M. (1978a), *I, Pierre Riviere*, Allen Lane

FOUCAULT, M. (1978b), 'Politics and the study of discourse', *Ideology and Consciousness*, no. 3, Spring, pp. 7–26

FOUCAULT, M. (1979), *The History of Sexuality*, vol. 1, Allen Lane

FREEDMAN, A. M., KAPLAN, H. I., and SADOCK, B. J. (1976), *Modern Synposis of 'Comprehensive Textbook of Psychiatry II'*, Maryland: Little, Brown

FREEDMAN, M. (1971), *Homosexuality and Psychological Functioning*, California: Wadsworth

FREEDMAN, M. (1975), 'Homosexuals may be healthier than straights', *Psychology Today*, March, pp. 28–32

FREEDMAN, M. and MAYERS, J. (1976), *Loving Men: A Photographic Guide to Gay Love-Making*, New York: Hark Publishing Co.

FREUD, S. (1977), *On Sexuality*, vol. 7, Penguin Freud Library, Penguin

FREUD, S. (1951), 'Letter to an American Mother', *American Journal of Psychiatry*, CV11, April, p. 787

FRIDAY, N. (1974), *My Secret Garden: Women's Sexual Fantasies*, New York: Pocket Books

FRIDAY, N. (1975), *Forbidden Flowers*, New York: Pocket Books

GAGNON, J. H. (1977), *Human Sexualities*, Illinois: Scott, Foresman & Co.

GAGNON, J. H., and SIMON W. S. (1967a) (eds.), *Sexual Deviance*, New York: Harper & Row

GAGNON, J. H., and SIMON, W. S. (1967b), 'Femininity in the lesbian community', *Social Problems*, vol. 15

GAGNON, J. H., and SIMON, W. S. (1973), *Sexual Conduct: The Social Sources of Human Sexuality*, Chicago: Aldine

GALANA, L., and COVINA, G. (1977), *The New Lesbians*, California: Moon Books

GARDE, N. I. (1964), *Jonathan to Gide: The Homosexual History*, New York: Vantage

GARFINKEL, H. (1967), *Studies in Ethnomethodology*, New Jersey: Prentice-Hall

GAYLIN, W. (1978), (ed.), *Doing Good: The Triumph of Benevolence*, New York: Pantheon

GIALLOMBARDO, R. (1966), *Society of Women*, New York: Wiley & Sons

GILBERT, A. N. (1974), 'The Africaine court martial', *Journal of Homosexuality*, vol. 1, pp. 111–22

GILBERT, A. N. (1976), 'Buggery and the British Navy 1700–1861', *Journal of Social History*, vol. 10

GILBERT, A. N. (1977), 'Social deviance and disaster during the Napoleonic wars', *Albion*, vol. 9

GILLIS, J. (1974), *Youth and History*, Academic Press

GLASER, B., and STRAUSS, A. (1965), *Awareness of Dying*, Weidenfeld and Nicolson

GLOVER, E. (1957), (ed.), 'The problem of homosexuality', memorandum presented to the departmental committee on Homosexual Offences and Prostitution by the Institute for the Study and Treatment of Delinquency

GOFFMAN, E. (1961), *Asylums: Essays on the Social Situation of Mental Patients and Other Inmates*, New York: Anchor Books, Doubleday

GOFFMAN, E. (1963a), *Behaviour in Public Places*, Macmillan

GOFFMAN, E. (1963b), *Stigma: Notes on the Management of Spoiled Identity*, New Jersey: Prentice-Hall

GOFFMAN, E. (1968), *Stigma: Notes on the Management of Spoiled Identity*, Penguin

GOODE, E., and HABER, L. (1977), 'Sexual correlates of homosexual experience: an exploratory study of college women', *Journal of Sex Research*, vol. 13, pp. 12–21

GOODE, E., and TROIDEN, R. (1974), *Sexual Deviance and Sexual Deviants*, New York: William Morrow

GORDON, C. (1979), 'Other inquisitions', *Ideology and Consciousness*, vol. 6, pp. 23–46

GORHAM, D. (1978), 'The "maiden tribute of modern Babylon" re-examined: child prostitution and the idea of childhood in late Victorian England', *Victorian Studies*, vol. 21

GORNICK, V. (1971), 'Women as outsiders', in V. Gornick and B. Moran (eds.), *Women in Sexist Society*, Mentor

GOULDNER, A. W. (1968), 'The sociologist as partisan: sociology and the welfare state', *American Sociologist*, vol. 3, pp. 103–16

GOVE, W. (1976), (ed.), *The Labelling of Deviance*, Wiley

GRAY, R. (1977), 'Bourgeois hegemony in Victorian Britain', in J. Bloomfield (ed.), *Class, Hegemony and Party*, Lawrence & Wishart

GREEN, R. (1969), 'Mythological, historical and cross-cultural aspects of transsexualism', in Green and Money (eds.) (1969)

GREEN, R. (1972), 'Homosexuality as mental illness', *International Journal of Psychiatry*, 10 March, pp. 77–128

GREEN, R., and MONEY, J. (1969), (eds.), *Transsexualism and Sex Reassignement*, Maryland: John Hopkins University Press

GREENBERG, D. F., and BYSTRYN, M. H. (1978), 'Social sources of the prohibition against male homosexuality', unpublished paper presented at the annual meeting of the SSSP, September

HAIST, M., and HEWITT, J. (1974), 'The butch-fem dichotomy in male homosexual behaviour', *Journal of Sex Research*, vol. 10, pp. 68–75

HALL, S. (1978), 'Some problems with the ideology/subject couplet', *Ideology & Consciousness*, no. 3, Spring, pp. 113–21

HALL, S. (1980), 'Reformism and the legislation of consent', in National Deviancy Conference (eds.), *Permissiveness and Control: The Fate of the Sixties Legislation*, Macmillan

HALL, S., CHRITCHER, C., JEFFERSON, T., CLARKE, J., and ROBERTS, B. (1978), *Policing the Crisis: Mugging, The State, and Law and Order*, Macmillan

HALL, S., and JEFFERSON, T. (1975), (eds.), *Resistance Through Rituals*, Hutchinson

HALMOS, P. (1979), *The Personal and The Political: Social Work and Political Action*, Hutchinson

HAMBURGER, C., STURUP, G., and DAHL-IVERSEN, E. (1953), 'Transvestism, hormonal, psychiatric and surgical treatment', *Journal of the American Medical Association*, vol. 152, pp. 391–6

HARE, E. H. (1962), 'Masturbatory insanity: the history of an idea', *Journal of Mental Science*, vol. 108, pp. 1–25

HARRY, J., and DEVALL, W. B. (1978), *The Social Organization of Gay Males*, New York: Praeger

HARVEY, A. D. (1978), 'Prosecutions for sodomy in England at the beginning of the nineteenth century', *The Historical Journal*, vol. 21, no. 47, pp. 939–48

HAUSER, R. (1962), *The Homosexual Society*, Bodley Head

HEDBLOM, J. H. (1973), 'Dimensions of lesbian sexual experience', *Archives of Sexual Behaviour*, vol. 2, no. 4, pp. 329–41

HENRIQUES, F. (1962), *Prostitution and Society*, vol. 1, MacGibbon & Kee, pp. 341–3

HERTOFT, P. (1976), 'Sexual minorities', in S. Crown (ed.), *Psychosexual Problems, Psychotherapy, Counselling and Behaviour*, Academic Press

HERTZ, J., TILLINGER, K., and WESTMAN, A. (1961), 'Transvestism', *Acta Psychiatrica Scandinavia*, vol. 37, pp. 283–94

HILL, W. W. (1935), 'The status of hermaphrodite and transvestite in Navaho culture', *American Anthropologist*, vol. 37, pp. 273–9

HIRSCHFELD, M. (1938), *Sexual Anomalies and Perversions*, Encyclopaedia Press

HIRSCHFELD, M. (1946), *Sexual Anomalies and Perversions*, Encyclopaedia Press

HISTORY WORKSHOP (1978), 'Editorial: history and theory', *History Workshop*, no. 6

HITE, S. (1976), 'The Hite report: a nationwide study of female sexuality', New York: Macmillan Publishing Co.

HMSO (1957), *The Report of the Committee on Homosexual Offences and Prostitution*, Command Paper 247

HOCQUENGHEM, G. (1978), *Homosexual Desire*, Allison & Busby

HOFFMANN, M. (1968), *The Gay World: Male Homosexuality and the Social Creation of Evil*, New York: Basic Books

HOOKER, E. (1956), 'A preliminary analysis of group behaviour of homosexuals', *Journal of Psychology*, vol. 42, pp. 217–25

HOOKER, E. (1958), 'Male homosexuality in the Rorscharch', *Journal of Projective Techniques*, pp. 33–54

HOOKER, E. (1965), 'Male homosexuals and their "worlds"', in J. Marmor (1965), pp. 83–107

HOOKER, E. (1967), 'The homosexual community', in Gagnon and Simon (1967a)

HOOKER, E. (1969a), 'Final report of the task force on homosexuality', *Homophile Studies*, vol. 13, no. 22, pp. 5–12

HOOKER, E. (1969b), 'Parental relations and male homosexuality in patient and nonpatient samples', *Journal of Consulting and Clinical Psychology*, vol. 33, no. 2, pp. 140–2

HOOKER, E. (1975), 'Facts that liberated the gay community: an interview', *Psychology Today*, 9 December, p. 52

HOOKER, E. (1978), 'An interview with Evelyn Hooker by Lord Humphreys', *Alternative Life-Style*, vol. 1, pp. 191–206

HORTON, C. B., and CLARK, E. K. (1931), 'Transvestism or eonism', *American Journal of Psychiatry*, vol. 10, pp. 1025–30

HOUSTON, R. (1978), 'The way we wear', *Gay News*, vol. 131, pp. 14–15

HOYER, N. (1933), *Man Into Woman*, Jarrolds

HUGHES, E. C. (1945), 'Dilemmas and contradictions of status', *American Journal of Sociology*, vol. 1, pp. 353–9

HUGHES, P., and BRECHT, G. (1976), *Vicious Circles and Infinity*, Cape

HUMPHREYS, L. (1971), 'New styles in homosexual manliness', *Trans-Action*, March–April, pp. 38–46

HUMPHREYS, L. (1972), *Out of the Closets: The Sociology of Homosexual Liberation*, New Jersey: Prentice-Hall

HUMPHREYS, L. (1975), *Tea-Room Trade*, 2nd edn. Chicago: Aldine

HUMPHREYS, L. (1979a), 'Being odd against all odds', in R. C. Federico, *Sociology*, Addison-Wesley, pp. 238–42

HUMPHREYS, L. (1979b), 'Exodus and identity: the emerging gay culture', in M. P. Levine (1979b)

HYDE, H. M. (1948), *The Trials of Oscar Wilde*, William Hodge

HYDE, H. M. (1970), *The Other Love: An Historical and Contemporary Survey of Homosexuality in Britain*, Heinemann

ISHERWOOD, C. (1954), *The World in the Evening*, Methuen

JAY, K., and YOUNG, A. (1979), *The Gay Report*, New York: Summit Books

JOHNSON, R. (1979), 'Histories of culture/theories of ideology: notes on an impasse', in M. Barrett (1979)

JOHNSTON, J. (1973), *Lesbian Nation*, New York: Touchstone

JORGENSEN, C. (1967), *A Personal Autobiography*, New York: Bantam Books

KARLEN, A. (1971), *Sexuality and Homosexuality: The Complete Account of Male and Female Sexual Behaviour and Deviation with Case Histories*, MacDonald

KATZ, J. (1976), *Gay American History: Lesbians and Gay Men in the U.S.A.*, New York: Thomas & Cromwell Co. Inc.

KEAT, R., and URRY, J. (1975), *Social Theory as Science*, Routledge & Kegan Paul

KELLY, D. (1979), 'The structuring and maintenance of a deviant

264 Bibliography

identity: an analysis of lesbian activity', in D. H. Kelly (ed.), *Deviant Behaviour*, New York: St. Martin's Press

KESSLER, W., and MCKENNA, E. (1978), *Gender: An Ethnomethodological Approach*, Wiley

KINSEY, A. C., POMEROY, W. B., and MARTIN, C. E. (1948), *Sexual Behaviour in the Human Male*, Philadelphia: W. B. Saunders

KINSEY, A. C., GEBHARD, P., POMEROY, W. B., and MARTIN, C. E. (1953), *Sexual Behaviour in the Human Female*, Philadelphia: W. B. Saunders

KITSUSE, J. I. (1962), 'Societal reaction to deviant behaviour: problems of theory and method', *Social Problems*, vol. 9, no. 3, pp. 247–56

KLEINBERG, S. (1978), 'Macho men: or where have all the sissies gone?' *Gay News*, vol. 142, pp. 16–18

KRAFFT-EBING, (1965), *Psychopathia Sexualis: A Mecido-Economic Study*, translated by M. E. Wedeck, New York: G. P. Putnam's & Sons

KUHN, A. (1978), 'Structures of patriarchy and capital in the family', in Kuhn and Wolpe (1978), pp. 42–67

KUHN, A., and WOLPE, A. M. (1978), *Feminism and Materialism: Feminism and Modes of Production*, Routledge & Kegan Paul

KUTCHINSKY, B. (1970), *Studies on Pornography and Sex Crimes in Denmark: A report on the U.S. Presidential Commission on Obscenity and Pornography*, Copenhagen: New Social Science Monographs

LACLAU, E. (1977), *Politics and Ideology in Marxist Theory*, New Left Books

LAFITTE, F. (1958–9), 'Homosexuality and the law', *British Journal of Delinquency*, vol. 9, pp. 8–19

LASCH, C. (1979), *The Culture of Narcissism: American Life in an Age of Diminishing Experience*, New York: W. W. Norton

LAURITSEN, J., and THORSTAD, D. (1974), *The Early Homosexual Rights Movement (1864–1935)*, New York: Times Change Press

LAVIN, N. I., THORPE, J. G., BARKER, J. C., BLAKEMORE, C. B., and CONWAY, C. O. (1961), 'Behaviour therapy in a case of transvestism', *Journal of Nervous and Mental Disease*, vol. 133, pp. 346–53

LAWS, J. L., and SCHWARTZ, P. (1977), *Sexual Scripts: The Social Construction of Female Sexuality*, Illinois: The Dryden Press

LEE, J. A. (1978), *Getting Sex*, Ontario: Musson Books

LEE, J. A (1979), 'The gay connection', *Urban Life*, vol. 8, pp. 175–98

LEHNE, G. K. (1976), 'Homophobia among men', in D. S. David and R. Brannon, *The Forty-Nine Percent Majority: The Male Sex Role*, Addison-Wesley, pp. 66–88

LEMERT, E. (1967), *Human Deviance, Social Problems and Social Control*, New Jersey: Prentice-Hall

LEVINE, M. P. (1979a), 'Gay ghetto', in M. P. Levine (1979b)

LEVINE, M. P. (1979b), *Gay Men: The Sociology of Male Homosexuality*, Harper & Row

LEVITT, E. E., and KLASSEN, D. (1974), 'Public attitudes toward homosexuality', in *Journal of Homosexuality*, vol. 1, no. 1

LEZNOFF, M. (1956), 'Interviewing homosexuals', *American Journal of Sociology*, vol. 62, no. 2, pp. 202–5

LEZNOFF, M., and WESTLEY, W. A. (1967), 'The homosexual community', in Gagnon and Simon (1967a)

LLOYD, R. (1977), *Playland: A Study of Boy Prostitution*, Blond & Briggs

LOVE, B. (1975), 'A case for lesbians as role models for healthy adults', in Vida (1978), p. 83

LUKIANOWICZ, N. (1959), 'Survey of various aspects of transvestism in the light of our present knowledge', *Journal of Nervous and Mental Disease*, vol. 133, pp. 346–53

LUMBY, M. E. (1976), 'Homophobia: the quest for a valid scale', *Journal of Homosexuality*, vol. 2, pp. 39–47

MACDONALD, A. P., and GAMES, R. G. (1974), 'Some characteristics of those who hold positive and negative attitudes towards homosexuals', *Journal of Homosexuality*, vol. 1, pp. 9–28

MARCUSE, H. (1969), *Eros and Civilization*, Sphere

MARMOR, J. (ed.), (1965), *Sexual Inversion: The Multiple Roots of Homosexuality*, New York: Basic Books

MARTIN, D., and LYON, P. (1972), *Lesbian/Woman*, New York: Bantam Books

MASTERS, W., and JOHNSON, V. (1966), *Human Sexual Response*, Boston: Little Brown & Co.

MASTERS, W., and JOHNSON, V. (1970), *Human Sexual Inadequacy*, Churchill

MASTERS, W., and JOHNSON, V. (1979), *Homosexuality in Perspective*, Massachusetts: Little, Brown

MATZA, D. (1961), 'Subterranean traditions of youth', *Annals of the American Academy of Political and Social Science*, vol. 338, pp. 102–18

MAY, G. (1930), *Social Control of Sex*, Allen & Unwin

MCCAGHY, C. H., and SKIPPER, J. K. (1969), 'Lesbian behaviour as an adaptation to the occupation of stripping', *Social Problems*, vol. 17, no. 2, pp. 262–70

MCINTOSH, M. (1965), 'The homophile movement and the homosexual's dilemma', unpublished Leicester University staff seminar paper

MCINTOSH, M. (1968), 'The homosexual role', *Social Problems*, vol. 16, no. 2, pp. 182–92

MEYER, J. K., and HOOPER, J. E. (1974), 'The gender dysphoria syndromes', *Plastic and Reconstructive Surgery*, vol. 54, pp. 444–51

MILLER, W. B. (1962), 'Lower class culture as a generating milieu of gang delinquency', in M. Wolfgang *et al.* (eds.), *The Sociology of Crime and Delinquency*, Wiley

MILLMAN, M. (1975), 'She did it all for love: a feminist view of the sociology of deviance', in M. Millman and R. Moss Kanter (eds.), *Another Voice: Feminist Perspectives on Social Life and Social Science*, pp. 251–79, New York: Doubleday

MILLS, C. W. (1940), 'Situated actions and vocabularies of motive', *American Sociological Review*, vol. 5, pp. 904–13

MITCHELL, J. (1974), *Psychoanalysis and Feminism*, Allen Lane

MONEY, J. (1973), 'Gender role, gender identity, core gender identity: usage and definition of terms', *Journal of the American Academy of Psychoanalysis*, vol. 1, pp. 397–403

MONEY, J., and SCHWARTZ, B. (1969), 'Public opinion and social issues in transsexualism: a case study in medical sociology', in Green and Money (1969)

MONEY, J., and TUCKER, P. (1977), *Sexual Signatures*, Abacus

MORGAN, R. (1978), *Going Too Far*, New York: Vintage

MORIN, S. F. (1977), 'Heterosexual bias in psychological research on lesbianism and male homosexuality', *American Psychologist*, vol. 32, pp. 629–37

MORIN, S. F., and SCHULTZ, S. J. (1978), The gay movement and the rights of children', *Journal of Social Issues*, vol. 34, pp. 137–49

MORRIS, J. (1974), *Conundrum*, Faber & Faber

MORRISON, D., and TRACEY, M. (1979), *Whitehouse*, Macmillan

MYRON, N., and BUNCH, C. (1975), *Lesbianism and the Womens Movement*, Maryland: Diana Press

NEWBY, H., and BELL, C. (1977), *Doing Social Research*, Allen & Unwin

NICHOLS, J. (1979), 'Butcher than thou: beyond machismo', in M. P. Levine (1979b)

NORTH, M. (1972), *The Secular Priests: Psychotherapists in Contemporary Society*, Allen & Unwin

OAKLEY, A. (1976), *Housewife*, Penguin

OLKON, D. M., and SHERMAN, I. C. (1944), 'Eonism with outstanding psychopathic features', *Journal of Nervous and Mental Disorders*, vol. 99, pp. 159–67

OPLER, M. K. (1965), 'Anthropological and cross cultural aspects of Homos', in Marmor (1965), pp. 108–23

OSTOW, M. (1953), Correspondence, *Journal of the American Medical Association*, vol. 152, p. 1553

OVESEY, L. (1969), *Homosexuality and Pseudohomosexuality*, New York: Science House

PARLIAMENTARY DEBATES (1885a), Hansard, vol. 296, col. 646 (26 March)

PARLIAMENTARY DEBATES (1885b), Hansard, vol. 300, cols. 1397–8 (27 July–12 August)

PARLIAMENTARY DEBATES (1885c), Hansard, vol. 300, col. 1551 (27 July–12 August)

PARLIAMENTARY DEBATES (1966–7a), Hansard, vol. 731, col. 262

PARLIAMENTARY DEBATES (1966–7b), Hansard, vol. 738, vol. 1082

PARLIAMENTARY DEBATES (1966–7c), Hansard, vol. 738, col. 1087

PARSONS, T. (1951), *The Social System*, New York: Free Press

PAULY, I. B. (1965), 'Male psychosexual inversion: transsexualism', *Archives of General Psychiatry*, vol. 13, August, pp. 172–81

PAULY, I. B. (1969), 'Adult manifestations of female transsexualism', in Green and Money (1969)

PEARCE, F. (1973), 'How to be immoral and ill, pathetic and dangerous, all at the same time: mass media and the homosexual', in S. Cohen and J. Young (eds.), *The Manufacture of News: Deviance, Social Problems and the Mass Media*, Constable

PEARCE, F., and ROBERTS, A. (1973), 'The social regulation of sexual behaviour and the development of industrual capitalism', in R. Bailey and J. Young (eds.), *Contemporary Social Problems in Britain*, Saxon House

PERSON, E., and OVESEY, L. (1974a), 'The transsexual syndrome in males; I primary transsexualism', *American Journal of Psychotherapy*, vol. 28, no. 1, pp. 4–20

PERSON, E., and OVESEY, L. (1974b), 'The transsexual syndrom in males; II secondary transsexualism', *American Journal of Psychotherapy*, vol. 28, no. 2, pp. 174–93

PETERSON, R. P., and LICATA, S. J. (1979), 'The collection and analysis of documents for the civil liberties and sexual orientation project', *Journal of Homosexuality*, vol. 4, pp. 277–82

PLUMMER, K. (1975), *Sexual Stigma: An Interactionist Account*, Routledge & Kegan Paul

PLUMMER, K. (1976), 'The homosexual taboo', *Gay News*, no. 106

PLUMMER, K. (1978), 'Men in love: observations on the gay couple', in M. Corbin (ed.), *The Couple*, Penguin

PLUMMER, K. (1979a), *Symbolic Interactionism and Sexual Differentation: An Empirical Investigation*, unpublished report to SSRC

PLUMMER, K. (1979b), 'Misunderstanding labelling perspectives', in D. Downes and P. Rock (eds.), *Deviant Interpretations*, Martin Robertson

PLUMMER, K. (forthcoming), *Documents of Life*, Allen & Unwin
PONSE, B. (1977), 'Secrecy in the lesbian world', in C. Warren (ed.), *Sexuality: Encounters, Identities and Relationships*, Sage
PONTE, M. R. (1974), 'Life in a parking lot: an ethnography of a homosexual drive-in', in J. Jacobs (ed.), *Deviance: Field Studies and Self Disclosures*, California: National
POSTER, M. (1978), *Critical Theory of the Family*, Pluto Press
PRINCE, C. V. (1957), 'Homosexuality, transvestism and transsexualism', *American Journal of Psychotherapy*, vol. 11, pp. 80–5

RADICALESBIANS (1970), 'The woman – identified woman', in K. Jay and A. Young (eds.), *Out of the Closets*, New York: Douglas Links
RADZINOWICZ, L. (1968), *A History of English Criminal Law (Vol. 4): Grappling for Control*, Stevens & Sons
RANDELL, J. B. (1959), 'Transvestism and transsexualism', British Medical Journal, 26 December, pp. 1448–52
RANDELL, J. B. (1973), *Sexual Variations*, Priory Press
RAYMOND, M. (1956), 'Case of fetishism treated by aversion therapy', *British Medical Journal*, vol. 2, pp. 235–40
REICH, W, (1969), *The Sexual Revolution*, New York: Farrar Strauss & Giroux
REICHE, R. (1970), *Sexuality and Class Struggle*, New Left Books
REICHE, R., and DANNECKER, M. (1977), 'Male homosexuality in West Germany – a sociological investigation', *Journal of Sex Research*, vol. 13, no. 1, pp. 35–53
REISS, A. J. (1962), 'The social integration of queers and peers', *Social Problems*, vol. 9, pp. 102–19
RIDDELL, C. (1971), 'Transvestism and the tyranny of gender', unpublished paper
RIEMER, J. W. (1977), 'Varieties of opportunistic research', *Urban Life*, vol. 5, pp. 467–77
ROBERTS, J. R. (1979), 'In America they call us dykes', in *Sinister Wisdom*, vol. 9, pp. 2–11
ROBINSON, P. (1976), *The Modernization of Sex*, Paul Elek
ROCK, P. (1974), 'Sociology of deviancy and conceptions of moral order', *British Journal of Criminology*, vol. 14, pp. 139–49
ROCK, P. (1976), 'Some problems of interpretative historiography', *British Journal of Sociology*, vol. 27, no. 3, pp. 353–69
ROCK, P. (1979), *The Making of Symbolic Interactionism*, Macmillan
RODGERS, B. (1972), *A Gay Lexicon*, Blond & Briggs
ROSEN, D. H. (1974), *Lesbianism: A Study of Female Homosexuality*, Charles C. Thomas
ROTENBERG, M. (1979), *Damnation and Deviance*, Free Press
ROWSE, A. L. (1977), *Homosexuals in History: A Study of Ambivalence in Society, Literature and the Arts*, Weidenfeld & Nicolson

RUITENBECK, H. M. (1963), *The Problem of Homosexuality in Modern Society*, New York: Dutton

RUSSELL, D. E. H., and VAN DE VEN, N. (eds.) (1976), *Proceedings of the International Tribunal on Crime Against Women*, California: Les Femmes

RUTH, B. (1977), 'Cathexis: on the nature of s and m', *Lesbian Tide*, May/June

SAGARIN, E. (1969), *Odd Man In*, Quadrangle Books

SAGARIN, E. (1970, 'Languages of the homosexual sub-culture', in *Medical Aspects of Human Sexuality*, April

SAGARIN, E. (1973), 'The good guys, the bad guys and the gay guys', *Contemporary Sociology*, vol. 2, no. 1

SAGARIN, E. (1975), *Deviants and Deviance: An introduction to the study of devalued people and behaviour*, New York: Praeger

SAGARIN, E. (1978), 'Transexualism: legitimation, amplification and exploitation of deviance by scientists and mass media', in C. Wilick (ed.), *Deviance and Mass Media*, Sage

SAGARIN, E., and KELLY, R. J. (1976), 'Sexual deviance and labelling perspectives', in W. Gove (1976), pp. 243–72

SAGHIR, M. T., and ROBINS, E. (1973), *Male and Female Homosexuality: A Comprehensive Investigation*, Maryland: Williams and Wilkins

SANG, B. (1978), 'Lesbian research: a critical evaluation', in G. Vida (ed.), *Our Right to Love: A Lesbian Resource Book*, New Jersey: Prentice-Hall

SCHAFER, S. (1976), 'Sexual and social problems of lesbians', *The Journal of Sex Research*, vol. 12, no. 1, pp. 50–69

SCHEFF, T. J. (1975), (ed.), *Labelling Madness*, New Jersey: Prentice-Hall

SCHOFIELD, M. (1965), *Sociological Aspects of Homosexuality*, Longman

SCHOFIELD, M. (1976), *Promiscuity*, Gollancz

SCHUR, E., and BEDAU, J. (1976), *Victimless Crime: Two Sides of a Controversy*, New Jersey: Prentice-Hall, Spectrum Books

SCHUR, E. M. (1965), *Crimes Without Victims – Deviant Behaviour and Public Policy: Abortion, Homosexuality, Drug Addiction*, New Jersey: Prentice-Hall

SCOTT, R. A. (1972), 'A proposed framework for analyzing deviance as a property of social order, in Scott and Douglas (1972), pp. 9–35

SCOTT, R. A., and DOUGLAS, J. D (1972) (eds.), *Theoretical Perspectives on Deviance*, Basic Books

SENNETT, R. (1974), *The Fall of Public Men*, Cambridge University Press

SHERFEY, J. J. (1973), *The Nature and Evolution of Female Sexuality* (1973), New York: Vintage

SHIVELY, M. G., and DE CECCO, J. P. (1977), 'Components of sexual identity', *Journal of Homosexuality*, vol. 3, pp. 41–9

SIGUSCH, C., and SCHMIDT, G. (1970), 'Sex differences in responses to psychosexual stimulation by films and slides', *Journal of Sex Research*, vol. 6, pp. 268–83

SIM, M. (1974), *Guide to Psychiatry*. 3rd edn, Churchill Livingstone

SIMON, W., and GAGNON, J. H. (1967), 'Homosexuality: the formulation of a sociological perspective', *Journal of Health and Social Behaviour*, vol. 8, September, pp. 177–84

SIMPSON, R. (1976), *From the Closets to the Courts*, Penguin

SMITH, F. B. (1976), 'Labouchere's Amendment to the Criminal Law Amendment Act', *Historical Studies*, vol. 17

SMITH-ROSENBERG, C. (1975), 'The female world of love and ritual: relations between women in nineteenth century America', *Signs*, vol. 1

SYNDER, C. C., and BROWNE, E. Z. (1977), 'Intersex problems and hermaphroditism', in J. M. Converse (ed.), *Reconstructive Plastic Surgery*, vol. 7, 2nd edn. Philadelphia: W. B. Saunders

SOCARIDES, C. W. (1969), 'The desire for sexual transformation: a psychiatric evaluation of transsexualism', *American Journal of Psychiatry*, vol. 125, no. 10, pp. 149–25

SOCARIDES, C. W. (1970), 'A psychoanalytic study of the desire for sexual transformation (transsexualism) the plaster-of-Paris man', *International Journal of Psychoanalysis*, vol. 51, pp. 341–9

SOCARIDES, C. W. (1978), *Homosexualty*, Jason Aronson

SONENSCHEIN, D. (1969), 'The homosexual's language', *Journal of Sex Research*, vol. 5, no. 4, pp. 281–91

SONTAG, S. (1967), 'Notes on camp', in S. Sontag, *Against Interpretation and Other Essays*, Eyre & Spottiswoode, pp. 275–92

SPADA, J. (1979), *The Spada Report*, New York: Signet

SPECTOR, M. (1976), 'Labelling theory in *Social Problems*, A young journal launches a new theory', *Social Problems*, vol. 24, pp. 69–74

SPECTOR, M. (1977), 'Legitimizing homosexuality', *Society*, July/August, pp. 52–6

SPECTOR, M., and KITSUSE, J. (1977), *Constructing Social Problems*, California: Wadsworth

STAFFORD-CLARK, C. D. (1964), 'Essentials of the clinical approach', in I. Rosen (ed.), *The Pathology and Treatment of Sexual Deviation*, Oxford University Press

STAMBOLIAN, G., and MARKS, E. (eds.) (1979), *Homosexualities and French Literature*, New York: Cornell University Press

STAMFORD, J. (1979), *Spartacus International Gay Guide*, Amsterdam

STANLEY, L. (1976), 'On the receiving end', *Out* (*Che* magazine), no. 1, pp. 6–7

STEAKLEY, J. D. (1975), *The Homosexual Emancipation Movement in Germany*, New York: Arno Press

STEFFENSMEIER, D., and STEFFENSMEIER, R. (1974), 'Sex differences in reactions to homosexuals: reseant continuities and further developments', *Journal of Sex Research*, vol. 10, no. 1, pp. 52–67

STEKEL, W. (1934), *Bisexual Love: Physicians and Surgeons*, Book Co.

STOLLER, R. J. (1964), 'A contribution to the study of gender identity', *International Journal of Psychoanalysis*, vol. 45, pp. 220–6

STOLLER, R. J. (1968), *Sex and Gender*, Hogarth Press

STOLLER, R. J. (1972), 'Transsexualism and transvestism', *Psychiatric Annals*, vol. 1, pp. 61–72

STOLLER, R. J. (1975), *Sex and Gender, vol. II: The Transsexual Experiment*, Hogarth Press

STOLLER, R. J. (1976), *Perversion: The Erotic Form of Hatred*, New York: Parthean

STONE, L. (1977), *The Family, Sex and Marriage*, Weidenfeld & Nicolson

STRAUSS, A. (1969), *Mirrors and Masks: The Search for Identity*, California: Sociology Press

STYLES, J. (1979), 'Outsider/insider: researching gay baths', *Urban Life*, vol. 8, pp. 135–52

SYMONDS, J. A. (1964), *Studies in Sexual Inversion, Embodying 'A Study of Greek Ethics' and 'A Study in Modern Ethics'*, New York: Medical Press

SZASZ, T. (1979), 'Getting away with murder', *Gay News*, no. 179

TANNER, D. (1978), *The Lesbian Couple*, Lexington

TAYLOR, G. R. (1965a), 'Historical and mythological aspects of homosexuality', in Marmor (1965)

TAYLOR, G. R. (1965b), *Sex in History*, Panther

TEAL, D. (1971), *The Gay Militants*, New York: Stein and Day

THOMPSON, E. P. (1979), *The Poverty of Theory*, Merlin

THOMPSON, P. (1978), *The Voice of the Past: Oral History*, Oxford University Press

TOLSON, A. (1977), *The Limits of Masculinity*, Tavistock

TRIPP, C. A. (1977), *The Homosexual Matrix*, Quartet

TRUMBACK, R. (1977), 'London's sodomites: homosexual behaviour and western culture in the 18th century', *Journal of Social History*, Fall, pp. 1–33

TURNER, R. (1962), 'Role-taking: process versus conformity' in A. Rose (ed.), *Human Behaviour and Social Process*, Routledge and Kegan Paul

VANCE, E. B., and WAGNER, N. M. (1976), Written descriptions of orgasm: a study of sex differences', *Archives of Sexual Behaviour*, vol. 6, pp. 87–98

VICTOR, J. (1978), 'The social psychology of sexual arousal: a symbolic interactionist interpretation', in N. K. Denzil (ed.), *Studies in Symbolic Interactionism*, vol. 1, Connecticut: JAI Press

VIDA, G. (1978) (ed.), *Our Right to Love: A Lesbian Resource Book*, New Jersey: Prentice-Hall

VIDICH, A. J., BENSMAN, J., and STEIN, M. R. (1964) (eds.), *Reflections on Community Studies*, New York: Harper & Row

WARD, E. (1896), *The Secret History of the London Clubs*, first published 1709, J. Dutton

WARREN, C. A. (1972), 'Observing the gay community', in Douglas, *Research on Deviance*, New York: Random House

WARREN, C. A. (1974), *Identity and Community in the Gay World*, Wiley

WARREN, C. A. (1977), 'Fieldwork in the gay world: issues in phenomenological research', *Journal of Social Issues*, vol. 33, pp. 93–107

WARREN, C., and PONSE, B. (1977), 'The existential self in the gay world', in J. Douglas and J. M. Johnson, *Existential Sociology*, Cambridge University Press, pp. 273–90

WEEKS, J. (1977), *Coming Out: Homosexual Politics in Britain from the 19th Century to the Present*, Quartet

WEEKS, J. (1978), 'Preface' to Hocquenghem (1978)

WEEKS J. (1979), 'Movements of affirmation: sexual meanings and homosexual identities', *Radical History Review*, vol. 20, pp. 164–80

WEEKS, J. (1980), 'Inverts, perverts and Mary Annes: male prostitution and the regulation of homosexuality in England in the 19th and early 20th centuries', *Journal of Homosexuality*, vol. 5

WEINBERG, G. (1973), *Society and the Healthy Homosexual*, New York: Anchor

WEINBERG, M. S. (1976) (ed.), *Sex Research; Studies from the Kinsey Institute*, Oxford University Press

WEINBERG, M. S., and WILLIAMS, C. J. (1974), *Male Homosexuals: Their Problem and Adaptation*, Oxford University Press

WEINBERG, M. S., and WILLIAMS, C. J. (1975), 'Gay baths and the social organization of impersonal sex', *Social Problems*, vol. 23, pp. 124–36

WEINBERG, M., and BELL, A. (1972), *Homosexuality: An Annotated Bibliography*, New York: Harper & Row

WEINBERG, T. (1978), 'On "doing" and "being" gay: sexual behaviour and homosexual male self identity', *Journal of Homosexuality*, vol. 4, pp. 143–56

WEST, D. J. (1955), *Homosexuality*, 1st edn, Duckworth

WEST, D. J. (1977), *Homosexuality Reassessed*, Duckworth

WESTERMARCK, E. (1906), *The Origin and Development of the Moral Ideas*, Macmillan

WESTPHAL, C. (1870), 'Die Contrare Sexualemphindung', *Archive fur Psychiatrie and Nervenkrankenheiten*, vol. 2, pp. 291–312

WESTWOOD, G. (1952), *Society and the Homosexual*, Golancz

WESTWOOD, G. (1960), *A Minority: A Report on the Life of the Male Homosexual in Great Britain*, Longman

WHITHAM, F. (1977), 'The homosexual role: a reconsideration', *Journal of Sex Research*, vol. 13, pp. 1–11

WHITHAM, F. (1980), 'The prehomosexual male child in three societies: the United States, Guatemala, Brazil', *Archives of Sexual Behaviour*, vol. 9, no. 2, pp. 87–99

WIEDEMAN, G. H. (1953), 'Correspondence', *Journal of the American Medical Association*, vol. 152, p. 167

WILLIAMS, C. J., and WEINBERG, M. S (1971), *Homosexuals and the Military: A Study of Less Than Honourable Discharge*, New York: Harper & Row

WILSON, E. (1977), *Women and the Welfare State*, Tavistock

WILLIS, P. (1977), *Learning to Labour*, Saxon House

WILLIS, P. (1978), *Profane Culture*, Routledge & Kegan Paul

WINCZE, J. P., HOON, P., and HOON, E. F. (1977), 'Sexual arousal in women: a comparison of cognitive and physiological responses by continuous measurement', *Archives of Sexual Behaviour*, vol. 6, pp. 121–33

WINTER, J. (1978), 'The rise and fall of gross indecency', *Q International*, vol. 2, no. 5, pp. 35–6

WOLF, D. G. (1979), *The Lesbian Community*, University of California Press

WOLFF, C. (1971), *Love Between Women*, Duckworth

WORSLEY, P. (1977) (ed.), *Introducing Sociology*, 2nd edn, Penguin

WORSLEY, T. C. (1967), *Flannelled Fool: A Slice of Life in the Thirties*, Alan Ross.

YAWGER, N. S. (1940), 'Transvestism and other cross-sex manifestations', *Journal of Nervous and Mental Disorders*, vol. 92, pp. 41–8

YORK, P. (1979), 'Machomania' *Harpers & Queen*, February

ZARETSKY, E. (1976), *Capitalism, the Family and Personal Life*, Pluto Press

ZIJDERVELD, A. (1971), *The Abstract Society*, Penguin

ZINNER, J. (1978), 'Review of *La Valonte de Savoir, Telos*, no. 36, pp. 215–25

ZURCHER, L. A. (1977), *The Mutable Self: A Self Concept for Social Change*, Sage

ZURCHER, L. A. JNR, and KIRKPATRICK, R. G. (1976), *Citizens for Decency: Anti-Pornography Crusades, a State of Defence*, University of Texas Press, Austin

Index